Adolescents in the Search for Meaning

Tapping the Powerful Resource of Story

Mary L. Warner

The Scarecrow Press, Inc.
Lanham, Maryland • Toronto • Oxford
2006

SCARECROW PRESS, INC.

Published in the United States of America
by Scarecrow Press, Inc.
A wholly owned subsidiary of
The Rowman & Littlefield Publishing Group, Inc.
4501 Forbes Boulevard, Suite 200, Lanham, Maryland 20706
www.scarecrowpress.com

PO Box 317
Oxford
OX2 9RU, UK

British Library Cataloguing in Publication Information Available

Library of Congress Cataloging-in-Publication Data

Warner, Mary L.
Adolescents in the search for meaning : tapping the powerful resource of story / Mary L. Warner.
p. cm.
Includes bibliographical references and index.
ISBN-13 978-0-8108-5430-7 (pbk. : alk. paper)
ISBN-10 0-8108-5430-9 (pbk. : alk. paper)
1. Teenagers—Books and reading—United States. 2. Young adult literature—Bibliography. 3. Young adult fiction—Bibliography. 4. Social problems—Juvenile fiction—Bibliography. 5. Teenagers in literature. 6. Adolescence—Bibliography. I. Title.
Z1037.W285 2006
028.5′5—dc22 2005023572

™ The paper used in this publication meets the minimum requirements of American National Standard for Information Sciences—Permanence of Paper for Printed Library Materials, ANSI/NISO Z39.48-1992. Manufactured in the United States of America.

To Dan, Brian, and Sarah; Paul, Mary Kate, Rachel, Jacob, and Luke; Denise and Travis; and Mark and Erin: my nieces and nephews, who continue to teach me about the world of young adults.

Contents

Foreword

Sue Ellen Bridgers

My childhood public library was comprised of several shelves in a small community building augmented by the monthly appearance of the bookmobile under my cousin's big oak tree in our little southern town. As much as we relied on those meager resources, my sister and I wanted to own what we read aloud and were delighted when a gift arrived that by shape and size just had to be a book. From our early volumes, many of which were poetry, we learned to appreciate the cadence of language and the sheer beauty of words. We experienced the uncanny twist of shared emotion when we heard A. A. Milne's "Rice Pudding," with its delightful refrain "What *is* the matter with Mary Jane?" or "Halfway Down," which expresses a child's need to have a thinking place, or "Lines and Squares," which gave voice to my own anxious nature. We loved Eugene Field, too, sad as he was, and of course, Robert Louis Stevenson, who understood the dream world of childhood as well as any psychologist might.

From our early fiction, we discovered the delights of the animal world (*Old Mother West Wind, The Wind in the Willows*), fairy tales that were companions to the darkness we felt in our own experiences, and family stories like *Little Women* and *The Five Little Peppers and How They Grew* that offered us siblings who shared sadness and misunderstandings but mostly affection. When we reached our early teens in the fifties, we found a gap in what was personally meaningful to us—we skipped from *My Friend Flicka* to *Jane Eyre*—but by high school, our reading was mostly from our grandmother's shelf (what a joy to discover *Gone with the Wind* there!), from the library in a neighboring city, and from paperback books which were just becoming popular and on which we spent our meager funds. We loved stories in whatever form they came—plays, films, popular music, ballet, opera—but our greatest pleasure was reading. Books taught and inspired us, but most of all they comforted us, in the sense both of solace and of strength. We were, without knowing it, being nourished and strengthened by what we read.

From my earliest years, I knew that important insights could be drawn from stories. My maternal grandmother was a great storyteller. From her we learned not only our family history but also life lessons which she couched in stories. I see now that she frequently told parables. After Grandmother's death, our mother took on the role of storyteller. In response to a simple question, she would say, "Now there's a story to tell about that," and off she would go, enriching the smallest incident with lovely details and succinct character studies.

As a reader and a writer, my youthful connection to stories and books gives me a special feeling for *Adolescents in the Search for Meaning: Tapping the Powerful Resource of Story*. Looking at Dr. Mary Warner's research into what young people find meaningful in literature is somewhat disheartening, and yet the untapped fiction available and recommended in this book is quite astounding. Dr. Warner provides guidance that can connect parents, teachers, and librarians to books that may help teenagers find meaning in life. There is no stronger incentive for beginning a book than a personal recommendation. "You might like this," are powerful words because they are the words of "gift giving." Not "you must read this" or "this book will change you, clarify, explain, expose your depths to you," but "you might *like* it."

Adolescents in the Search for Meaning explores the unsettling world of the young adult. We all want to say to them, "Hold on!" A wise friend of mine says in times of difficulty, "It came to pass, not to stay," but teenagers live in the pain of the moment and it's hard for them to see beyond it. They don't always ask for help or see the available resources, which accounts for the high suicide rate in their age group. They need hope and, since earliest speech, stories have provided insight and given hope.

As Ernest Kurtz and Katherine Ketcham write in their book *The Spirituality of Imperfection*:

> What can we do, in order to be? Yet again, an ancient answer echoes across the centuries: *Listen! Listen to stories!* For what stories do, above all else, is hold up a mirror so that we can see ourselves. Stories are mirrors of human be-ing, reflecting back our very essence. In a story, we come to know precisely the both/and, mixed-up-ed-ness of our very being. In the mirror of another's story, we can discover *our*

> tragedy and *our* comedy—and therefore our very *human*-ness, the ambiguity and incongruity that lie at the core of the human condition. (Kurtz and Ketcham 1992, 63)

As a writer of young adult literature, I am grateful for the information this book provides. Calling attention to the importance of helping young people find meaning through books is a worthwhile endeavor in and of itself. In the hands of parents, teachers, and librarians willing to say, "you might like this one," it provides a valuable step toward connecting young people with books. Story is a powerful resource, one of the most enduring tools we have for exploration and understanding. It is a gift for a lifetime. Readers of this book will gain information and inspiration to help make that gift a reality in the lives of many young people.

Preface

The Power of Story

Some evenings ago, I read *A Ring of Endless Light* by Madeleine L'Engle. This book, published in 1980, is early in the young adult (YA) literature genre, but it identifies exactly why I'm writing a book about adolescents in the search for meaning. As I read *A Ring of Endless Light* and watched the main character struggle with death and loss, Vicky's story reminded me of the sudden death of my oldest brother in an accident that happened when I was 18. I had a number of "life guides" to help me through, but most importantly I remember a teacher/mentor who shared her own story of loss and suggested that I read *The Bridge of San Luis Rey* by Thorton Wilder. I want to return the favor of that teacher and suggest books and stories of other human beings—real and fictional—as powerful resources to meet the crush of pressures that young adults feel, since these stories show characters facing similar experiences and convey how the characters work through their difficulties. The gift of story is precisely what we as teachers, mentors, librarians, and parents can give to the teens of the early twenty-first century who are dealing with any of life's challenges.

Katherine Paterson, author of numerous books for young people, encourages the reading of fiction. Through fiction, she asserts, young readers can experience life at a safe distance while preparing themselves for later experiences in their own lives. These readers learn about characters by knowing their souls and by experiencing their lives at a safe and neutral distance, where danger does not threaten. Paterson aims to write a story so its characters have a life of their own; many teens respond to her believable and well-developed characters, whose stories are honest and true to life. One of her best-known books, *Bridge to Terabithia* (one that teens in my survey recommended) was Paterson's response to dealing with the death of a friend of hers who had been struck by lightning (see www.terabithia.com).

Robert Coles, social scientist, humanist, psychiatrist, and in many ways a storyteller, also conveys much about the importance of story in his book *The Call of Stories*. Coles relates insights he learned from physician and poet William Carlos Williams during his internships in psychological counseling: "Their [patients'] story, yours, mine—it's what we all carry with us on this trip we take, and we owe it to each other to respect our stories and learn from them" (Coles 1989, 30).

As young adulthood places unique demands on teenagers—they are establishing independent identities and separating from family and parents, while attempting to develop strong peer relationships—they have a particular need for story. They are old enough to grasp many of the general life realities—economic, social, physical, and psychological—but they have not had the life experience, which can offer reassurance that they will live through these realities. The late twentieth century and the opening decade of the twenty-first have heightened the challenges. We have terrorism; biological weapons; increasing threats to the environment and limited natural resources; growing disparity between rich and poor; and less stability in family, national, and world structures. Frequently adolescents have not established the sources of meaning that can help them both survive and thrive; without sources of meaning or fulfillment and under significant pressure, many teens seek compensation, consciously or unconsciously, in destructive ways. What I find in L'Engle's novel and the many wonderful YA novels available are stories to which teens can relate, but all too often these stories remain untapped resources.

YA literature, including works by Ted Hipple, Gary Salvner, Virginia Monseau, Joan Kaywell, and so many others who have followed the genre since the early novels, has come "of age through themes that matter not just to teens struggling with adolescence but to all of us—the quest for justice, the savagery of war and hatred; and the struggles for love, acceptance, and understanding . . ." (Monseau and Salvner 2000, ix).

In *Adolescents in the Search for Meaning: Tapping the Powerful Resource of Story*, a number of YA authors talk about their books and their stories, and about why they believe writing for young adults is so vital. *A Ring of Endless Light* shows L'Engle's protagonist, Vicky Austin, facing the huge pressures of death and loss on several fronts: from being a companion to her grandfather who is dying of leukemia to supporting three young men who have all themselves experienced death. The novel opens with a funeral, and throughout the book Vicky grieves, struggles, befriends, and survives—all because of a number of significant support structures. She is lucky to be surrounded by supportive family members and to possess a good deal of maturity as well as a somewhat uncanny sense for communing with nature, as she does with the dolphins who are part of Adam's summer research project (Adam is a young marine biologist). Further, Vicky's grandfather feels a special kinship with her, possibly because both share a love of poetry and poets, and her ability to express her feelings in poetry grounds her. Grandfather is truly wise, willing to share his experiences of dying with his family, particularly with Vicky.

Vicky, again, has something not shared by many young adults facing death; she has family and friends with whom she can talk about the great mystery of the ending of life and about how to continue to live fully. From her grandfather, Vicky is given poets' words, specifically the words of Henry Vaughn: "I saw Eternity the other night, / Like a great ring of pure and endless light . . ." (L'Engle 1980, 64). From Vaughn's poem, she comes to understand that she cannot stay in "the dazzling darkness." In Vicky's numbness after actually holding death in her arms, she is challenged by her grandfather to her greatest "letting go": "You are to be a light-bearer. You are to choose the light" (L'Engle 1980, 318). Just as these words from literature help Vicky as well as other young adults to find strength in poetry, it is for us as teachers, librarians, and other adults significant in the lives of teens to foster the story's potential for meaning.

What L'Engle gives the reader, and what she gave me, is a powerful portrayal of an adolescent who does choose the light despite numerous painful reasons to choose darkness. This gift of L'Engle's, this ability to relate so completely (because in so many ways Vicky's story is my story), is my purpose in writing for adolescents in the search for meaning; I want them to know of books like *A Ring of Endless Light*, where they can meet characters who live through the painful and joyful realities of life and can learn from their peers in the literature. I want young adults to understand that they need not float in a world of meaninglessness and cope by inflicting violence on themselves or others. I'm passionate about the power of story, particularly the stories of adolescents relayed so well through literature, to be a life-changing, life-saving medium that we as parents, teachers, librarians, and writers can give to young adults.

Works Cited

Coles, Robert. *The Call of Stories*. Boston: Houghton Mifflin, 1989.
L'Engle, Madeleine. *A Ring of Endless Light*. New York: Farrar, Straus and Giroux, 1980.
Monseau, Virginia R., and Gary M. Salvner, eds. *Reading Their World: The Young Adult Novel in the Classroom*. 2nd ed. Portsmouth, NH: Boyton/Cook Heinemann, 2000.

~

Acknowledgments

This book has involved so many people who deserve recognition and appreciation. First of all, I thank Gary Salvner and the ALAN (Assembly on Literature for Adolescence of the National Council of Teachers of English) Research Grant committee for the funding that supported my research with adolescents.

I appreciate the over 1400 young adults who responded to the YA literature survey and the teachers and parents who encouraged their participation. The responses from these young adults are vital to this book because I wanted to hear primarily from the teens themselves about their search for meaning. Because the survey didn't ask for names, the teen respondents are mainly anonymous, but I do know most of the English teachers who conducted the survey; thanks to each of you. Pamela Sissi Carroll, former editor of the *ALAN Review*, Kim Bowen, K–12 Language Arts Consultant for the North Carolina Department of Public Instruction, and other ALAN and NCTE members helped publicize the Survey; without their help, I wouldn't have been able to reach all the teens I did.

Sue Ellen Bridgers, a young adult author and personal friend, has provided ongoing support in many ways. Her foreword to the book describes her commitment to young adults; her many presentations with me at NCTE, ALAN, and North Carolina English Teachers Association conferences have furthered my thinking and understanding of the importance of young adult literature. She also read numerous drafts of the book's manuscript as she prepared to write the Foreword, and she gave me editorial and authorial advice.

I'm also grateful to each of the young adult authors who were able to answer the YA authors' survey that comprises chapter 3 of the book. These authors are Laurie Halse Anderson, Ann Angel, Jan Cheripko, Chris Crutcher, Karen Cushman, Don Gallo, Karen Hesse, Norma Fox Mazer, Shelley Fraser Mickle, Han Nolan, Katherine Paterson, Gary Paulsen, Rodman Philbrick, Marilyn Reynolds, Jerry Spinelli, Ruth White, and Jane Yolen. Indirectly, Madeleine L'Engle and the late Robert Cormier participated in the author survey as well through previous interviews, as did L'Engle through her words in a special commemorative edition of *An Acceptable Time*.

A host of people have assisted me with the compilation and presentation of the data from the survey. Laura Chapman, Faith Dabney, David Dameron, Noelle Kehrberg, Amanda Riddle, Beth Kefauver, Nancy DeSain, and Matt Brigner and others from Instructional Technology at Western Carolina University; Jean Shirota of San Jose State University; and Martin Dillon of Scarecrow Press have all worked with the data presentation, providing immense technological assistance.

I also acknowledge the support of Donna Fisher, retired high school teacher and librarian, who helped with annotations and teaching resources for books featured in chapters 4 through 8.

I express gratitude as well to my family members, to friends, and to the School Sisters of Notre Dame, especially of the Mankato, Minnesota province, for their moral support, encouragement, and prayer.

Finally, I appreciate the effort of Martin Dillon at Scarecrow Press for his guidance throughout this project.

Introduction

Contemporary Realities

Recently, when I told one of my nieces, an almost 20-year-old in her second year in college, that I was writing a book on adolescents in the search for meaning, she commented that it seemed a semi-depressing topic and wondered how I had been inspired to tackle such a project. Her comment evoked a response that leads to a discussion of my overall purpose for this book. Yes, I have been among those many adults in the United States who have been continually alarmed at the violence among adolescents and caused by adolescents, particularly high-profile school shootings. But most of my questions at the time of the Columbine shootings were about what Eric Harris and Dylan Klebold read or didn't read and what happened in their lives that caused them to act with such violence. While undoubtedly their actions cannot be explained by one single reason, it is conceivable that the loss of meaning or inability to find meaning played a role. Fourteen of the books frequently cited by teens in my survey deal specifically with violence; two—*Rachel's Tears* and *She Said Yes*—are the stories of teen victims of Columbine.

A book by Scarecrow Press, *Life Is Tough: Guys, Growing Up, and Young Adult Literature* (Rachelle Lasky Bilz), was published in late 2004. An ongoing series by the same press, edited by Arlene Hirschfelder, is entitled "It Happened to Me"; this series is designed for teens searching for answers about certain illnesses, social issues, or lifestyle interests. Greenwood Press has published a series, Using Literature to Help Troubled Teenagers, with volumes published to date addressing end-of-life, health, societal, identity, abuse, and family issues. The more than 40 books annotated in chapters 4 through 8 of this book also specifically speak to the topics of violence and loss of meaning. The number of these books is just one indicator of the role story can play in addressing adolescents and violence.

Violence is only one of the many symptoms of a lack of meaning. It is precisely this hopelessness or inability to find reasons to live—and to live happy and fulfilling lives—that I suggest can be addressed through reading about the stories of others, through literature. The power of others' stories to suggest meaning for our own life stories impels me to suggest that we need to tap the resource of story. YA author Gary Paulsen frequently discusses the role reading played in his life. In his answers to the YA author questionnaire I sent to him, Paulsen said, "At least in my case, reading saved my life. I was a terrible student, hated school, failed the ninth grade, and a librarian I didn't even know gave me a library card and then handed me a book. That one woman helped me find a place where it didn't hurt, a place where I fit in, a place where I belonged—the pages of a book."

Psychologists posit that adolescence is distinguishable from other growth periods in that the biological changes accompanying puberty both influence and are influenced by psychology, behavior, and society (Lerner, Easterbrooks, and Mistry 2003, 296). They further suggest that adolescents possess the cognitive development to comprehend such realities as death, separation and divorce, ridicule and prejudice, peer pressure, and identity issues. But cognitive development is only a part of the total human psyche, particularly that of adolescents.

The contemporary movement toward holistic living—evident in everything from the rise of health food stores and vegetarianism, to the trend toward low-carb diets, to interest in meditation and yoga, to magazines such as *Holistic Living* and *Parabola*, to numerous websites such as Mind/Body Control: Holistic Online.com (which recognizes the total human person—physically, emotionally, psychologically, and spiritually)—emphasizes that human beings are complex, existing at multiple levels from the biological-physical to the societal-historical. There are even websites, such as www.-mimbres.com/holp/bib/blk_r.htm, which provide bibliographies for the "holistic path." And while adults often bring to these multiple levels of existence a maturity and life experience that help them process meaning and live through a range of challenges integral to human existence from birth through death, adolescents rarely have that cache of resources. Further, young adulthood is a period fraught with identity issues, shifts in relationships from parental figures to peers, and questions about the future. Teenagers want to know who they are and what life holds for them, and they are in the search for and development of identity with peers who are equally adrift. Ironically, although adolescents are in the journey together, they are not always the most supportive of each other. Peer pressure, harassment, and bullying barrage the vulnerable inner world of many teenagers—survey respondents listed peer pressure as the number one issue they face.

This inner world of humans holds the most fragile and yet most crucial component of our being—the spirit.

> Whatever the expression, everyone is ultimately talking about the same thing—an unquenchable fire, a restlessness, a longing, a disquiet, a hunger, a loneliness, a gnawing nostalgia, a wildness that cannot be tamed, a congenital all-embracing ache that lies at the center of human experience and is the ultimate force that drives everything else. This dis-ease is universal. Desire gives no exemptions. (Rolheiser 1999, 4)

What Rolheiser suggests, after identifying the drives universal to humans, is that spirituality is "what we do with that desire"(Rolheiser 1999, 5); however, adolescents face such a variety of pressures, many far more external than internal, that they are not necessarily attuned to their inner world. And while organized religion grounds the spirituality of many adults, teenagers frequently are reevaluating and questioning the religion or spirituality that parents or adults in their lives embrace.

For adolescents, in particular, what we—caring adults—need to address is their human spirit, where they have the disquiet, the restlessness, and the ache, but need guidance regarding what to "do" with the feelings. They are human beings with the same unanswerable questions about death, suffering, and an afterlife that older human beings have, but adolescents' resources are more limited. An amazing number of books do have stories of young adults in the search and facing the realities that disquiet; one of the purposes of this book is to help teenagers know these books exist.

In the excellent series published by Greenwood Press, Using Literature to Help Troubled Teenagers, the many contributors acknowledge the realities that adolescents experience. Pamela S. Carroll, drawing on realities prevalent in 1994, listed seven of the myriad problems that teenagers need to negotiate:

1. Teenage sexual activity, and pregnancies for teens 15 years old and younger
2. Drug and alcohol abuse, with adolescent use of marijuana beginning by

tenth grade, and binge drinking and intoxication growing most rapidly among young adolescent females
3. Obesity, eating disorders, and poor physical fitness, and resulting low self-esteem
4. Delinquency and violence, not only among poor dropout teens, but now affecting teens from mainstream communities, and with the incidence of rape, robbery, and assault about twice as high as the rate for people age 20 and older
5. Serious injuries, including injuries that cause 57 percent of all deaths of adolescents who are 10–14 years old
6. Suicides among adolescents, with greatest increases among white males, and with those who are intoxicated seven times more likely than other victims to use a gun
7. Single-parent families and stepfamilies, with poverty more closely associated with single-parent families than with two-parent families (Carroll 1999, 9)

Possibly even more troubling than the data listed above are data related to adolescent suicide, a major indicator of the inability to find meaning in life. Keith Valone, Ph.D., Psy. D., a licensed psychologist, submits these facts in his presentations on the prevention of adolescent suicide:

- Somewhere in the United States, a teenager commits suicide every two hours
- Suicide kills more teens than any disease or natural cause
- Over 5,000 youth commit suicide every year
- Over 50,000 youth attempt suicide every year

Valone's statistics are verified by data provided by the American Pediatric Society & Society for Pediatric Research, the National Adolescent Health Information Center, the National Institute of Mental Health, and the National Mental Health Association (see websites listed below). These institutes add:

- Suicide is the leading cause of death for youth 15–19 years old
- Suicide is the fourth leading cause of death for children 10–14 years old
- Suicide is the second leading cause of death among college-age youth

Now some 10 years since the report from which the above data were taken, the problems are no less prevalent; the opening decade of the twenty-first century has added to the list terrorism and new wars, increasing issues related to technology, the further disintegration of the nuclear family, and more instances of violence. The statistics included above are not limited to those teens sometimes referred to as "at-risk" because of socioeconomic realities. And particularly because it is almost impossible to describe any teen or family setting as "normal," many more than those teenagers labeled (inappropriately or not) as "at risk" are affected.

As I mention in the opening statement of this introduction, this book is built on the premise that it is important to hear what adolescents say about their lives. I attempted to hear the voices of 13- to 18-year-olds by surveying them. Since late November 2001, nearly 1400 respondents have responded to the following questions:

1. What are the major issues you face in your life (e.g., peer pressure, separation of parents)?
2. Where do you go to get advice or guidance for dealing with the issues listed above?
3. Have you ever read a book or some type of writing that helped you with the issues that challenge you? Name that book or work(s).
4. What are some books or other writings that you'd recommend to your peers to read for finding advice or guidance?

What the teenagers themselves identify as the biggest issues in their lives shows that all of them struggle with a range of issues, but the survey reinforces that not all young adults are prone to violence or as self-focused as they have been portrayed. Carol Tell, in "Generation What? Connecting with Today's Youth," conveys that same notion in the words of an anonymous twelfth-grade student:

> "More than anything, our youth culture responds to positive feedback from the media and adults. Often the only feedback we're getting is negative. I have many friends who feel like they're taken for granted, because the troublemakers get all the attention. The people who are doing what they should be doing are just overlooked."—Twelfth-grade girl (Tell 1999/2000, 13)

There are millions whose lives have the ordinary and private tragedies of "normal" adolescence; unfortunately, the teenagers we "know" best are frequently those who make headlines, like John Lee Malvo, teenage sniper suspect in the Washington D.C. sniper deaths.

One group that has already responded and continues to respond to adolescents is comprised of the authors of young adult literature. Many of these authors have parented teenagers, many have been or are teachers, and most have been "that one significant adult" who has made a difference in the life of an adolescent. These authors, and so many other authors, have known the impact of their stories on the lives of young adults—often they receive poignant letters from teens chronicling the book's influence. Joan Kaywell's forthcoming *Letters of Hope: Young Adult Authors Respond to Teens in Trouble* is a collection of many of these letters.

The late Robert Cormier, whose numerous novels have had a major impact on adolescent (and adult) readers, expresses the passion of many YA authors. In his letter to readers, cited in *Using Literature to Help Troubled Teenagers Cope with End-of-Life Issues*, Cormier says:

> I've always believed that a writer's job is simply to bring up questions—because nobody has the answers to life-and-death mysteries—but I think it's important to provide hints to the answers . . . (Allen 2002, xix–xx)

Cormier admits "The hint of an answer" is all we really have. He reminds us, though, that we can draw comfort from the hints, the comfort of knowing we are part of the whole, part of all humanity. "In this link with other people, this sharing of our futures, we can somehow find a bit of solace, a sweet slant of light in all the darkness" (Allen 2002, xix–xx). Cormier goes on to comment that "light" for many, including for him, is God, but acknowledges that for others, "light" may be something else. He implies, as I've stated above, that participation in organized religion may not be the route many adolescents go. The larger issue is that adolescents keep searching, find some way to live with the unknowns, and realize they are not alone in their search.

Sue Ellen Bridgers, writer of several YA novels, all based in family life, shares Cormier's commitment to adolescents. In an essay called "Stories My Grandmother Told Me: Part Two" for the *ALAN Review*, Bridgers writes that we are all caught in our culture, searching for sense in the confusion, but she suggests that no one is more trapped than teenagers who are faced with the problems of daily life:

> The tremendous freedom they have, the problems of ecology and economy, the real and oppressive fear of nuclear holocaust—they have more need for interdependence than ever before. (Kelly 1999, 33)

As Bridgers has demonstrated through her novels:

> [Adolescents] need to share their mutual concerns with adults . . . They need to know we are with them and that they have ideas and visions and love to share that we adults are in true need of. They need books that reflect both the confusion and the calm, books that speak to the basic human need for companionship, books that portray family life in such a way that young people see the possibility of commitments to it that can sustain rather than destroy them. (Kelly 1999, 33)

Because hearing others' experiences and stories of life so often lends perspective to our own life, literature and story may actually be a means of "saving lives," particularly the kind of literature that Cormier and Bridgers, two significant YA literature authors, suggest. Writers of fiction create whole worlds with people and events, with values, ideas, and worldviews. These worlds can broaden our perspectives and in this way, teach us. Arthur Lerner discusses the emotional impact of story, speaking of how fiction presents characters facing the most tragic experiences and feeling the most harrowing emotions; at the same time, readers see the characters surviving conflicts and coming to resolution. The fictional world allows readers to experience vicariously and in a sense, safely, some of what real life does not allow (Lerner and Mahlendorf 1992, x).

The power of story—to heal, to teach, to motivate, to transform—is timeless. From fairy tales to biblical parables to folk tales to Alcoholic Anonymous and other 12-step programs to "witnesses" at religious gatherings to accounts of survivors of the Shoah (Holocaust), instances of storytelling abound. Frequently high schools host speakers at assemblies and the student body hears someone's story and recovery. An NBC evening news broadcast in recent months highlighted how telling one's story can serve as restitution for involuntary manslaughter. In this particular story, an adolescent driving while intoxicated killed a man's wife and child. The husband/father of the victims did not press for imprisonment for the teen; instead, the husband and the adolescent travel as a team to high schools and the adolescent tells his story: an example of the cathartic and healing power of story, one teenagers grasp.

Michael Ryan reports an even more interesting study in "Read a Book—Or Go to Jail" (1995). A district court judge in New Bedford, Massachusetts, began this experiment in January 1992 when he told repeat offender Don Ross, "Go to school and read books—or go to jail." Ross started to participate in a 12-week literature seminar led by English professor Robert Waxler at the University of Massachusetts, Amherst. Participants are serious offenders; the average participant has 16 prior offenses. Waxler, believing in the transformative power of stories, started by assigning short stories and then progressing to novels of increasing difficulty. He looked for materials that would address issues of violence, identity, and the individual's relationship to society. The first four years the seminar was in operation, 19 percent of participants were rearrested, but this compares to 45 percent of a similar group (matched by age, race, income, neighborhood, and offense), based on a study done by professors at the University of Massachusetts, Amherst, and the University of Indiana.

Particularly for young adults then, the emotional safety of seeing their real-life experiences mirrored in fiction or in someone else's story gives books the power to reach these adolescents not only intellectually, but also emotionally. When gripped by characters and their experiences—as I was with Vicky Austin in *A Ring of Endless Light*—readers, especially adolescents facing a complex of issues, can grow in understanding of and sensitivity toward themselves and others. Their worldviews can be broadened and opinions enlightened in a far less threatening way than in settings with adults with whom they may or may not be able to communicate.

I see additional purposes, maybe tangential, for this book as well. Reports on reading comprehension nationwide continue to show a decline; most often, the decline is seen in data on adolescents. For "bibliophiles," comprehension comes automatically, but what about those who seldom read or dislike reading? This dilemma plagues educators; perhaps simply identifying more books that teenagers want to read (because the books address teens' lives) will contribute to improved comprehension. We do have evidence of the millions of readers who have become hooked on the Harry Potter series, even if the books are well over 500 pages.

Another focal issue in public education is character education. The character education movement has been one attempt to respond to violence and abusive behaviors in schools. In reading about others, in learning about their lives, we are changed. Sometimes a formal, structured program doesn't achieve all that is desired precisely because it *is* so structured. For example, proponents of cultural diversity comment that a single month devoted to a specific cultural group, such as African American History Month, actually limits the growth of diversity because such a celebration isolates recognition to a particular time period, a month out of the year.

Day to day reading, such as might grow among teenagers who see more purpose in reading when books are connected to the teens' life issues, could shore up the efforts of the organized character education programs. Young adults can be changed by books that "show them their lives," by books that teach them they are not alone in fears, dreams, hopes, and anxieties. As adolescents find meaning, they need not resort to harmful ways to be fulfilled or to antisocial behaviors. An extensive list of resources for character education, compiled by Midge Frazel, is available at midgefrazel.net/character .html. In addition, numerous resources are included in the Works Cited and Character Education Resources following this introduction.

Many of the teaching ideas connected to the books annotated in chapters 4 through 8 offer suggestions for using the novel in connection with character education. Teachers could build entire units around YA literature.

Adolescents in the Search for Meaning: Tapping the Powerful Resource of Story is written to and for parents, teachers, librarians, and anyone wanting to respond to the adolescents of our world, the adults of the twenty-first century. Is my goal of reaching so many too idealistic or too broad? If even one adolescent is "saved" by a book, I think not.

Works Cited

Allen, Janet, ed. *Using Literature to Help Troubled Teens Cope with End-of-Life Issues*. Westport, CT: Greenwood Press, 2002.

American Pediatric Society & Society for Pediatric Research. www.aps-spr.org.

Carroll, Pamela S. *Using Literature to Help Troubled Teenagers Cope with Societal Issues*. Westport, CT: Greenwood Press, 1999.

Frazel, Midge. midgefrazel.net/character.html.

Kelly, Patricia P., and Robert C. Small Jr., eds. *Two Decades of "The ALAN Review."* Urbana, IL: NCTE, 1999.

Lerner, Arthur, and Ursula R. Mahlendorf. *Life Guidance through Literature*. Chicago: American Library Association, 1992.

Lerner, Richard M., M. Ann Easterbrooks, and Jayanthi Mistry, eds. *Handbook of Psychology: Developmental Psychology*. Vol. 6. Hoboken, NJ: John Wiley & Sons, 2003.

National Adolescent Health Information Center. nahic.ucsf.edu.

National Institute of Mental Health. www.nimh.nih.gov.

National Mental Health Association. www.nmha.org/infoctr/factsheets/82.cfm.

Rolheiser, Ronald. *The Holy Longing*. New York: Doubleday, 1999.

Ryan, Michael. "Read a Book—Or Go to Jail." *Parade Magazine*, February 5, 1995, 16–17.

Tell, Carol. "Generation What? Connecting with Today's Youth." *Educational Leadership* 57, no. 4 (1999/2000): 8–13.

Valone, Keith. www.sanmarino.k12.ca.us/~smhs/FacultyResources/documents/TeenSuicidePrev/tsl d003.htm. PowerPoint presentation on teen suicide prevention.

Character Education Resources

B., Kathy. www.desertskyone.com/character/books.html.

Braman, Amy. www.marcias-lesson-links.com/CharacterEd.html.

Children's Literature and Character Education. www.indiana.edu/~reading/ieo/bibs/chil itchar.html.

Education World Curriculum: One Character Education Program. www.education-world .com/a_curr/curr114.shtml.

Montgomery County Public Schools: Selected Secondary Literature. www.mcps.k12.md .us/departments/publishingservices/PDF/CharSec.pdf.

The School for Ethical Education. www.ethicsed.org/resources/resource.htm.

www.indiana.edu/~reading/chared/rsrchschol.html.

PART ONE

INTRODUCTION

Adolescents in the Search for Meaning: Tapping the Powerful Resource of Story builds on the important premise that young adults are searching for meaning and their voices need to be heard. Chapters 1 and 2 summarize the data, which I gathered throughout 2001–2003 from over 1400 teens.

Chapter 1, "Young Adults Sharing Their Perspectives," presents the actual survey, provides general comments based on the demographic information participants gave, and presents data compiled in response to two questions: "What are major issues you face in your life?" and "Where do you go for sources of guidance on these issues?" Much of the data is presented on charts that examine the data according to respondent's age and gender as well as demographics such as school size, type, and location.

Chapter 2, "Young Adults Sharing Reading Choices," addresses Questions 3 and 4 from the survey: "Have you ever read a book or some type of writing that helped you with the issues that challenge you?" and "What are some books or other writings that you'd recommend to your peers?" This chapter has tables showing the books that teens identified as helping them and which they'd recommend. It also includes charts showing what males and females, according to age groups, have read and suggest to others to read.

In addition to hearing what young adults themselves have to say, I also wanted to explore what authors of YA literature say about writing for teens. Chapter 3, "YA Authors Describe Their Commitment to Adolescents" presents responses from about 20 writers about how they began writing for teens, why writing for teens is important, what books/readings the authors found helpful in their lives, and what these authors would suggest teens read.

Based on the issues the teens identified as most significant in their lives and building from the books they suggested, the remainder of *Adolescents in the Search for Meaning: Tapping the Powerful Resource of Story* presents books for adolescents. Each book entry includes publication information, a brief summary of the book, teaching ideas and resources, and a section entitled "Why You Should Give this Book to Teens." For many of the books, I have also given additional titles by the author for further reading. Following a brief introduction, chapters 4 through 8 annotate books in the following categories:

Chapter 4: Books about Real-Life Experiences
Chapter 5: Books about Facing Death and Loss
Chapter 6: Books about Identity, Discrimination, and Struggles with Decisions
Chapter 7: Books about Courage and Survival
Chapter 8: Books on Allegory, Fantasy, Myth, and Parable

Following the chapters is an appendix, a list of annotated books. Then, because no book could ever include all of the literature that teens should read or every writing that might help in the search for meaning, following the appendix is a bibliography that also includes additional print and electronic resources for YA literature.

CHAPTER ONE

Young Adults Sharing Their Perspectives

From the time of Columbine and even earlier, I had been struggling with the question of what teachers and other adults who are significant in the lives of teenagers could do to address the deeper issues that are frequently masked by the surface actions of teens. Primarily I wanted to find out what could give these young adults meaning. Similar to the situation of children with learning disabilities that are not visible—such as dyslexia and attention deficit disorder—the situation of young adults searching for meaning calls for probing that goes beyond the surface level of their actions, violent or destructive as these actions sometimes are. I knew I wanted to hear from young adults themselves, to get their answers to questions of meaning in their lives and to discover what blocks their search for meaning. This chapter and chapter 2 present the response from the young adults themselves and anticipate the books that are annotated in chapters 4 through 8.

I had done research for my doctoral dissertation that examined how literature, specifically texts designated as sacred, could offer stories and words that speak to some of the deeper issues of the human spirit. In creating a curriculum of "sacred texts of literature," I read many books, poems, plays, and short stories; such writings have touched the human spirit of adults for centuries. These writings address the "large questions" that adults face—illness, death, violence, suffering, "bad things happening to good people." But these large questions are not the property of adults alone. Adolescents—as anyone who teaches them or works with them knows only too well—face these same issues, but seldom are adolescents equipped with the resources to deal with these questions. For one, they simply have not lived long enough to have the advantage of life experience. Additionally, teenagers confront many pressing issues related to identity, acceptance, their future, and adulthood. Could story bring meaning to the voids they face? Provide answers for them in this all too fragile period of their lives? What literature could touch their spirits?

Hearing what teenagers themselves say about their lives is crucial in knowing what issues they face, who they seek out for guidance, and what they might want to read, since all too often we as parents, teachers, or other older adults operate on what we think adolescents are experiencing. Building from this belief that the voices of teenagers need to be heard, in summer 2001, I applied for and received an ALAN (Assembly for the Literature of Adolescents of NCTE—National Council of Teachers of English) Research Grant to help me conduct a survey and compile the response of young adults, thirteen to eighteen. I created the survey shown in figure 1.1. I put the survey online—on a website that could be accessed only through a designated URL

Survey for Adolescent Readers in the Search for Meaning

Please tell us about yourself

Your age:

Gender: Male Female

Type of High School: Public Private Parochial

School is in what kind of area: Rural Urban

Size of high school:
Under 500 students
500 to 1000 students
1001 to 2000 students
More than 2000 students

1. What are the major issues you face in your life? (i.e. peer pressure, separation of parents)
2. Where do you go to get advice or guidance for dealing with the issues listed above?
3. Have you ever read a book or some type of writing that helped you with the issues that challenge you? If so, name that book(s) or work(s):
4. What are some books or other writings that you'd recommend to your peers to read for finding advice or guidance?

Figure 1.1 Survey

that I distributed—because I did not want to be influenced or biased by postmarks that indicated a specific city, state, or part of the nation. I also wanted student anonymity as much as possible, so the only identifying demographic information requested was respondent gender and age, and type, location, and size of school. These demographics help in making observations about the data, particularly as they reveal distinctions in choices of books (by gender, for example).

I did, however, conduct the survey working primarily through English teachers, who presented the survey to their students and frequently monitored student response. By way of introduction, I included a letter to teachers explaining the research project, providing the URL where the survey was located, giving all contact information for me (including the website that explained the ALAN Research Grant), and expressing my appreciation for participation.

I noted in the letter that I created a permission form for administrators and parents to avoid any concerns either group might have about students in their school or their children participating. I sent the survey first to a network of teachers in western North Carolina and to schools where my students were doing Internship I and II. Many of my former students, then beginning English teachers, also had their students respond to the survey. The survey was published in a few public venues: the North Carolina English Language Arts Newsletter, the *ALAN Review* (Vol. 30, Fall 2002), a newsletter for the School Sisters of Notre Dame throughout the United States and Canada, and the newsletter for the Dakota Writing Project. I also worked with teachers and contacts I had from presentations at NCTE National Conventions as well as the teenagers from my family and of the families of former students in Minnesota, South Dakota, Nebraska, and other areas in the Midwest. All those participating in the survey were contacted directly or indirectly by me and needed access to the web URL to find the survey. Because participants had to know the online site of the survey or receive hard copies, I am reasonably certain there were few "crank" respondents.

I did not attempt to specify particular student groups—honors or Advanced Placement students, for example—because again, I wanted to hear from the "average" teenager. Thus I do not know specifically if respondents are reluctant readers or nonreaders or avid readers. However, from the responses to the question about what they might recommend to others to read, I did see many who commented, "I don't read." My goal was not only to find out what books these young adults do find significant, but also to go beyond their suggestions to make available to teachers, librarians, and parents more titles of powerful, relevant stories to offer to teens. In selecting books to include in chapter 4 through 8, I used the titles that the student respondents gave and built on the information they shared about the issues in their lives and the sources of guidance they seek when making choices of their own.

Demographic Information and General Comments

The survey became available online in late 2001. I continued to collect data through the summer of 2003. I got approximately 800 surveys in hard copy form; the other approximately 600 surveys were done online, primarily in the school setting. The data analysis in this chapter reflects the responses of 1406 individuals; the numbers below indicate how many respondents were part of each age group and the percentage, based on the 1392 participants who gave their age. Though I primarily aimed for responses from 13- to 18-year-olds, some respondents were younger than 13, some older than 18. The first part of the survey solicited demographic information; the second part presented four open-ended questions. The demographic information is shown in table 1.1.

Several charts are included within this chapter, detailing the results of the survey. For the purpose of compiling information and presenting it on these charts, the 10–13 year olds form one group; 14-year-olds, 15-year-olds, 16-year-olds are each separate groups; and those 17 and older are a group. The school demographic breakdowns were by type, location, and size. Table 1.2 indicates the type of school and the number of respondents for each type,

Table 1.1. Number of Respondents by Age

Age	*Responses*	*Percent*
10-year-olds	3	0.2%
11-year-olds	7	0.5%
12-year-olds	75	5.4%
13-year-olds	172	12.4%
14-year-olds	377	27%
15-year-olds	269	19%
16-year-olds	190	13.6%
17-year-olds	239	17.2%
18-year-olds	56	4%
19-year-olds	3	0.2%
21-year-old	1	.07%
Totals	1392	100%

Table 1.2. Type of School and Number of Respondents

Type of school	*Responses*	*Percent*
Parochial	320	23%
Private	249	18%
Public	837	59%
Totals	1406	100%

table 1.3 shows the location of school and the numbers for each, and table 1.4 indicates the size of school and the numbers for each.

Questions 1 and 2 allow for multiple answers and thus require some description or qualitative analysis as well as the quantitative. To address the multiple answers given by many respondents, I have done a tally of the first issue (Question 1) and first guidance source (Question 2) cited by respondents; in a separate tally I have accounted for second issues and second sources of guidance from responses to these questions. There are participants who listed more than two issues as major in their lives and/or listed more than two sources of guidance. These are not reflected in the figures; I note the number of respondents who did cite more issues and/or sources of guidance in tables 1.6 and 1.8 (described in more detail below). In any case, the data are presented primarily to let us know what these young adults are experiencing and to hear how they describe their worlds.

Table 1.3. Location of School and Number of Respondents

Location of school	*Responses*	*Percent*
Rural	1151	82%
Urban	255	18%
Totals	1406	100%

Table 1.4. Size of School and Number of Respondents

Size of school	*Responses*	*Percent*
Under 500	543	39%
500–1000	177	13%
1001–2000	582	42%
Over 2000	74	6%
Totals	1376	100%

For the purpose of data analysis, I also grouped the issues, guidance sources, and types of books that respondents listed. The groupings regarding the major issues respondents face are:

- Separation of parents/divorce
- Illness and death of family members/friends
- Peer pressure: drinking, drugs, sex, weapons; moral and ethical choices
- Acceptance/self-esteem/being popular; getting made fun of/teased
- Family issues: parental expectations, abuse, alcoholism, fighting/conflicts
- School-related issues: academic achievement, grades, homework, extracurriculars, sports/winning, holding a job while attending school
- Emotional issues: stress, pressure, depression, suicide, bulimia/anorexia, addictions, dealing with the future, moving, finding free time
- Friendships/relationships/dating/conflicts
- War, terrorism, safety of family/country, poverty/money, social conditions, teen parents
- God/faith/religious affiliation

Survey Results

Question 1: What are the major issues you face in your life?

Table 1.5 summarizes the number of times each issue in Question 1 was listed first—in other words, how often it was the student's primary issue. The order of the issues listed below follows the categories numbered above. The percent is based on 1375 responses, since some participants did not list any issues.

Table 1.5. Primary Issues and the Number of Responses for Each

Issue	*Responses*	*Percent*
Separation of parents/divorce	113	8.2%
Illness/death of family members/friends	51	3.7%
Peer pressure	464	34%
Acceptance	74	5.4%
Family issues	97	7%
School issues	254	18.5%
Emotional issues	100	7.3%
Friendships	102	7.4%
Social conditions	20	1.5%
Faith	3	0.2%

The charts in figures 1.2 and 1.3 present the breakdown of primary issues connected to gender and age.

Note that for both females and males between 10 and 16, peer pressure ranked the highest. Since adolescent psychology indicates that in the early teen years the search for identity is a primary focus, the high percentage of respondents identifying peer pressure as their primary issue is not a surprise. Because peer pressure and school issues are those ranked highest, many books annotated in chapters 4 through 8 relate to these topics. Some of the books included there may seem more applicable to adult readers, but if several respondents named the book as helpful, I usually included it. Alternately, some books listed by participants may seem too "young" for 13- to 18-year-olds. Again, because I believe in the importance of taking the responses from survey respondents seriously, I have included books like *Tuck Everlasting* or *A Wrinkle in Time* or *The Giver*. As many of us who teach literature know, these books, which are allegorical, can be read on many levels and by readers of many ages. For *The Giver* in particular, the book with its utopist world holds much more meaning for older adolescents and young adults than for readers under 13.

What could be disturbing is that this category of peer pressure included the pressures to drink, use and abuse drugs, be sexually active, and make moral/ethical choices, indicating that many students as young as 13 are dealing with these issues. Ironically for males, by the time they are 16, 17, or older, peer pressure becomes far less of an issue; at the same time, they are gaining the maturity that might make drug and alcohol use and sexual activity somewhat more "safe." In females, the drop in the importance of peer pressure doesn't begin as noticeably until age 17 or older.

A second observation from the data, which again is not necessarily a surprise, is the emphasis for females 16 and older on school-related issues. This category includes acceptance into colleges and academic achievement, as well as the time management issue of juggling "extracurriculars," homework, and sports. Many respondents spoke of the stress of winning or doing well both academically and athletically as peers and family might expect. Males ages 17 and up show a jump in this category as well. Once again, this pressure to perform and succeed is a major theme in many of the books included in chapter 4. Another component of the school issues category was holding a job while attending school. Many students are affected by trying to work up to 40 hours a week and still manage coursework. Even having the energy to stay awake in classes when working an outside job becomes a factor.

For females, the next most important issue (though significantly fewer

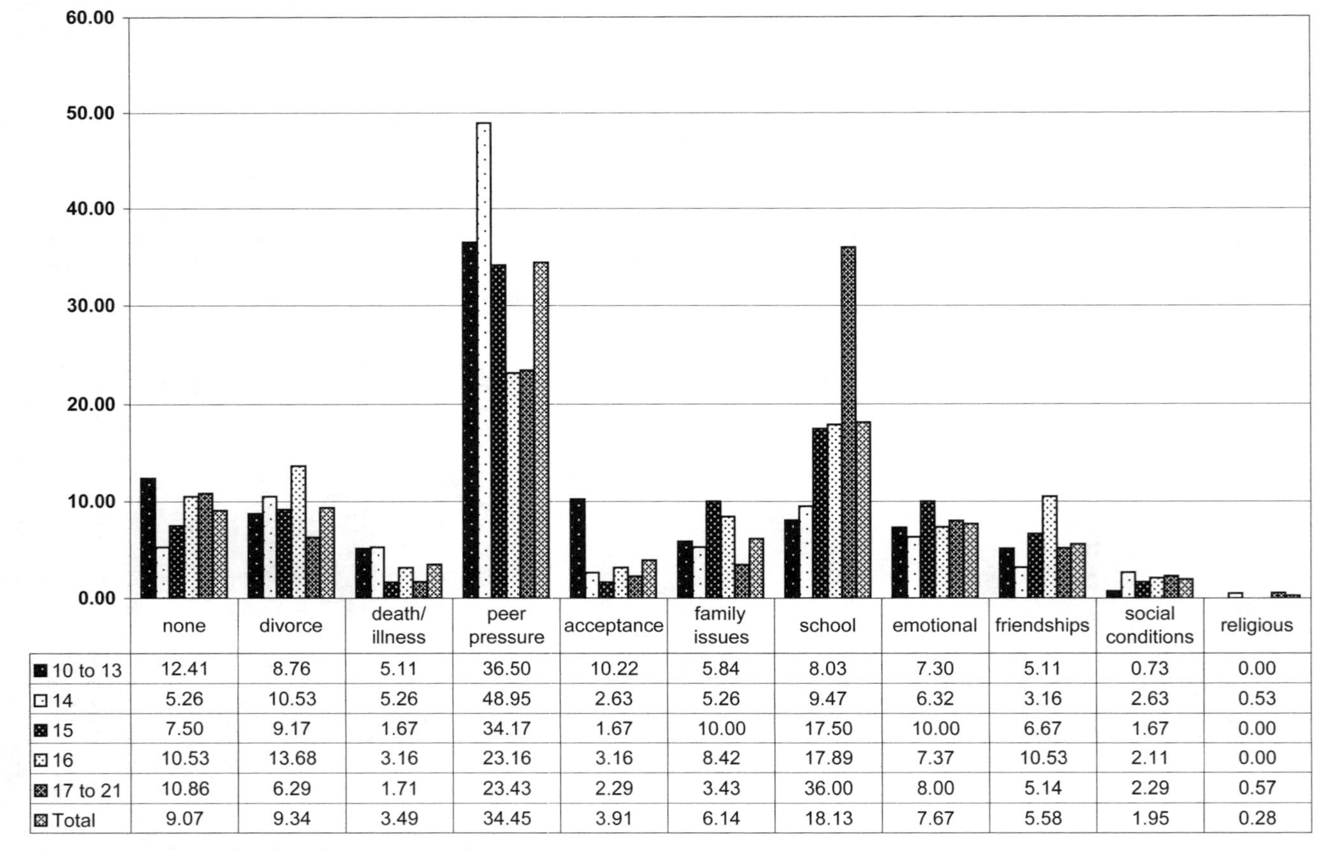

	none	divorce	death/ illness	peer pressure	acceptance	family issues	school	emotional	friendships	social conditions	religious
10 to 13	12.41	8.76	5.11	36.50	10.22	5.84	8.03	7.30	5.11	0.73	0.00
14	5.26	10.53	5.26	48.95	2.63	5.26	9.47	6.32	3.16	2.63	0.53
15	7.50	9.17	1.67	34.17	1.67	10.00	17.50	10.00	6.67	1.67	0.00
16	10.53	13.68	3.16	23.16	3.16	8.42	17.89	7.37	10.53	2.11	0.00
17 to 21	10.86	6.29	1.71	23.43	2.29	3.43	36.00	8.00	5.14	2.29	0.57
Total	9.07	9.34	3.49	34.45	3.91	6.14	18.13	7.67	5.58	1.95	0.28

Figure 1.2. Chart of Males, First Issue (% of 726)

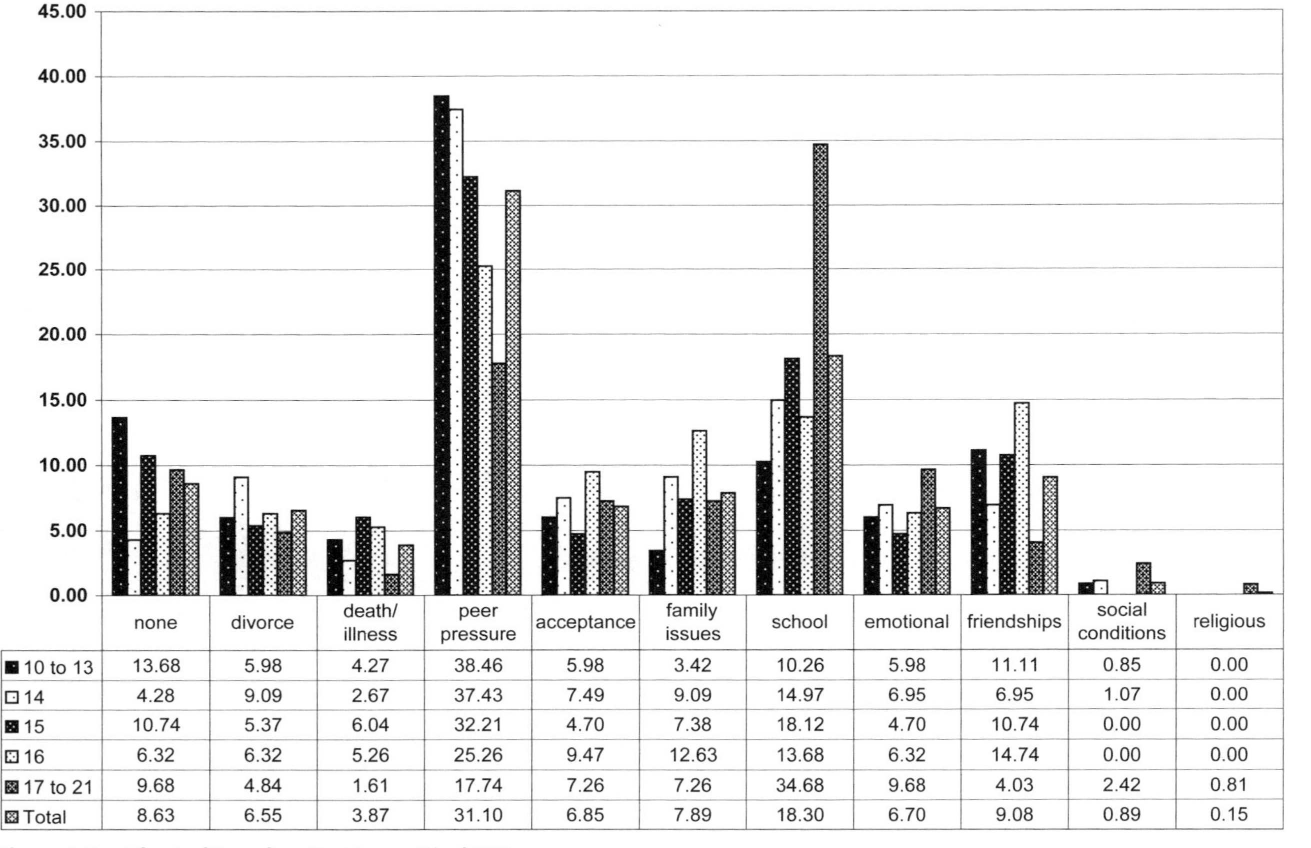

	none	divorce	death/ illness	peer pressure	acceptance	family issues	school	emotional	friendships	social conditions	religious
10 to 13	13.68	5.98	4.27	38.46	5.98	3.42	10.26	5.98	11.11	0.85	0.00
14	4.28	9.09	2.67	37.43	7.49	9.09	14.97	6.95	6.95	1.07	0.00
15	10.74	5.37	6.04	32.21	4.70	7.38	18.12	4.70	10.74	0.00	0.00
16	6.32	6.32	5.26	25.26	9.47	12.63	13.68	6.32	14.74	0.00	0.00
17 to 21	9.68	4.84	1.61	17.74	7.26	7.26	34.68	9.68	4.03	2.42	0.81
Total	8.63	6.55	3.87	31.10	6.85	7.89	18.30	6.70	9.08	0.89	0.15

Figure 1.3. Chart of Females, First Issue (% of 680)

respondents indicate this) is friendships/relationships and dating. Sixteen-year-old females are the ones of all the age groups who rank this area highest. Once again, the data are consistent with developmental stages and the psychology of adolescents. Sixteen-year-old males also rank relationships higher than other male age groups do. It was interesting to see that an issue ranking higher overall for males than friendships/relationships is emotional issues. More often than not, American culture still promotes images of tough males and "men don't cry," thus this higher rating of emotional issues could signal what teen males are actually experiencing, whether their experiences are being addressed or not. I made a conscious effort to consider books that would appeal to male teen readers; fortunately, many authors of young adult literature—Chris Crutcher, Gary Paulsen, and Robert Cormier to name a few—have written and continue to write books featuring attractive male protagonists with great appeal.

If we were to combine the percentages for the issues of divorce/separation of parents and family issues, these issues would actually rank higher than (or at least on par with) the issues related to school. Many of the books the respondents listed relate to family issues; I see this as directly related to the percentages of respondents ranking these two issues higher than several of the other issues. This category of family and parental issues is a focus of many books included in chapter 4.

The charts in figures 1.4 and 1.5, which show issues ranked second by the respondents, also reveal some insightful data. Fourteen-year-old females ranked peer pressure, school-related issues, and family-related issues significantly higher as a second issue than did their male counterparts. Peer pressure remains a dominant issue for 14-year-old and younger females, but school-related issues rate more important in the secondary issues than they did in the primary issues for females. Fifteen-year-old males ranked school-related issues and friendships/relationships highest for their second issue. This may be because, compared to 14-year-old males, more 15-year-old males are participating in athletics and are beginning dating. While 16-year-old males ranked school-related issues lower than others, they also indicated that peer pressure and friendships/relationships are greater concerns for them. Those females 16, 17, and older are clearly focused on school-related issues and friendships/relationships, while these same issues rank fairly evenly for males of the same ages. Females 16, 17, and older ranked emotional issues much higher than their male counterparts as well. The category of emotional issues includes the following: stress, pressure, depression, suicide, bulimia/anorexia, addictions, dealing with the future, moving, and finding free time.

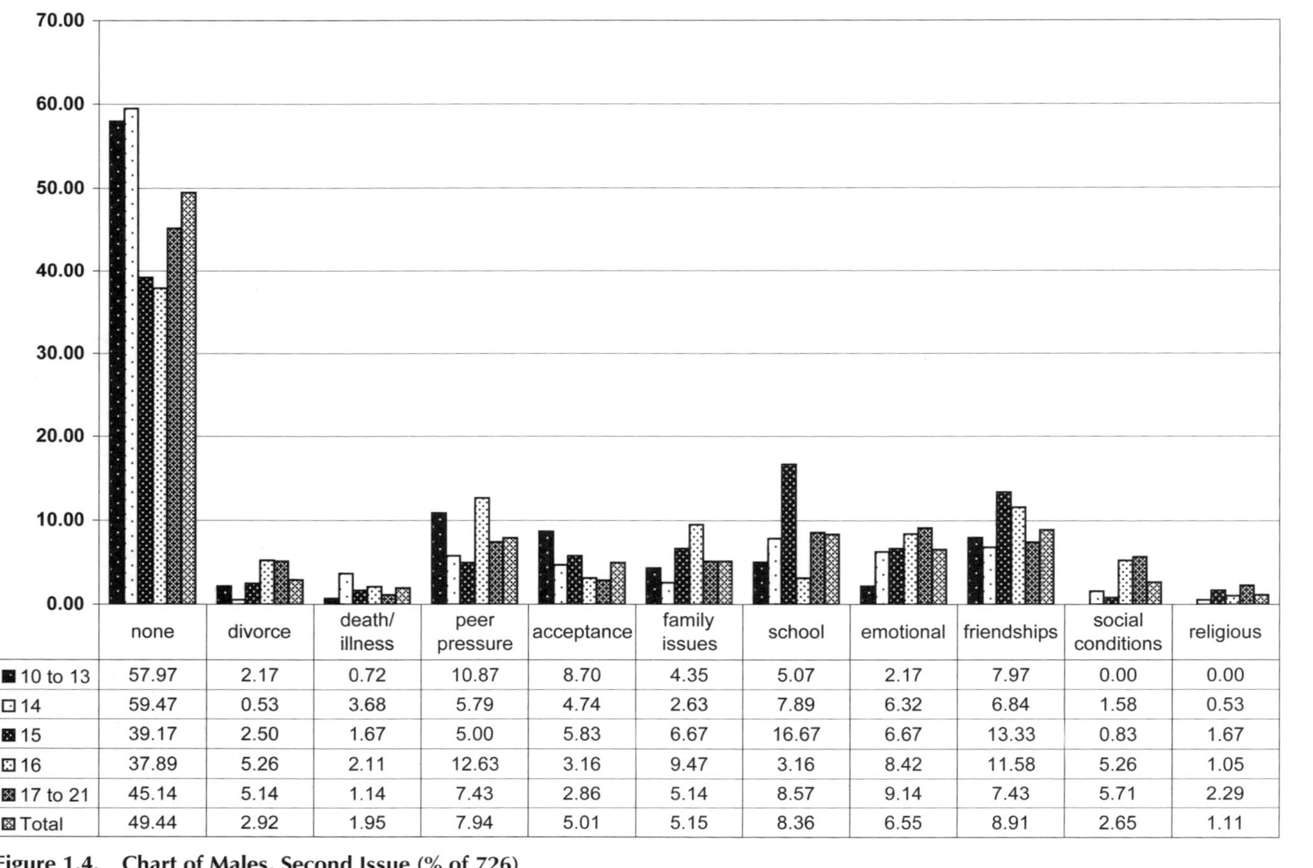

	none	divorce	death/ illness	peer pressure	acceptance	family issues	school	emotional	friendships	social conditions	religious
10 to 13	57.97	2.17	0.72	10.87	8.70	4.35	5.07	2.17	7.97	0.00	0.00
14	59.47	0.53	3.68	5.79	4.74	2.63	7.89	6.32	6.84	1.58	0.53
15	39.17	2.50	1.67	5.00	5.83	6.67	16.67	6.67	13.33	0.83	1.67
16	37.89	5.26	2.11	12.63	3.16	9.47	3.16	8.42	11.58	5.26	1.05
17 to 21	45.14	5.14	1.14	7.43	2.86	5.14	8.57	9.14	7.43	5.71	2.29
Total	49.44	2.92	1.95	7.94	5.01	5.15	8.36	6.55	8.91	2.65	1.11

Figure 1.4. Chart of Males, Second Issue (% of 726)

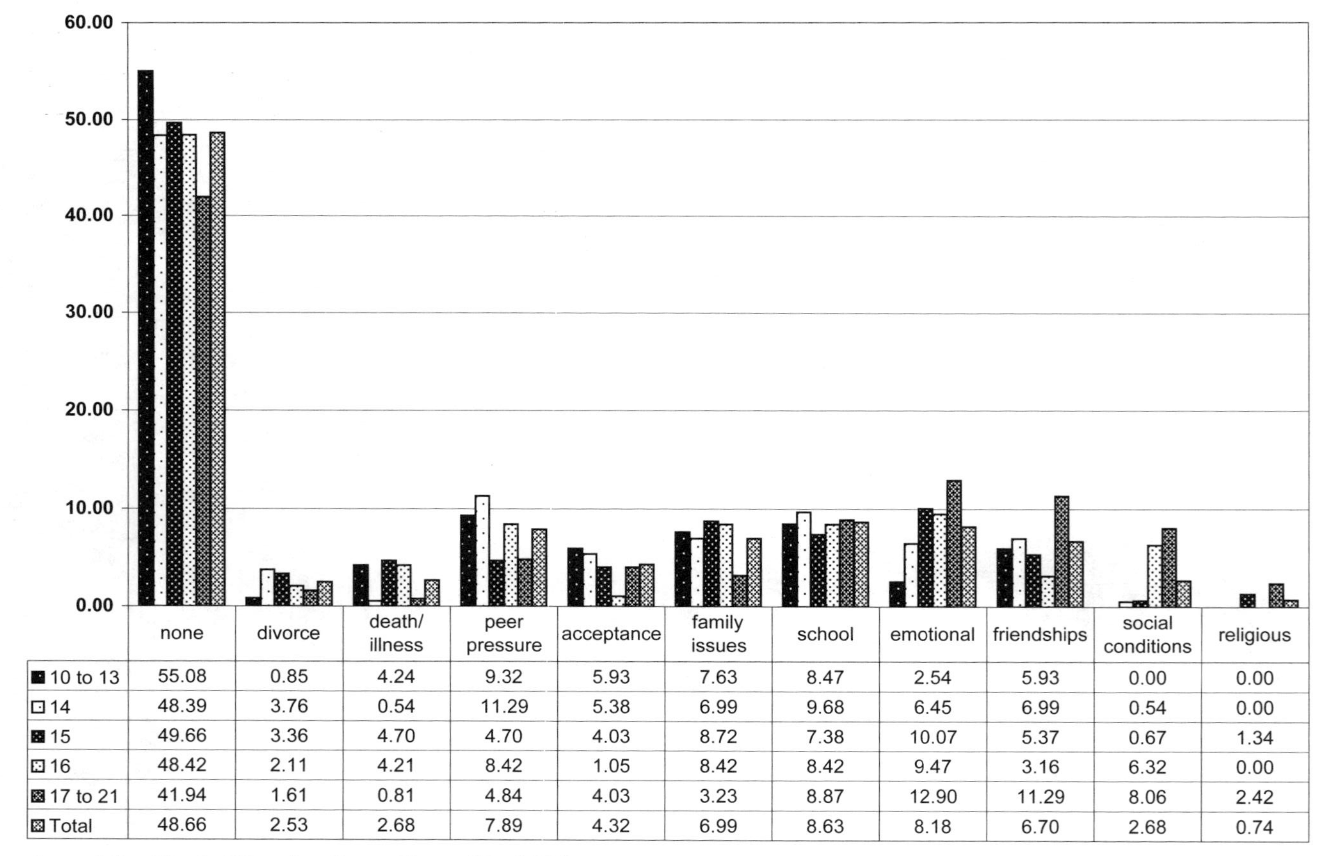

	none	divorce	death/ illness	peer pressure	acceptance	family issues	school	emotional	friendships	social conditions	religious
10 to 13	55.08	0.85	4.24	9.32	5.93	7.63	8.47	2.54	5.93	0.00	0.00
14	48.39	3.76	0.54	11.29	5.38	6.99	9.68	6.45	6.99	0.54	0.00
15	49.66	3.36	4.70	4.70	4.03	8.72	7.38	10.07	5.37	0.67	1.34
16	48.42	2.11	4.21	8.42	1.05	8.42	8.42	9.47	3.16	6.32	0.00
17 to 21	41.94	1.61	0.81	4.84	4.03	3.23	8.87	12.90	11.29	8.06	2.42
Total	48.66	2.53	2.68	7.89	4.32	6.99	8.63	8.18	6.70	2.68	0.74

Figure 1.5. Chart of Females, Second Issue (% of 680)

It is not unexpected that these issues would be of concern to females 16 and older when American culture so heavily emphasizes body image.

These charts show by gender and age what respondents listed as their first and second issues. I did not prioritize issues as I tabulated the data: whatever the respondent listed first became issue one, and so forth. The data in table 1.6 summarize responses from those who listed three or four issues.

The charts displaying the percentages for the first issue according to age groups and school size (see later in this chapter) reveal some age-specific insights. For the 10- to 13-year-olds, peer pressure ranks high regardless of size school, but in the smaller schools, presumably more rural, the issue of friendships/relationships is not as significant as it is when school size increases. One possible reason for this difference could be that in the smaller schools, students may know each other better. Fourteen-year-olds, regardless of school size, indicate throughout that peer pressure is a major issue in their lives, though the percentage is particularly high in schools under 500 and those with 1001–2000 students. The data also show that divorce/separation of parents is significant, particularly in schools of 500–1000 students. All other issues for 14-year-olds were scored as nearly negligible. Fifteen-year-olds show a rise in the school-related issues as school size increases; this result may mean that individuals know each other less and that the pressure to belong to some group is greater as school size increases.

The 16-year-olds present one striking difference from the other age groups. In schools under 500, for 16-year-olds, family issues rank nearly as high as peer pressure. If family issues were combined with divorce/separation, the percentage would actually be higher than the percent indicating peer pressure. Once again, the rural setting might influence this percentage. In many rural settings, particularly in western North Carolina, one of the primary locations from which respondents came, families are close-knit and

Table 1.6. Third and/or Fourth Issues

Ages	*Total responses*	*More than 2 issues*
12-year-olds	75	10
13-year-olds	172	24
14-year-olds	373	62
15-year olds	268	45
16-year olds	190	33
17-year-olds	239	18
18-year-olds +	60	6

important, but they also have many of the problems that families in more isolated geographical regions have. Friendships/relationships rated fairly high as an issue for the teens from schools with under 500 students and with 500–1000 students; this factor might indicate that dating is on the rise from age 16 on.

Not all that surprising, for those 17 and older the primary issue is school-related. This is the age group who are moving to college and who are confronting life after high school. The percentage of those 17 and older indicating the school-related issues rises with school size as well.

When comparing the school types, one obvious difference is the higher ranking of school-related issues for those in private or parochial schools. This factor may reflect the quality of the private and parochial schools, which focus more specifically on the college-bound. Also given that public schools are tuition free, more students from lower socioeconomic situations attend. For some of these students, education after high school is not an option or possibility. Families who send their children to private or parochial schools frequently have higher expectations of their children; for many of these adolescents, their parents have invested so much in tuition at the high school level that the parents demand their children perform well. Pressure to get good grades and to excel in sports and other extracurricular events was one of the school-related issues, and the high percentages for school-related issues bear this out.

Much of the information revealed by these various combinations of age groups, school size, and school type is not surprising. The variations in presentation of the data by combining different components, however, offer different perspectives, which is why I have included several different combinations of factors such as type of school to present the statistics. Readers should feel free to examine in detail those charts they find more relevant to the adolescents they meet and in their particular school contexts.

Question 2: Where do you go to get advice or guidance for dealing with the issues listed above?

The second question of the survey sought to identify where the teens went for sources of guidance on the issues they face. Again, I combined a range of sources into individual categories in order to process the data. Figures 1.6 to 1.9 delineate the primary and secondary sources respondents listed; the numbers for those who listed three or more sources of guidance will be cited similar to the ones above for issues. The categories for guidance sources and the

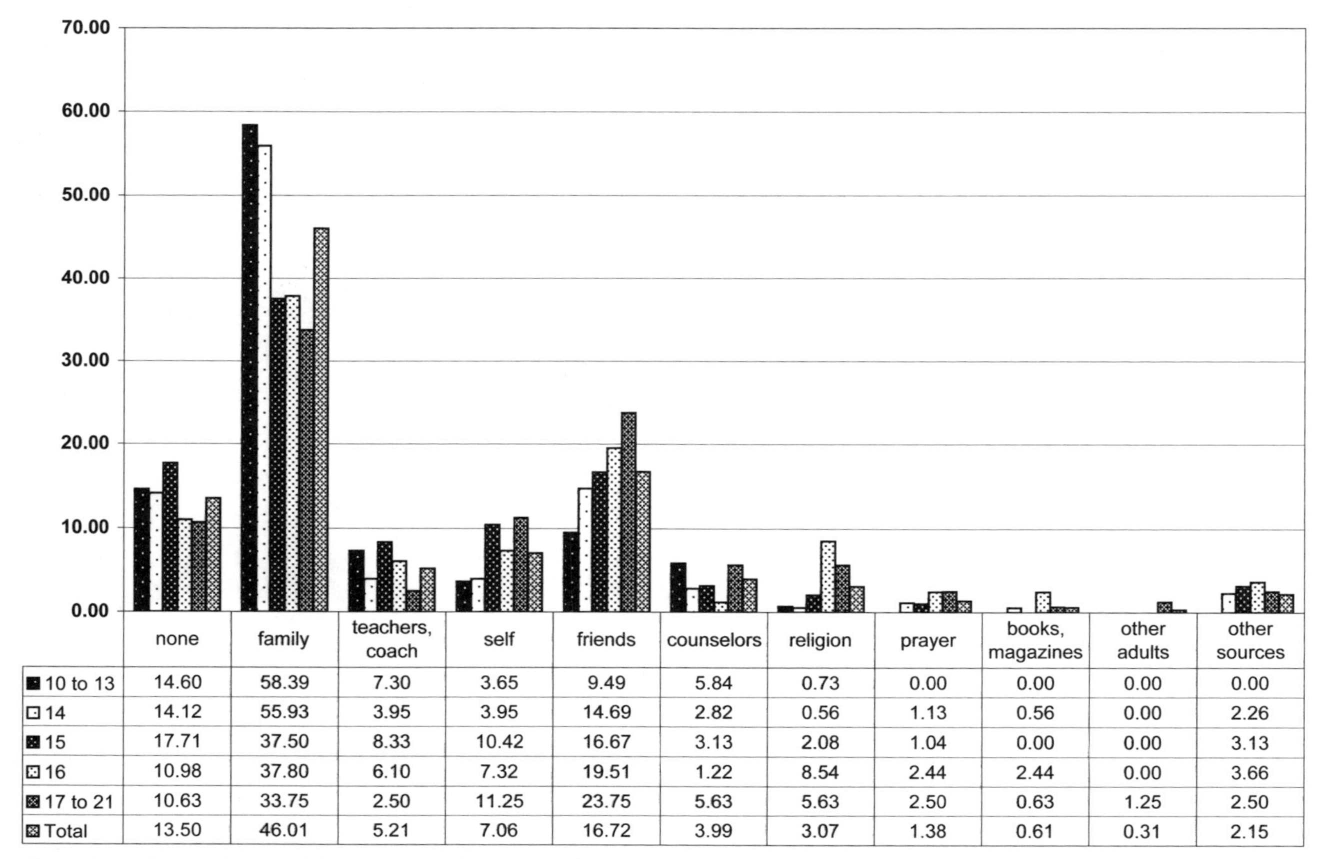

	none	family	teachers, coach	self	friends	counselors	religion	prayer	books, magazines	other adults	other sources
10 to 13	14.60	58.39	7.30	3.65	9.49	5.84	0.73	0.00	0.00	0.00	0.00
14	14.12	55.93	3.95	3.95	14.69	2.82	0.56	1.13	0.56	0.00	2.26
15	17.71	37.50	8.33	10.42	16.67	3.13	2.08	1.04	0.00	0.00	3.13
16	10.98	37.80	6.10	7.32	19.51	1.22	8.54	2.44	2.44	0.00	3.66
17 to 21	10.63	33.75	2.50	11.25	23.75	5.63	5.63	2.50	0.63	1.25	2.50
Total	13.50	46.01	5.21	7.06	16.72	3.99	3.07	1.38	0.61	0.31	2.15

Figure 1.6. Chart of Males, First Guidance Source (% of 720)

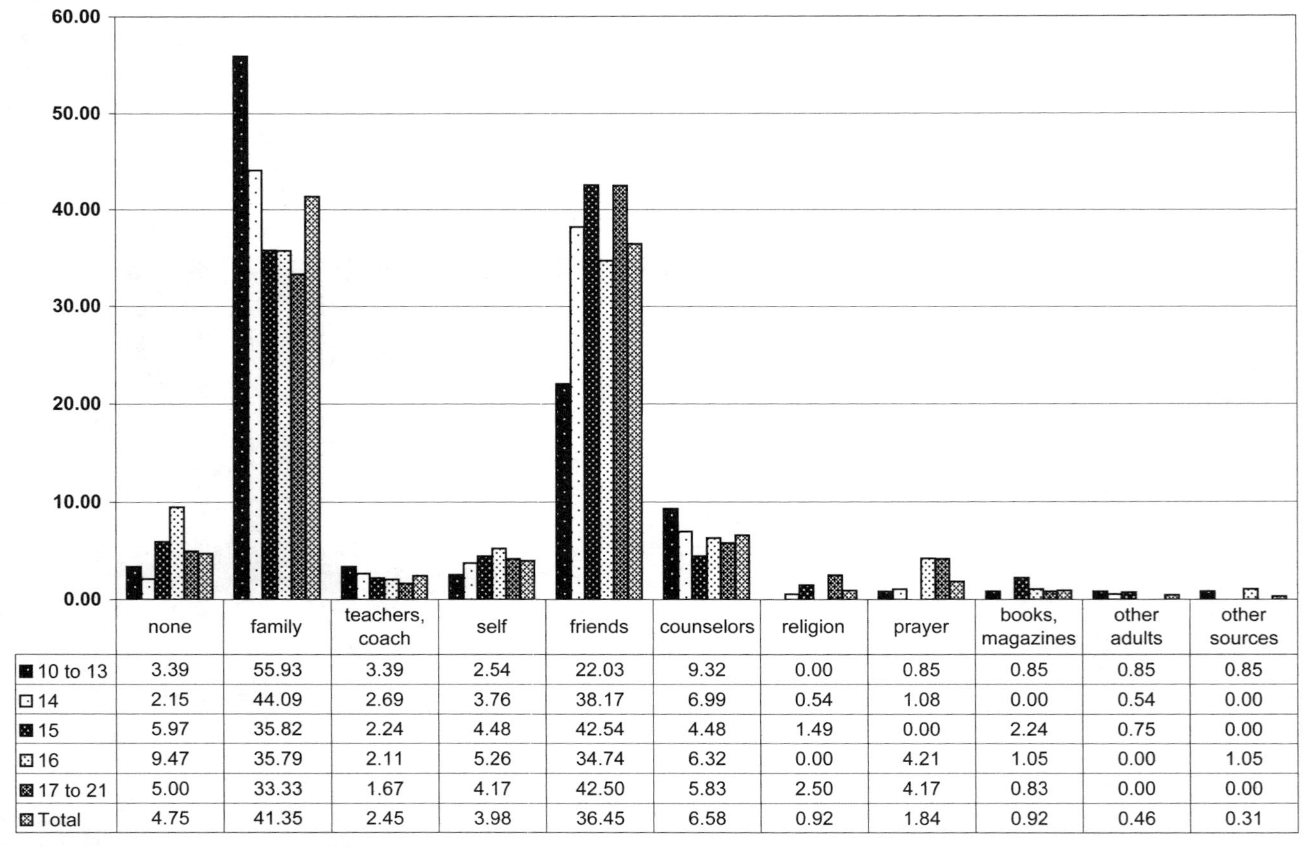

	none	family	teachers, coach	self	friends	counselors	religion	prayer	books, magazines	other adults	other sources
10 to 13	3.39	55.93	3.39	2.54	22.03	9.32	0.00	0.85	0.85	0.85	0.85
14	2.15	44.09	2.69	3.76	38.17	6.99	0.54	1.08	0.00	0.54	0.00
15	5.97	35.82	2.24	4.48	42.54	4.48	1.49	0.00	2.24	0.75	0.00
16	9.47	35.79	2.11	5.26	34.74	6.32	0.00	4.21	1.05	0.00	1.05
17 to 21	5.00	33.33	1.67	4.17	42.50	5.83	2.50	4.17	0.83	0.00	0.00
Total	4.75	41.35	2.45	3.98	36.45	6.58	0.92	1.84	0.92	0.46	0.31

Figure 1.7. Chart of Females, First Guidance Source (% of 680)

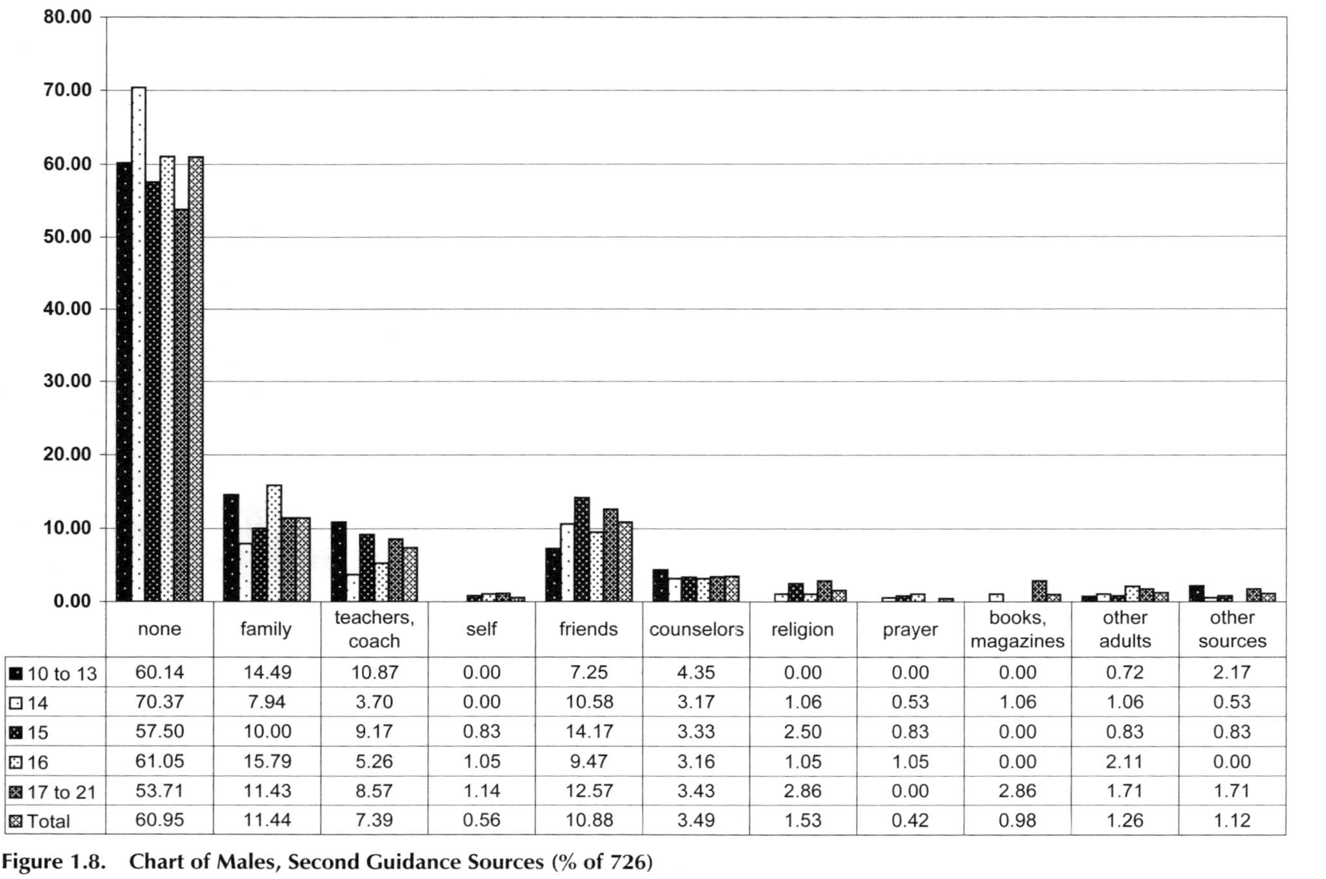

	none	family	teachers, coach	self	friends	counselors	religion	prayer	books, magazines	other adults	other sources
10 to 13	60.14	14.49	10.87	0.00	7.25	4.35	0.00	0.00	0.00	0.72	2.17
14	70.37	7.94	3.70	0.00	10.58	3.17	1.06	0.53	1.06	1.06	0.53
15	57.50	10.00	9.17	0.83	14.17	3.33	2.50	0.83	0.00	0.83	0.83
16	61.05	15.79	5.26	1.05	9.47	3.16	1.05	1.05	0.00	2.11	0.00
17 to 21	53.71	11.43	8.57	1.14	12.57	3.43	2.86	0.00	2.86	1.71	1.71
Total	60.95	11.44	7.39	0.56	10.88	3.49	1.53	0.42	0.98	1.26	1.12

Figure 1.8. Chart of Males, Second Guidance Sources (% of 726)

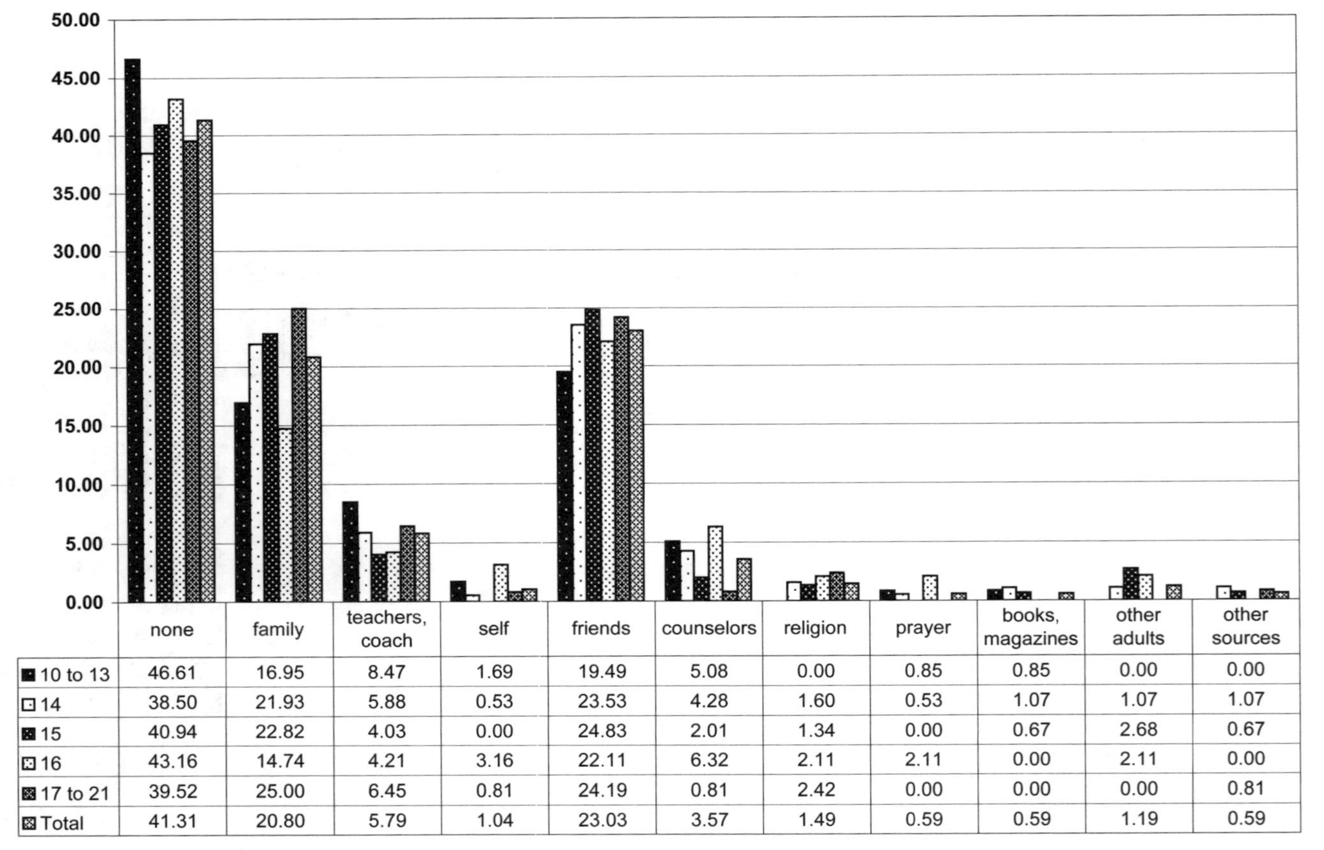

	none	family	teachers, coach	self	friends	counselors	religion	prayer	books, magazines	other adults	other sources
10 to 13	46.61	16.95	8.47	1.69	19.49	5.08	0.00	0.85	0.85	0.00	0.00
14	38.50	21.93	5.88	0.53	23.53	4.28	1.60	0.53	1.07	1.07	1.07
15	40.94	22.82	4.03	0.00	24.83	2.01	1.34	0.00	0.67	2.68	0.67
16	43.16	14.74	4.21	3.16	22.11	6.32	2.11	2.11	0.00	2.11	0.00
17 to 21	39.52	25.00	6.45	0.81	24.19	0.81	2.42	0.00	0.00	0.00	0.81
Total	41.31	20.80	5.79	1.04	23.03	3.57	1.49	0.59	0.59	1.19	0.59

Figure 1.9. Chart of Females, Second Guidance Source (% of 680)

overall number of respondents indicating each category as the primary source of guidance are listed in table 1.7.

Figures 1.6 through 1.9 do not denote the number of respondents who said they have no source of guidance or do not choose to go to any particular guidance source, though there were some respondents stating they did not go to any source for guidance. For both males and females, family members (not solely parents, though parents were listed frequently) are the first source for guidance. As might be expected, 10- to 13-year-olds, regardless of gender, most frequently listed parents and family as the first choice for guidance; friends as a primary source of guidance is the next highest, though the percentage is significantly lower than for family. For all older adolescents, the difference between the percentages for "family" and "friends" is less significant. Again, adolescent psychology suggests that later adolescence is the stage when teens are moving toward greater independence from parents, so the percentage change is consonant with psychological studies.

Regarding type of school and the guidance sources selected, it is important to take into account that far more respondents attend public schools than private or parochial schools (refer back to table 1.2). For certain age groups, however, there are some differences. For example, the number of 15-year-olds who indicate family as their first guidance source is significantly lower for those in public schools than for those 15-year-olds in parochial schools. Thirteen-year-olds in public schools rated family much higher than friends/

Table 1.7 Categories of Guidance Sources and Number Indicating Category as a Primary Source of Guidance

Type of guidance	*Primary source*
Parents, siblings, grandparents/relatives	574
Teachers, coaches, principals	51
Self	72
Friends, peers	350
Guidance or professional counselors	69
Church, the Bible, pastors/ministers/priests, youth ministers, DARE	27
Jesus/God, prayer	21
Books, journaling, magazines	10
Neighbors, older adults, someone who can be trusted, scout leaders	5
Others: Internet, newscasts, TV, music, movies, running, solitude time, pets, plants	17
Total	1196

peers as sources of guidance compared to their counterparts in either private or parochial schools. Again, these additional combinations of data are provided to give more perspectives on the data.

Many respondents listed only one source of guidance, which accounts for the high percentages of "none" in figures 1.8 and 1.9 presenting the second listed guidance sources. Many teens of all ages indicated they almost equally would go to family or friends for guidance. Sixteen-year-old females go to friends more often than to family. The number of males listing only one source of guidance is higher than for females, which is evident in the high percentage for "None" in figure 1.8.

The number of respondents within each age group that listed more than two sources of guidance is shown in table 1.8. For example, 75 12-year-olds participated in the survey and 11 gave more than two sources of guidance.

The data from Questions 1 and 2 are presented in several other combinations to allow for other interpretations. Readers are encouraged to explore the charts (figures 1.10 through 1.23) that most interest them. The data combined in figures 1.10–1.12 are type of school, age group, and percent of respondents identifying each issue as their primary issue. The data presented in figures 1.13–1.16 show school size, age group, and percent of respondents identifying each issue as their primary issue. These figures present type of school, age group, and first guidance source. The data combined in figures 1.20–1.23 are size of school, age group, and first guidance source.

Table 1.8. Those Listing More Than Two Guidance Sources

Ages	*Participants*	*More than two sources*
12-year-olds	75	11
13-year-olds	172	24
14-year-olds	373	54
15-year-olds	268	25
16-year-olds	190	23
17-year-olds	239	37
18-year-olds +	60	11

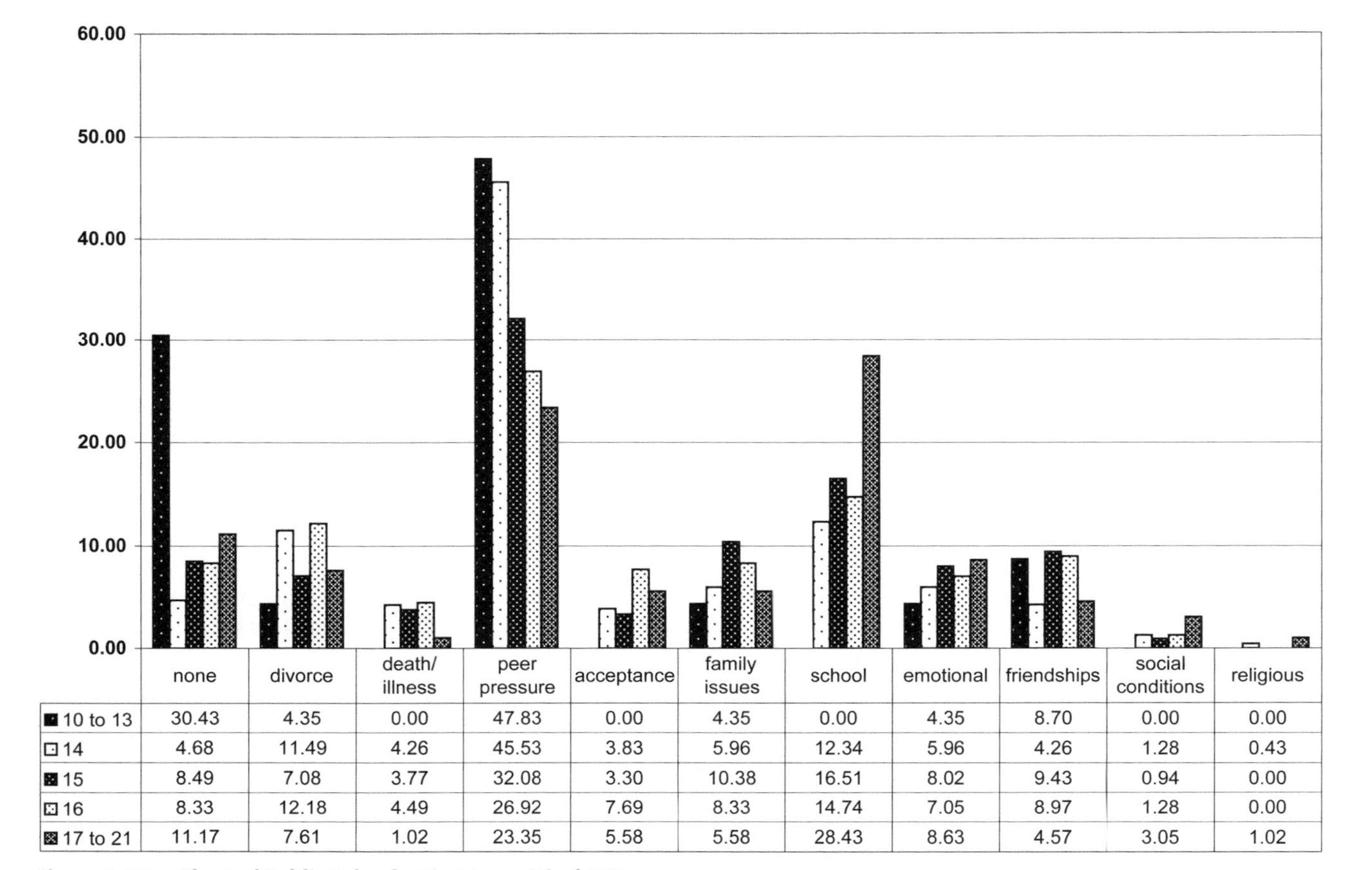

	none	divorce	death/ illness	peer pressure	acceptance	family issues	school	emotional	friendships	social conditions	religious
10 to 13	30.43	4.35	0.00	47.83	0.00	4.35	0.00	4.35	8.70	0.00	0.00
14	4.68	11.49	4.26	45.53	3.83	5.96	12.34	5.96	4.26	1.28	0.43
15	8.49	7.08	3.77	32.08	3.30	10.38	16.51	8.02	9.43	0.94	0.00
16	8.33	12.18	4.49	26.92	7.69	8.33	14.74	7.05	8.97	1.28	0.00
17 to 21	11.17	7.61	1.02	23.35	5.58	5.58	28.43	8.63	4.57	3.05	1.02

Figure 1.10. Chart of Public Schools, First Issue (% of 837)

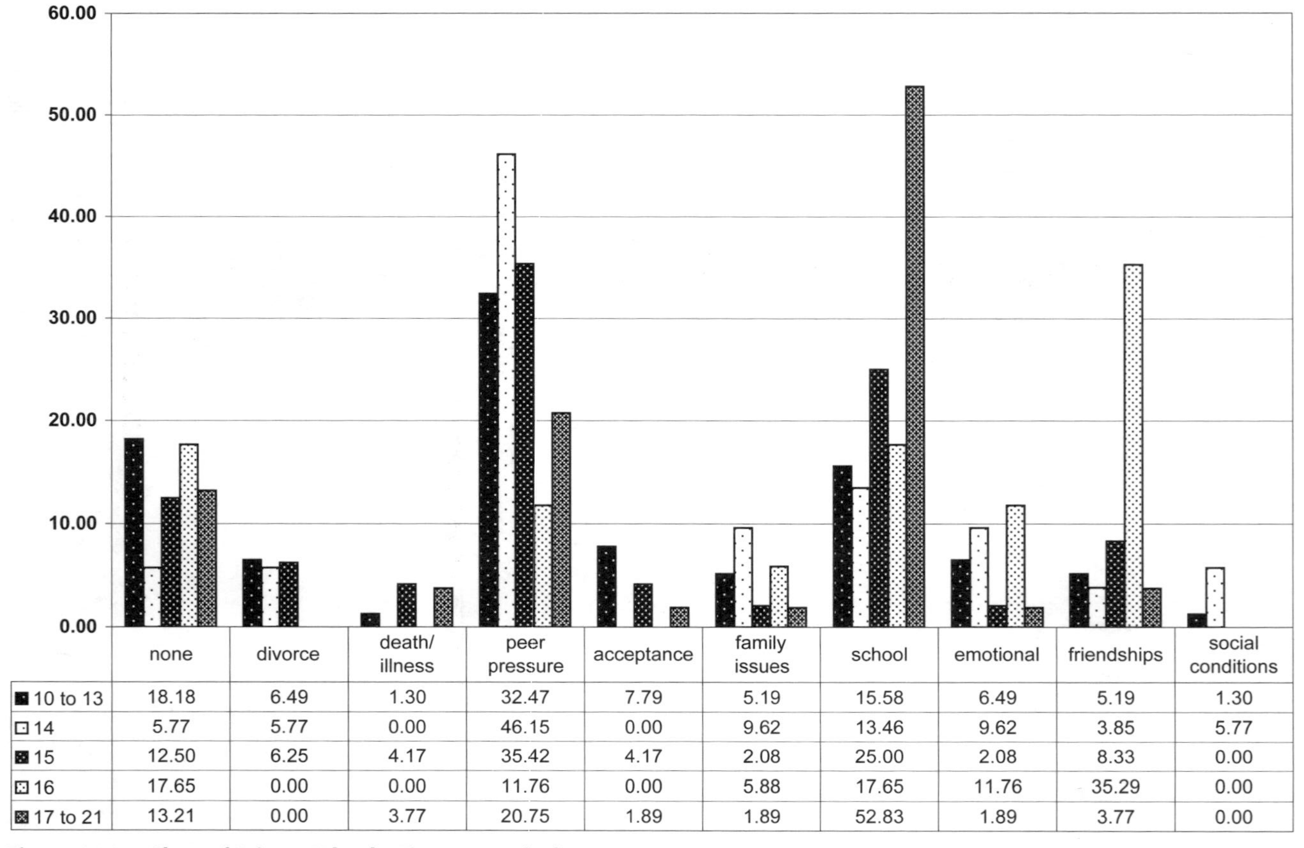

	none	divorce	death/ illness	peer pressure	acceptance	family issues	school	emotional	friendships	social conditions
10 to 13	18.18	6.49	1.30	32.47	7.79	5.19	15.58	6.49	5.19	1.30
14	5.77	5.77	0.00	46.15	0.00	9.62	13.46	9.62	3.85	5.77
15	12.50	6.25	4.17	35.42	4.17	2.08	25.00	2.08	8.33	0.00
16	17.65	0.00	0.00	11.76	0.00	5.88	17.65	11.76	35.29	0.00
17 to 21	13.21	0.00	3.77	20.75	1.89	1.89	52.83	1.89	3.77	0.00

Figure 1.11. Chart of Private Schools, First Issue (% of 249)

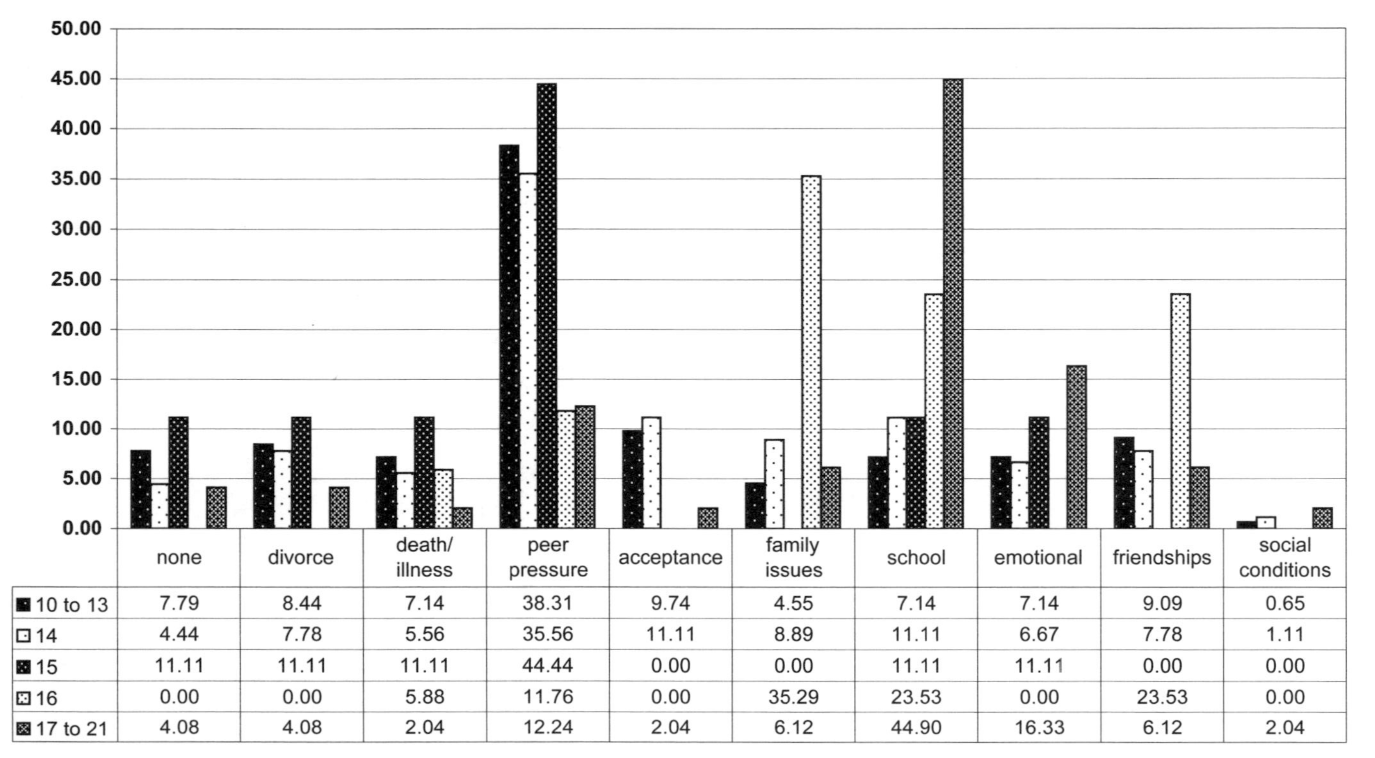

	none	divorce	death/ illness	peer pressure	acceptance	family issues	school	emotional	friendships	social conditions
10 to 13	7.79	8.44	7.14	38.31	9.74	4.55	7.14	7.14	9.09	0.65
14	4.44	7.78	5.56	35.56	11.11	8.89	11.11	6.67	7.78	1.11
15	11.11	11.11	11.11	44.44	0.00	0.00	11.11	11.11	0.00	0.00
16	0.00	0.00	5.88	11.76	0.00	35.29	23.53	0.00	23.53	0.00
17 to 21	4.08	4.08	2.04	12.24	2.04	6.12	44.90	16.33	6.12	2.04

Figure 1.12. Chart of Parochial Schools, First Issue (% of 320)

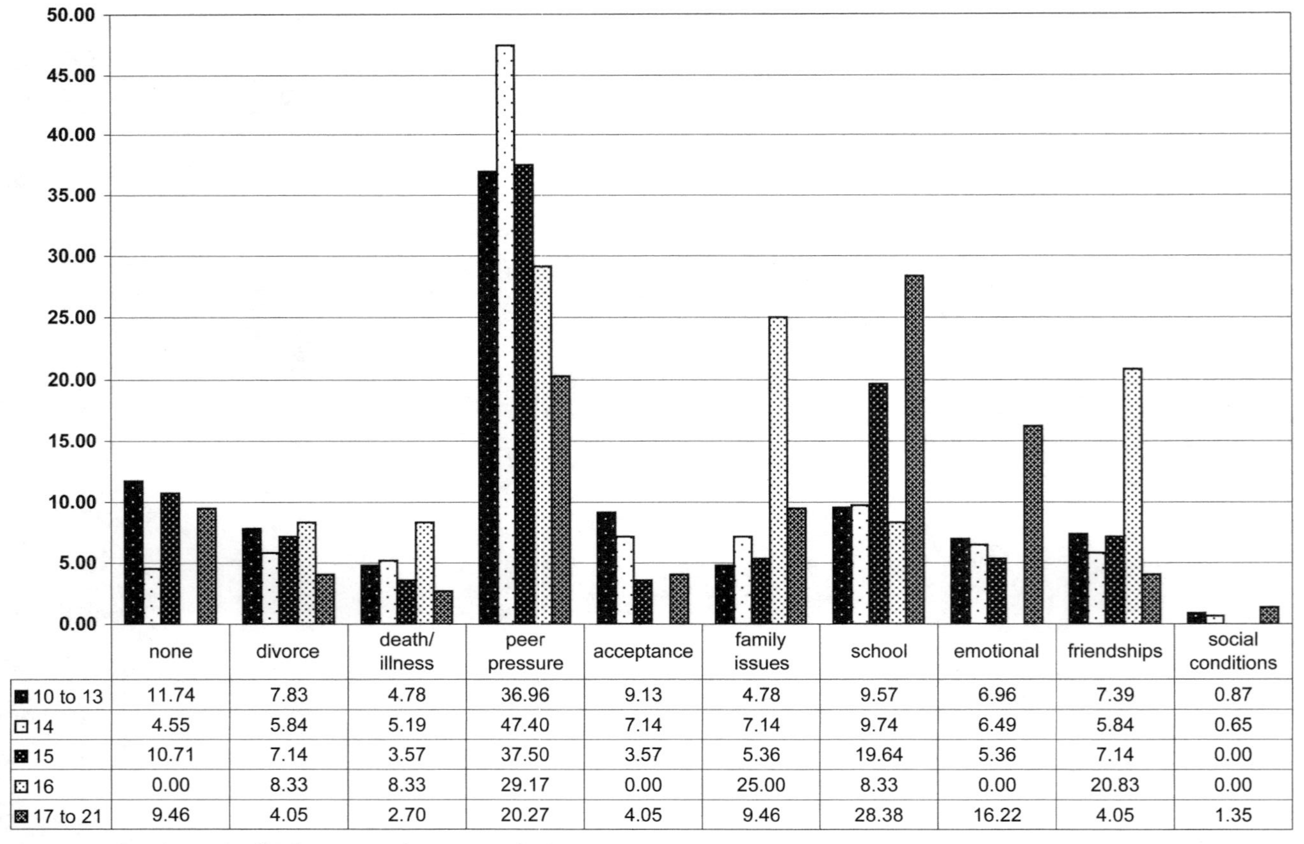

	none	divorce	death/ illness	peer pressure	acceptance	family issues	school	emotional	friendships	social conditions
10 to 13	11.74	7.83	4.78	36.96	9.13	4.78	9.57	6.96	7.39	0.87
14	4.55	5.84	5.19	47.40	7.14	7.14	9.74	6.49	5.84	0.65
15	10.71	7.14	3.57	37.50	3.57	5.36	19.64	5.36	7.14	0.00
16	0.00	8.33	8.33	29.17	0.00	25.00	8.33	0.00	20.83	0.00
17 to 21	9.46	4.05	2.70	20.27	4.05	9.46	28.38	16.22	4.05	1.35

Figure 1.13. Chart of Schools < 500, First Issue (% of 543)

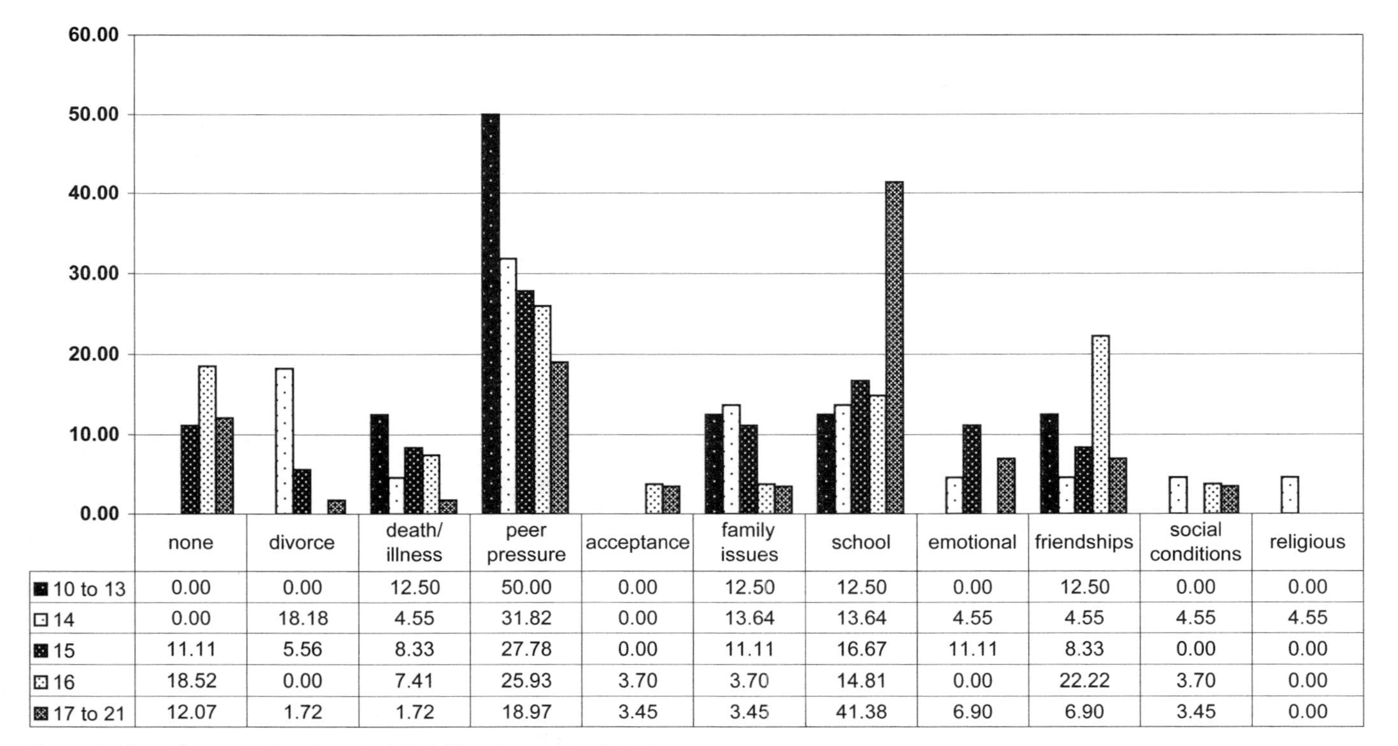

	none	divorce	death/ illness	peer pressure	acceptance	family issues	school	emotional	friendships	social conditions	religious
10 to 13	0.00	0.00	12.50	50.00	0.00	12.50	12.50	0.00	12.50	0.00	0.00
14	0.00	18.18	4.55	31.82	0.00	13.64	13.64	4.55	4.55	4.55	4.55
15	11.11	5.56	8.33	27.78	0.00	11.11	16.67	11.11	8.33	0.00	0.00
16	18.52	0.00	7.41	25.93	3.70	3.70	14.81	0.00	22.22	3.70	0.00
17 to 21	12.07	1.72	1.72	18.97	3.45	3.45	41.38	6.90	6.90	3.45	0.00

Figure 1.14. Chart of Schools 500–1000, First Issue (% of 543)

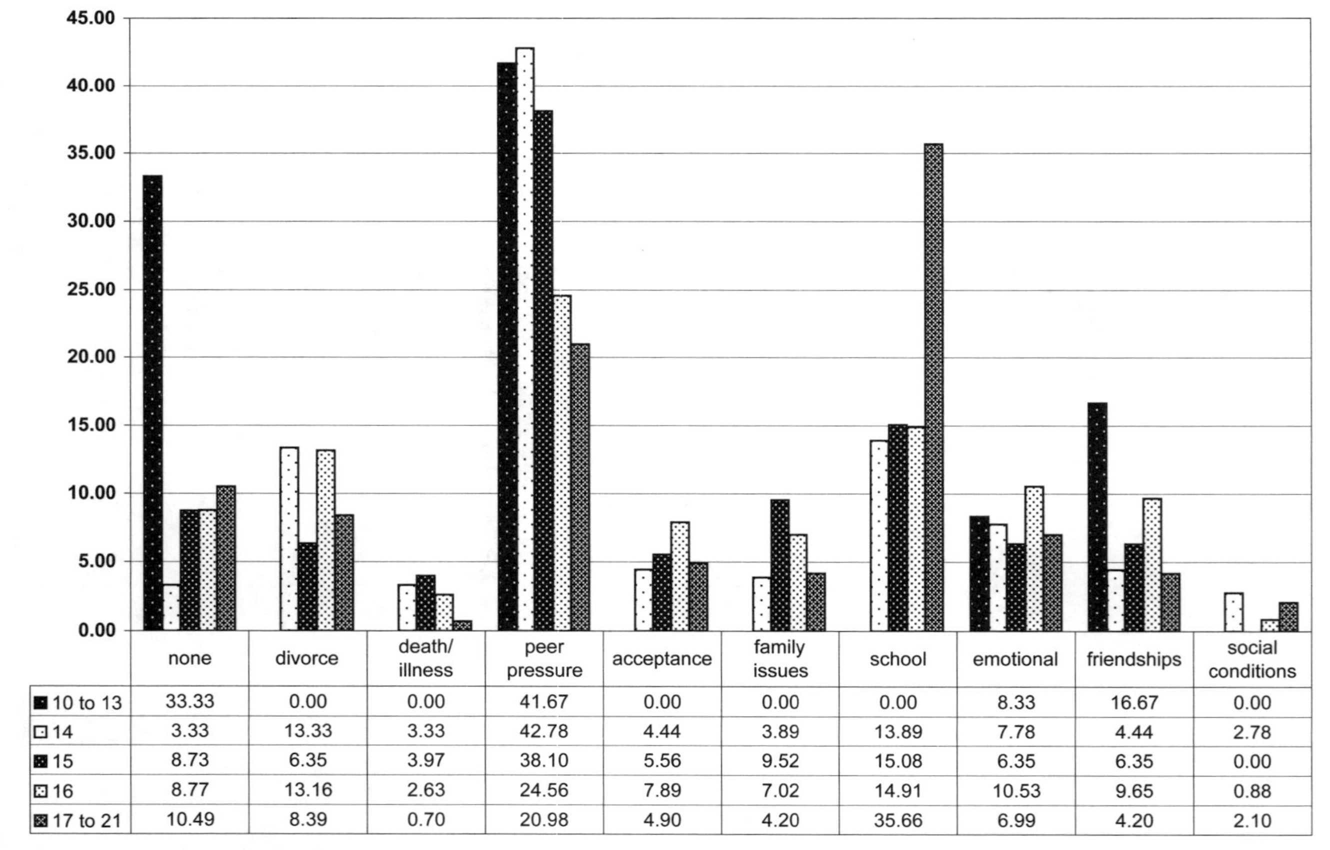

	none	divorce	death/ illness	peer pressure	acceptance	family issues	school	emotional	friendships	social conditions
10 to 13	33.33	0.00	0.00	41.67	0.00	0.00	0.00	8.33	16.67	0.00
14	3.33	13.33	3.33	42.78	4.44	3.89	13.89	7.78	4.44	2.78
15	8.73	6.35	3.97	38.10	5.56	9.52	15.08	6.35	6.35	0.00
16	8.77	13.16	2.63	24.56	7.89	7.02	14.91	10.53	9.65	0.88
17 to 21	10.49	8.39	0.70	20.98	4.90	4.20	35.66	6.99	4.20	2.10

Figure 1.15. Chart of Schools 1001–2000, First Issue (% of 543)

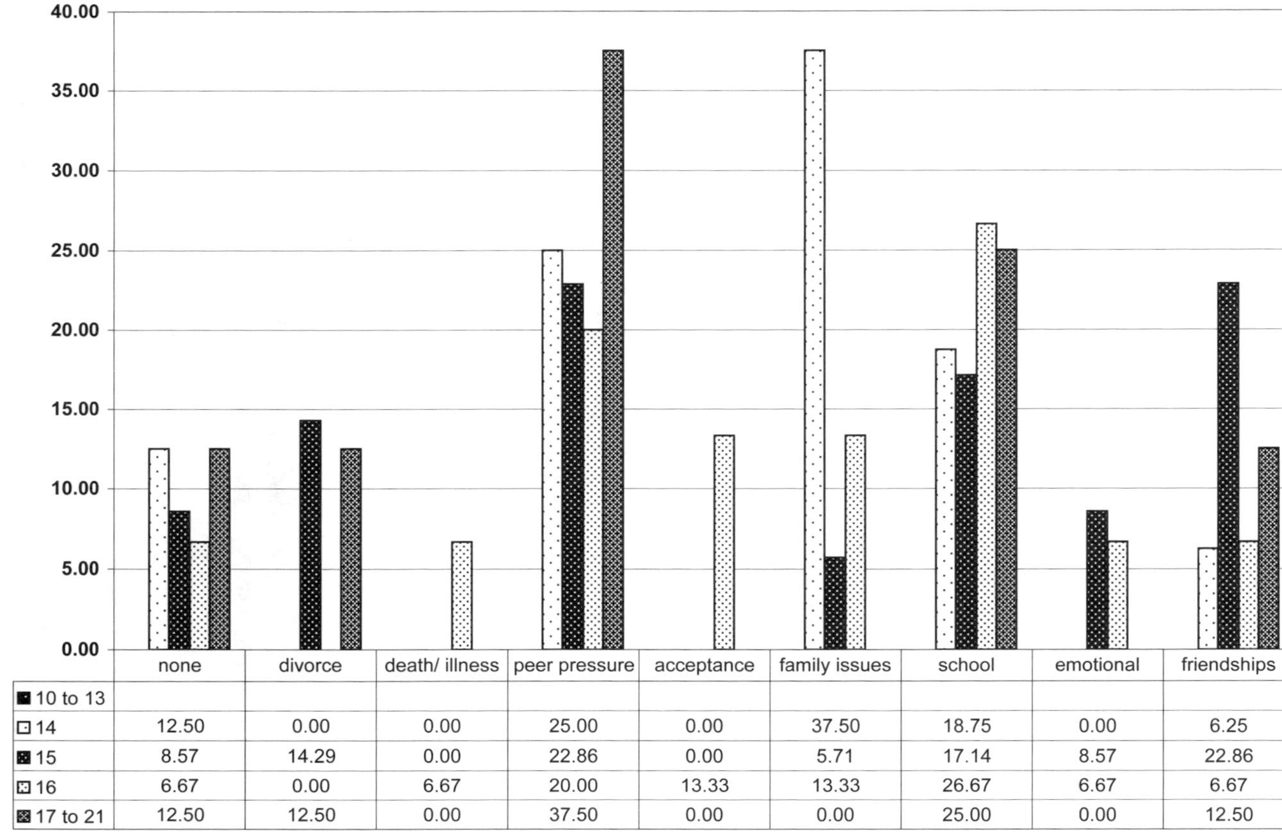

	none	divorce	death/ illness	peer pressure	acceptance	family issues	school	emotional	friendships
10 to 13									
14	12.50	0.00	0.00	25.00	0.00	37.50	18.75	0.00	6.25
15	8.57	14.29	0.00	22.86	0.00	5.71	17.14	8.57	22.86
16	6.67	0.00	6.67	20.00	13.33	13.33	26.67	6.67	6.67
17 to 21	12.50	12.50	0.00	37.50	0.00	0.00	25.00	0.00	12.50

Figure 1.16. Chart of Schools > 2000, First Issue (% of 543)

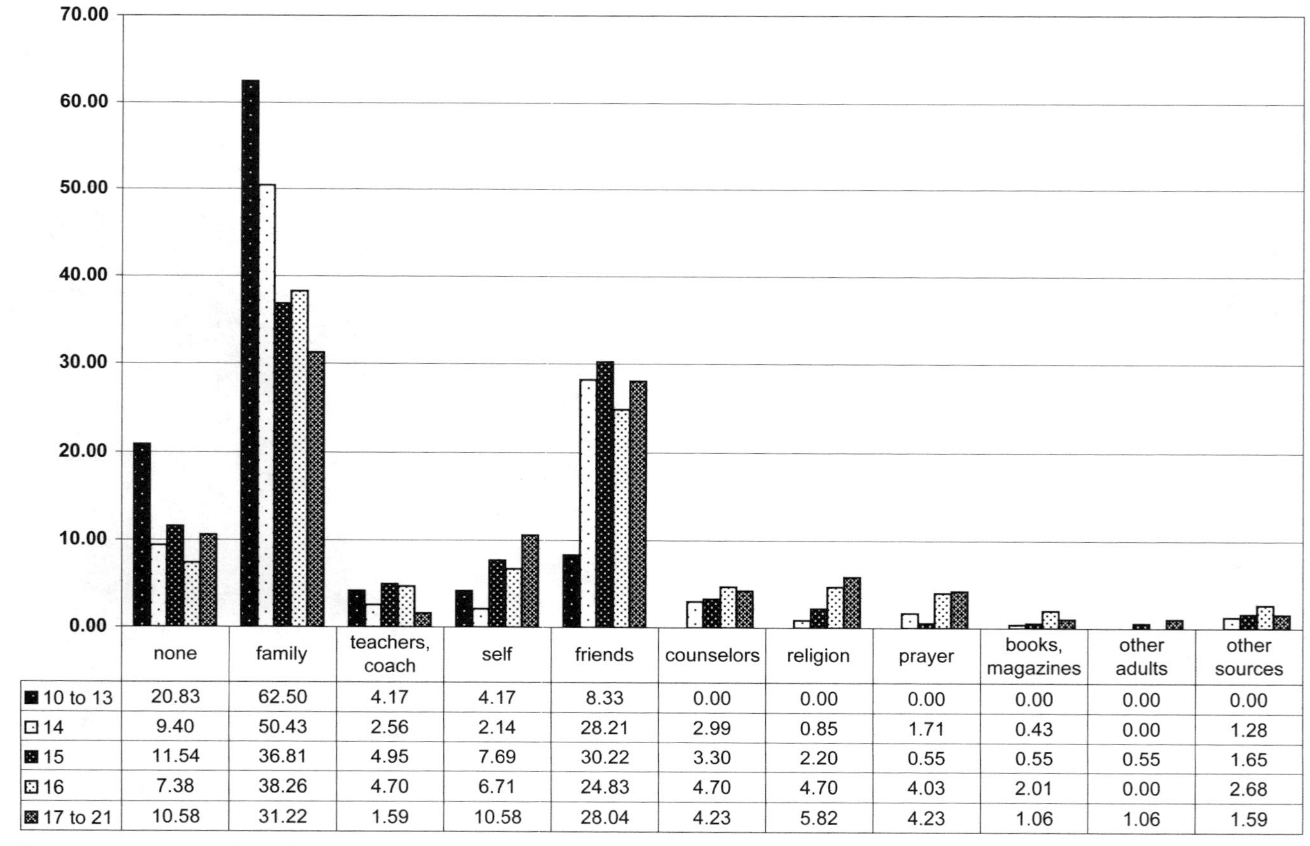

	none	family	teachers, coach	self	friends	counselors	religion	prayer	books, magazines	other adults	other sources
10 to 13	20.83	62.50	4.17	4.17	8.33	0.00	0.00	0.00	0.00	0.00	0.00
14	9.40	50.43	2.56	2.14	28.21	2.99	0.85	1.71	0.43	0.00	1.28
15	11.54	36.81	4.95	7.69	30.22	3.30	2.20	0.55	0.55	0.55	1.65
16	7.38	38.26	4.70	6.71	24.83	4.70	4.70	4.03	2.01	0.00	2.68
17 to 21	10.58	31.22	1.59	10.58	28.04	4.23	5.82	4.23	1.06	1.06	1.59

Figure 1.17. Chart of Public Schools, First Guidance Source (% of 837)

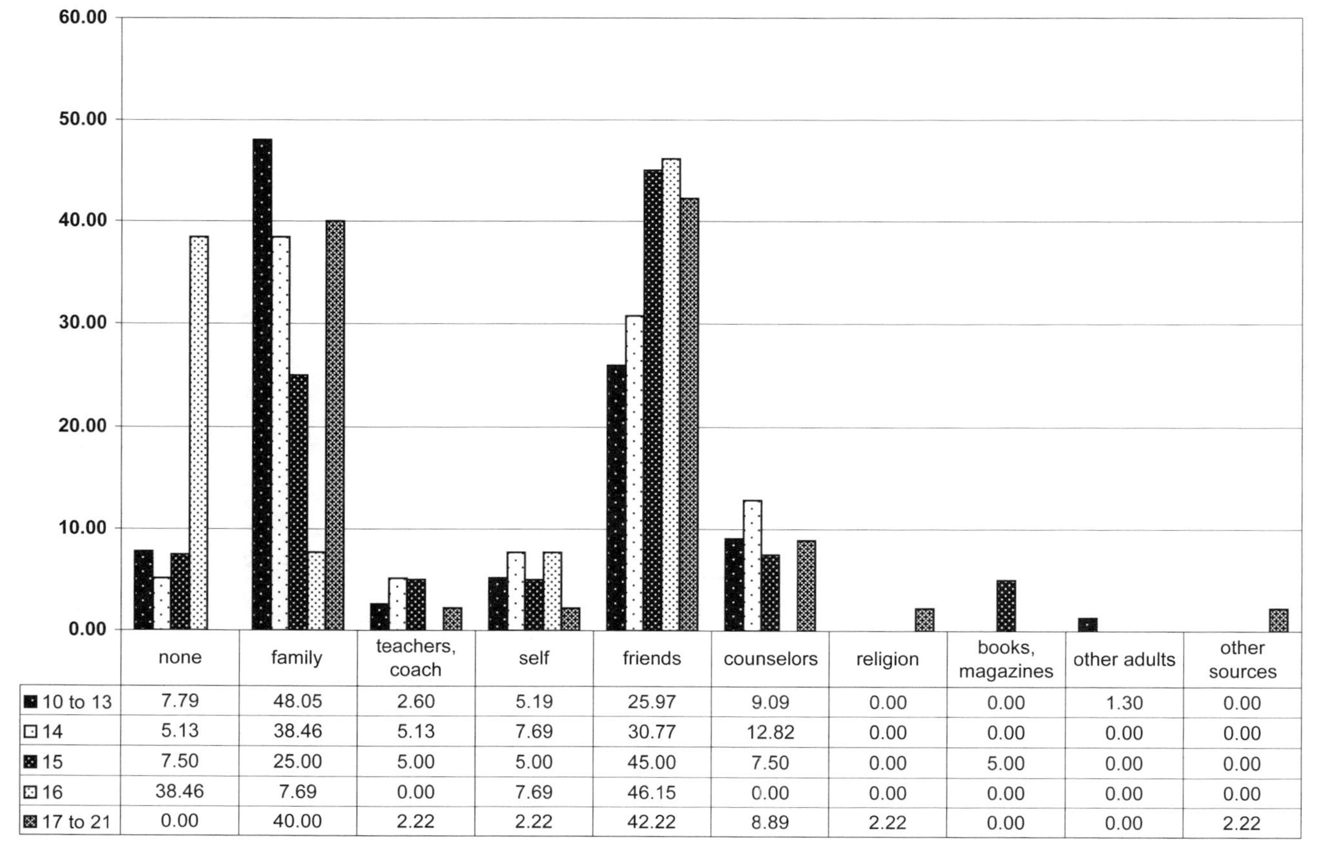

	none	family	teachers, coach	self	friends	counselors	religion	books, magazines	other adults	other sources
10 to 13	7.79	48.05	2.60	5.19	25.97	9.09	0.00	0.00	1.30	0.00
14	5.13	38.46	5.13	7.69	30.77	12.82	0.00	0.00	0.00	0.00
15	7.50	25.00	5.00	5.00	45.00	7.50	0.00	5.00	0.00	0.00
16	38.46	7.69	0.00	7.69	46.15	0.00	0.00	0.00	0.00	0.00
17 to 21	0.00	40.00	2.22	2.22	42.22	8.89	2.22	0.00	0.00	2.22

Figure 1.18. Chart of Private Schools, First Guidance Source (% of 249)

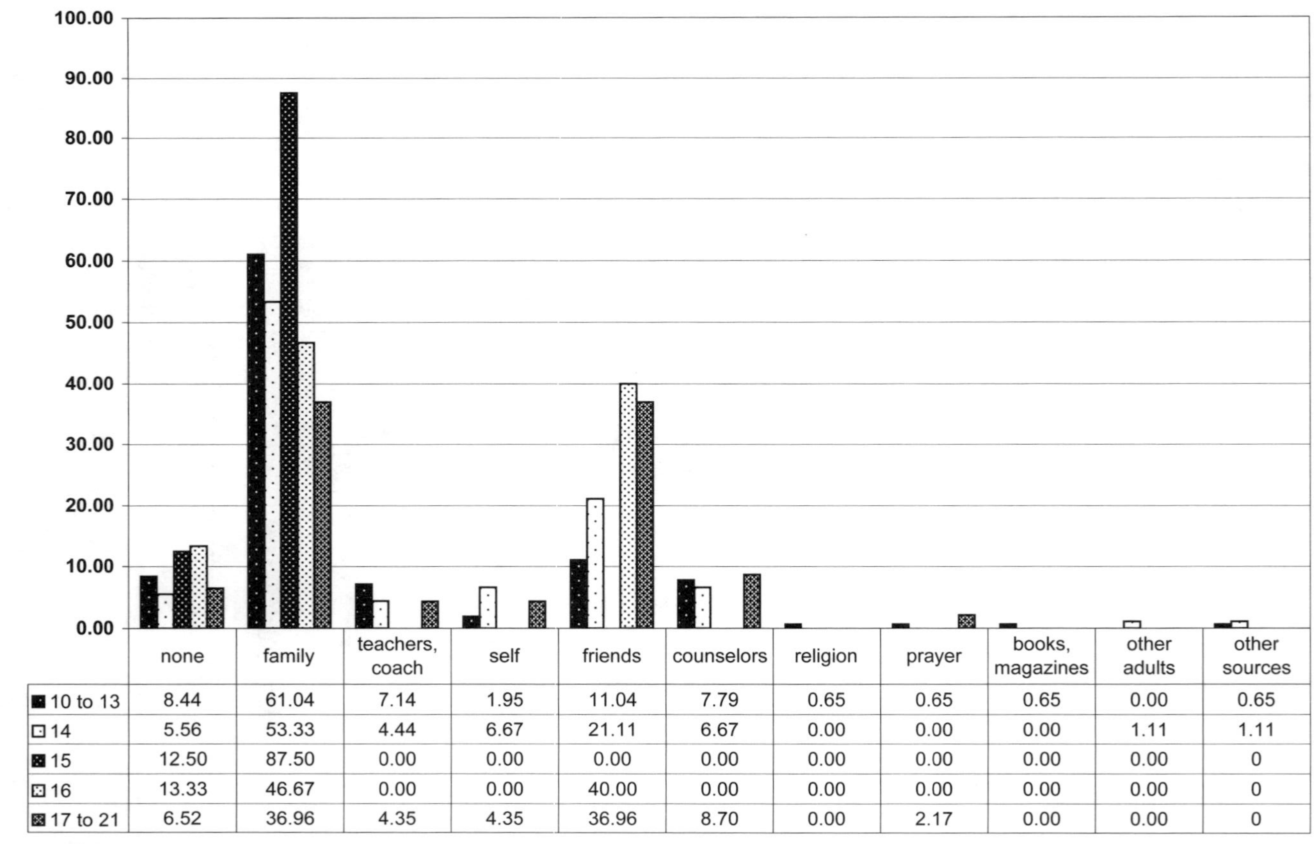

	none	family	teachers, coach	self	friends	counselors	religion	prayer	books, magazines	other adults	other sources
10 to 13	8.44	61.04	7.14	1.95	11.04	7.79	0.65	0.65	0.65	0.00	0.65
14	5.56	53.33	4.44	6.67	21.11	6.67	0.00	0.00	0.00	1.11	1.11
15	12.50	87.50	0.00	0.00	0.00	0.00	0.00	0.00	0.00	0.00	0
16	13.33	46.67	0.00	0.00	40.00	0.00	0.00	0.00	0.00	0.00	0
17 to 21	6.52	36.96	4.35	4.35	36.96	8.70	0.00	2.17	0.00	0.00	0

Figure 1.19. Chart of Parochial Schools, First Guidance Source (% of 320)

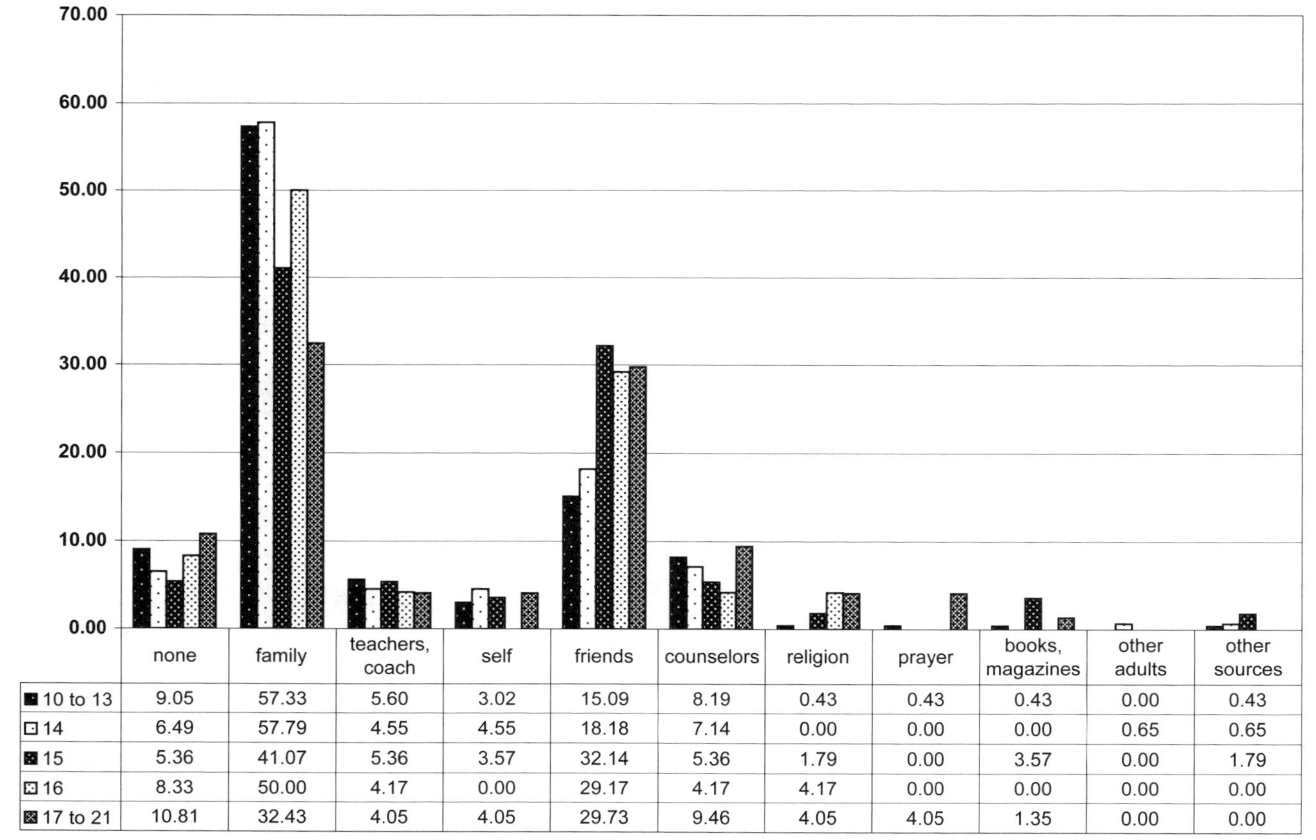

	none	family	teachers, coach	self	friends	counselors	religion	prayer	books, magazines	other adults	other sources
10 to 13	9.05	57.33	5.60	3.02	15.09	8.19	0.43	0.43	0.43	0.00	0.43
14	6.49	57.79	4.55	4.55	18.18	7.14	0.00	0.00	0.00	0.65	0.65
15	5.36	41.07	5.36	3.57	32.14	5.36	1.79	0.00	3.57	0.00	1.79
16	8.33	50.00	4.17	0.00	29.17	4.17	4.17	0.00	0.00	0.00	0.00
17 to 21	10.81	32.43	4.05	4.05	29.73	9.46	4.05	4.05	1.35	0.00	0.00

Figure 1.20. Chart of Schools < 500, First Guidance Source (% of 543)

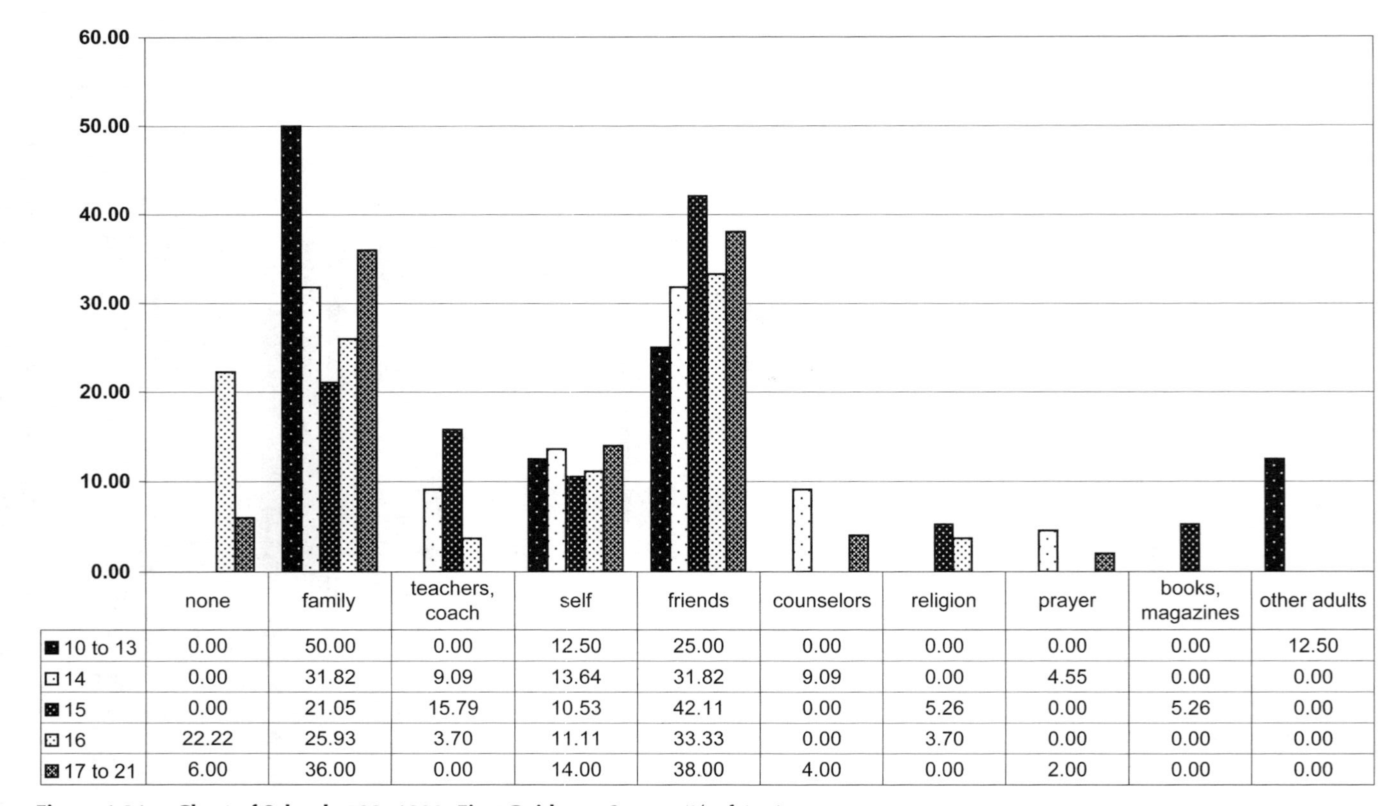

	none	family	teachers, coach	self	friends	counselors	religion	prayer	books, magazines	other adults
10 to 13	0.00	50.00	0.00	12.50	25.00	0.00	0.00	0.00	0.00	12.50
14	0.00	31.82	9.09	13.64	31.82	9.09	0.00	4.55	0.00	0.00
15	0.00	21.05	15.79	10.53	42.11	0.00	5.26	0.00	5.26	0.00
16	22.22	25.93	3.70	11.11	33.33	0.00	3.70	0.00	0.00	0.00
17 to 21	6.00	36.00	0.00	14.00	38.00	4.00	0.00	2.00	0.00	0.00

Figure 1.21. Chart of Schools 500–1000, First Guidance Source (% of 177)

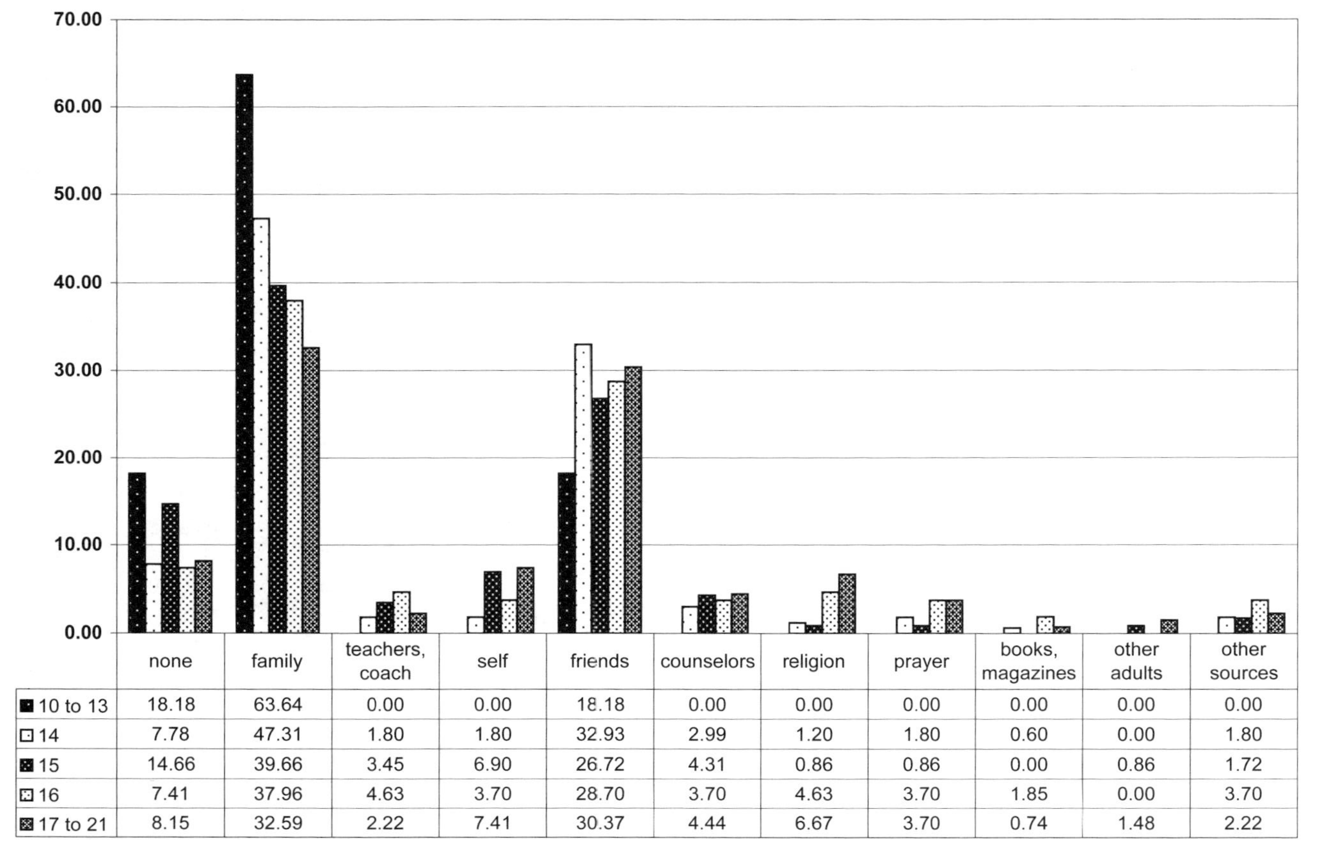

	none	family	teachers, coach	self	friends	counselors	religion	prayer	books, magazines	other adults	other sources
10 to 13	18.18	63.64	0.00	0.00	18.18	0.00	0.00	0.00	0.00	0.00	0.00
14	7.78	47.31	1.80	1.80	32.93	2.99	1.20	1.80	0.60	0.00	1.80
15	14.66	39.66	3.45	6.90	26.72	4.31	0.86	0.86	0.00	0.86	1.72
16	7.41	37.96	4.63	3.70	28.70	3.70	4.63	3.70	1.85	0.00	3.70
17 to 21	8.15	32.59	2.22	7.41	30.37	4.44	6.67	3.70	0.74	1.48	2.22

Figure 1.22. Chart of Schools 1001–2000, First Guidance Source (% of 582)

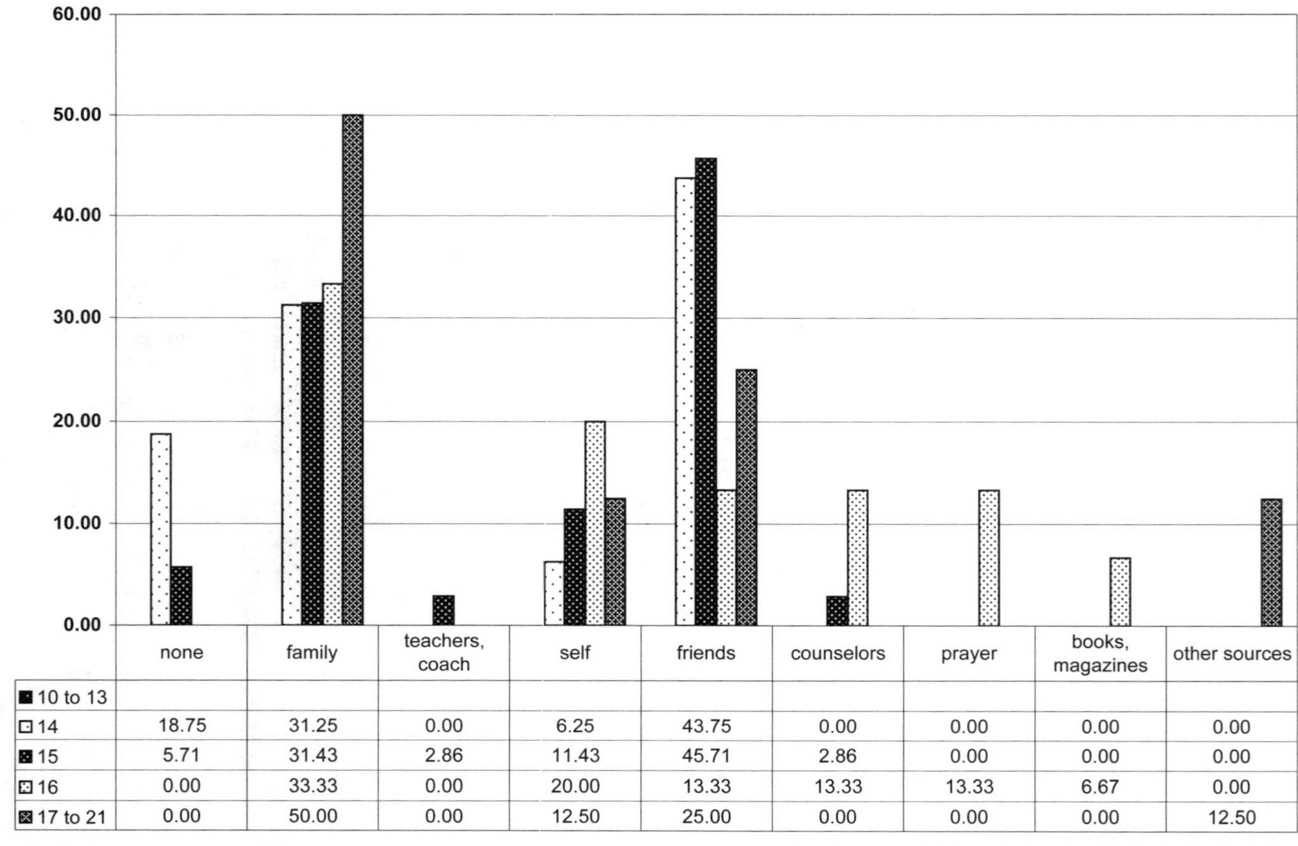

	none	family	teachers, coach	self	friends	counselors	prayer	books, magazines	other sources
10 to 13									
14	18.75	31.25	0.00	6.25	43.75	0.00	0.00	0.00	0.00
15	5.71	31.43	2.86	11.43	45.71	2.86	0.00	0.00	0.00
16	0.00	33.33	0.00	20.00	13.33	13.33	13.33	6.67	0.00
17 to 21	0.00	50.00	0.00	12.50	25.00	0.00	0.00	0.00	12.50

Figure 1.23. Chart of Schools > 2000, First Guidance Source (% of 74)

CHAPTER TWO

Young Adults Sharing Reading Choices

Survey Results

In this chapter, I will discuss the responses to Questions 3 and 4 of the survey.

Question 3: Have you ever read a book or some type of writing that helped you with the issues that challenge you? Name that book(s) or work(s).

Of all the survey questions, Question 3 is the one of greatest interest to English teachers and librarians, and it is most central to the purpose of this book. When viewing the tables below, it might be easy on first read to despair about the number of respondents who indicate "none" regarding a book that might have helped them with the issues in their lives. Possibly respondents felt they could list a book only if it directly helped them with one of the issues they cited in response to Question 1. I am aware of responses that said, "I have never read a book that helped me with these issues." At the same time, the number of respondents who listed the Bible or various books in the Chicken Soup series indicates that some respondents might have interpreted the question about issues in their lives more literally than I intended. Nonetheless, I see the high number of "none" responses and the number of Chicken Soup and Bible responses as a signal that young adults can use some help from teachers and librarians about connecting reading more closely to their lives and experiences. This connection can include the literature and other books they read as part of coursework or in school-related contexts as well as the reading they do on their own.

Some might wonder why I include in my lists a title that is suggested by only one teen. First of all, many titles listed by a single respondent in an age group—13-year-olds, for example—are listed in other age groups. Also in the interest of allowing the voices of the teen participants to be "heard," I wanted to be sure all titles or categories named by the teens would show up.

Here again books are categorized, as shown in table 2.1, and the number following each descriptor is the overall number from the possible 1416 respondents on what they had read that helped them. Looking at the books/readings that helped teens according to gender reveals some interesting insights, as shown in figures 2.1 and 2.2.

One obvious conclusion from figures 2.1 and 2.2 is that females have read more than males. This is not an unusual insight; most teachers are well aware of this situation in their classrooms. The fact remains, though: adolescent males have many challenging issues in their lives. Thus the task for teachers, librarians, and parents is to direct males to books that will engage and help them. Also, the high-profile school violence cases of recent years more often involve males than females. Some of what has been learned from the male offenders relates to loss of meaning or inability to feel accepted, and a major premise of this book is that adolescents can find meaning in stories and in the broad spectrum of YA literature. Chapters 4 through 8 list many books with appeal to male readers, as the annotations make clear; there are also specific book lists included at the end of the chapter directed primarily to adolescent males.

The actual titles are of greatest interest though, and these are shown in tables 2.2 through table 2.12 in alphabetical order by title. There may be

Table 2.1. Books That Helped Teens (1401 Responses)

Categories of Books	*Responses*	*Percent*
None	722	51.5%
Chicken Soup series	143	10%
Bible	124	9%
Self-help	100	7%
YA titles	116	8%
"Classics"	46	3.3%
Magazines, movies, music, newspaper, the Internet	76	5%
Poetry	6	0.4%
Contemporary bestsellers	33	2.3%
Couldn't remember the title	35	2.5%
Totals	1401	100%

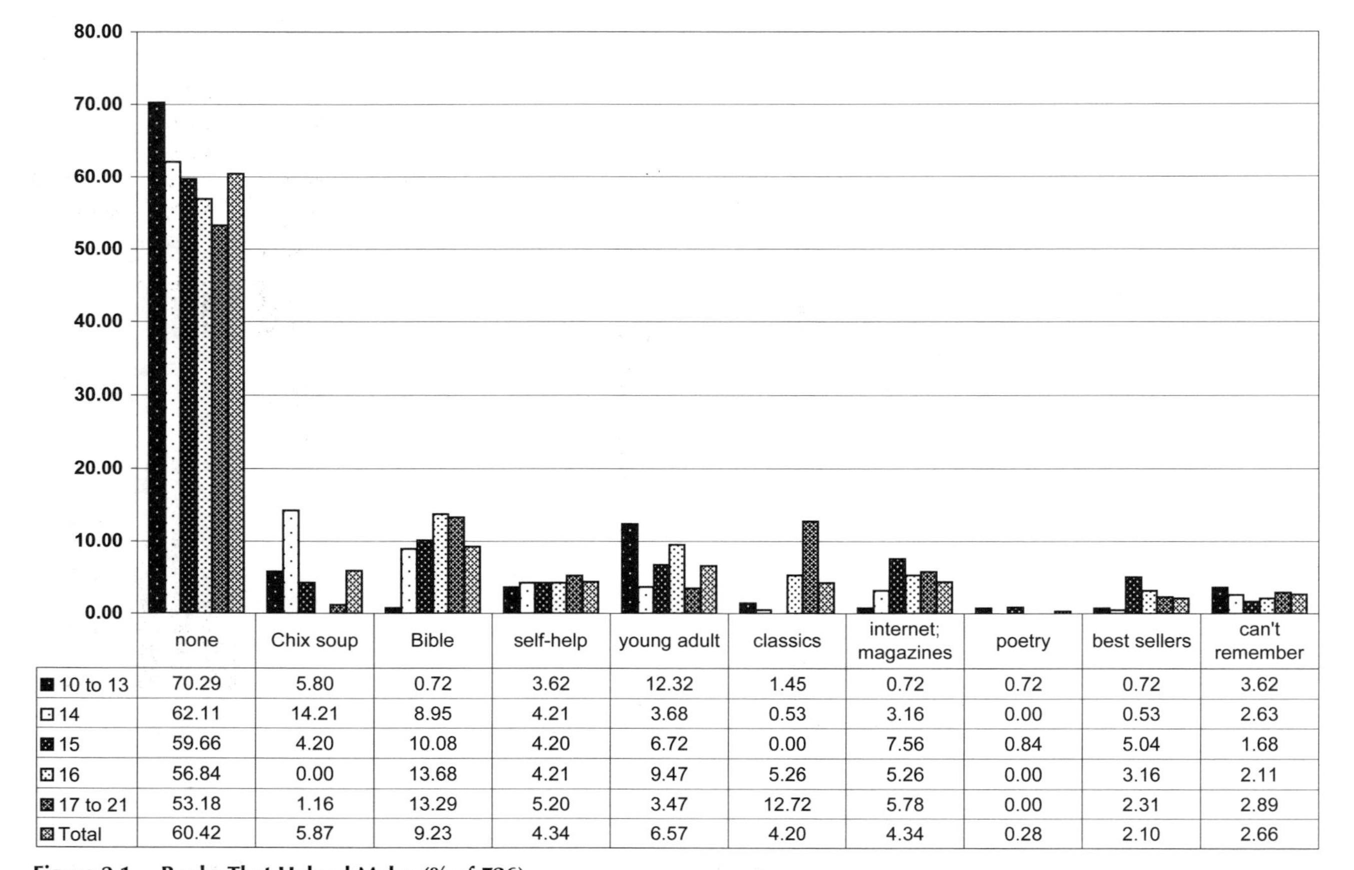

	none	Chix soup	Bible	self-help	young adult	classics	internet; magazines	poetry	best sellers	can't remember
10 to 13	70.29	5.80	0.72	3.62	12.32	1.45	0.72	0.72	0.72	3.62
14	62.11	14.21	8.95	4.21	3.68	0.53	3.16	0.00	0.53	2.63
15	59.66	4.20	10.08	4.20	6.72	0.00	7.56	0.84	5.04	1.68
16	56.84	0.00	13.68	4.21	9.47	5.26	5.26	0.00	3.16	2.11
17 to 21	53.18	1.16	13.29	5.20	3.47	12.72	5.78	0.00	2.31	2.89
Total	60.42	5.87	9.23	4.34	6.57	4.20	4.34	0.28	2.10	2.66

Figure 2.1. Books That Helped Males (% of 726)

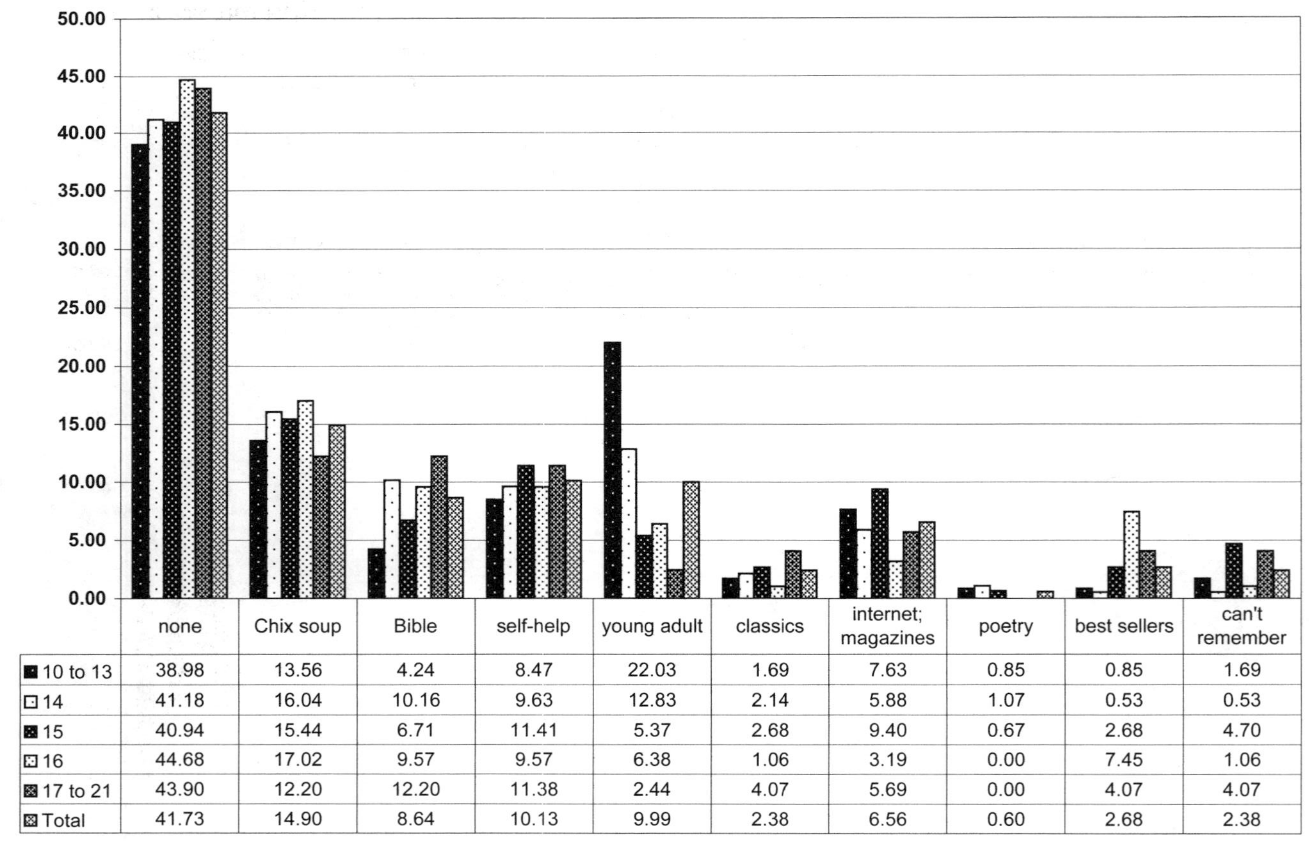

	none	Chix soup	Bible	self-help	young adult	classics	internet; magazines	poetry	best sellers	can't remember
10 to 13	38.98	13.56	4.24	8.47	22.03	1.69	7.63	0.85	0.85	1.69
14	41.18	16.04	10.16	9.63	12.83	2.14	5.88	1.07	0.53	0.53
15	40.94	15.44	6.71	11.41	5.37	2.68	9.40	0.67	2.68	4.70
16	44.68	17.02	9.57	9.57	6.38	1.06	3.19	0.00	7.45	1.06
17 to 21	43.90	12.20	12.20	11.38	2.44	4.07	5.69	0.00	4.07	4.07
Total	41.73	14.90	8.64	10.13	9.99	2.38	6.56	0.60	2.68	2.38

Figure 2.2. Books That Helped Females (% of 680)

some errors in titles; I have recorded exactly what respondents listed unless I could identify an obvious spelling error or incorrect wording in a title. Also, because those 12 and under had listed a significant number of books, I have included these in separate tables. For every age group, there are books to which parents of respondents of a particular age might object. Again, I have accurately recorded the information respondents provided. An authentic part of "listening to the adolescents" requires that we—teachers, parents, librarians, and other concerned adults—respect what the teens list. Often while teens won't reveal in any public forum an issue of concern in their lives, they will seek out other sources of information. Most of the books listed are among the safest ways of finding information and meaning. Most often when respondents have cited music, they are referring to the lyrics of songs that they've found helpful.

A number of titles listed throughout the age groups are "classics" or obviously literature that the teens have read in school. I find this a positive factor; if teens *are* finding meaning and making connections from the literature read for coursework, teachers will know they've achieved a major objective. And if the title of a "classic" work was all the respondent could remember, that still is a positive factor—at least the literature made enough of an impact to be remembered.

The number of references to the books in the Chicken Soup series rises from 12-year-olds (see table 2.2) through 16-year-olds, but then drops and few of the respondents in the 18–21-year-old category list these. It is also evident that the books these older teens suggest differ from those suggested by younger teens. Those 18 and older, for example, do not cite books in the Harry Potter and Lord of the Rings series. Generally, from age 17 on, respondents cite more books related to American and British literature and philosophy; these books align with coursework and may be an indication of these teens having less time for reading outside of school requirements.

In addition to the books cited by those 12 years old and younger, two participants listed magazines. There are a couple of notable differences between those 12 and under and the 13-year-old respondents. Twelve-year-olds are the only group where the Bible is listed only once. The surprising response from 12-year-olds, as noted by a participant at a workshop where I was recently sharing this data, is that one person listed *The Godfather*. I have no particular answer for why younger adolescents would name a book like *The Godfather* except to note that the books listed indicate that teens both read "up"—read what some adults might think are too difficult for a particular age level—as well as "down"—teens return to something they read when

Table 2.2. Books That Helped 12-Year-Olds (75 Responses)

Books	*Responses*
None	33
Chicken Soup books	9
Harry Potter books	2
Monster	2
Roll of Thunder, Hear My Cry	2
A Walk to Remember	2
All American Girl	1
Angus, Thongs, and Full-Frontal Snogging	1
Are You There God? It's Me Margaret	1
Bible	1
Cages	1
DARE pamphlet	1
Divine Secrets of the Ya-Ya Sisterhood	1
Girl Gets Real: A Teenage Guide to Life	1
The Girls	1
Go Ask Alice	1
Hoops	1
Keeping the Moon	1
Left Behind	1
Let the Circle Be Unbroken	1
Lizzy at Last	1
Mandy	1
Missing Since Monday	1
Nancy Drew books	1
Popular	1
Sisterhood of the Traveling Pants	1
Speak	1
Stormbreaker	1
Strategies for Teens	1
Summer of My German Soldier	1

younger, no doubt because they see this book from a new sense of maturity. Some examples of the "reading down" category include *The Little Engine that Could* and *Scrawny the Duck*, which appear on the list for 13-year-olds. But even more, the Harry Potter books or *The Hobbit* or *A Wrinkle in Time* appear on lists of those from 13 and up (table 2.3).

The additional categories that 13-year-olds gave included *Teen* magazine, music, Garfield comics, and the TV program *Seventh Heaven*. With the 13-year-olds, we find the first reference to *A Child Called It* or to other of the David Peltzer books. It is interesting that these titles are cited by every group,

Table 2.3. Books That Helped 13-Year-Olds (172 Responses)

Books	*Responses*
None	115
Chicken Soup books	18
Bible	5
Holes	4
Alice series	2
Are You There God? It's Me Margaret	2
Books by Gary Paulsen	2
The Diary of Anne Frank	2
Go Ask Alice	2
Hoop Dreams	2
Poems by Emily Dickinson	2
A Ring of Endless Light	2
Slam	2
Artemis Fowl	1
Biography of Martin Luther King Jr.	1
Biography of Michael Jordan	1
A Child Called It	1
Child of the Wolves	1
Coming Clean	1
Divine Secrets of the Ya-Ya Sisterhood	1
Don't Sweat the Small Stuff for Teenagers	1
Far Apart, Yet So Close	1
Georgia series	1
Girl's Guide to Growing Up	1
Girl's Guide to Life	1
The Godfather	1
God's Little Book of Devotionals	1
Harry Potter books	1
Hoops	1
I Know Why the Caged Bird Sings	1
Just Ella	1
The Little Engine That Could	1
Make Lemonade	1
Midnight for Charlie Bone	1
My America series	1
Of Mice and Men	1
Phoenix Rising	1
Phyllis Naylor books	1
Poems such as "Making Sara Cry"	1
Pony Pals	1
River Boy	1
Scrawny, the Classroom Duck	1
The Seven Habits of Highly Successful Teens	1
She Said Yes	1

even those 18 and older. Peltzer's story is horrific, but because the teens themselves have named his books and, once again, teachers who have seen this data verify how many of their students read Peltzer's books, I believe we have to take the listing of these titles seriously.

Beginning with the 14-year-olds (see tables 2.4 and 2.5), more books that might be considered "classics" or at least part of the typical high school English curriculum begin to show up. Works such as *Of Mice and Men*, *To Kill a Mockingbird*, *Night*, and *Cyrano de Bergerac*, for example, appear fairly consistently from the 14-year-old selections up. If respondents actually found what they were reading "officially" in English classes connected to their lives, this is a very positive factor. Also evident in the lists for those 14- through 17-years old are an increasing number in "the self-help" category (see tables 2.6 through 2.11).

Two other categories that 18- to 21-year-olds indicated are music—specifically the lyrics of songs—and journaling. The books chosen by those 18 and older (see table 2.12) do not hold many surprises; teachers who have seen the results seem to agree that the responses are typical even when they are from regions of the country where I probably did not have survey participants. When I shared these survey responses with teachers at a California English teachers' conference, their responses showed much commonality between selections appearing on the survey and what selections they thought their students might have indicated.

Survey Question 4 shifts focus from what teens read to what they would recommend to their peers:

Question 4: What are some books or other writings that you'd recommend to your peers to read for finding advice or guidance?

Table 2.13 gives the overall totals by category of the books that teens would recommend. The percentage of respondents having no recommendations is 7 percent lower than those saying "None" in response to Question 3 about having read a book that helped them. In addition, the percentages of respondents who would recommend the Bible or books in the Chicken Soup series are slightly higher than the percentages who say these books have helped them. More respondents recommend books in the self-help and YA literature categories than say they have been helped by books in these two categories. The rest of the percentages are nearly the same for both books read and books recommended. Figures 2.3 and 2.4 present a composite of data, by gender and age groups, on the books recommended.

Table 2.4. Books That Helped 14-Year-Olds (377 Responses)

Books	*Responses*
None	186
Chicken Soup books	57
Bible	38
A Child Called It	6
Books by Lurlene McDaniel	3
Daily Devotionals	3
Harry Potter books	3
Lord of the Rings trilogy	3
Seven Habits of Highly Effective People	3
She Said Yes	3
To Kill a Mockingbird	3
A Walk to Remember	3
Alice series	2
Be An Eleven	2
Catcher in the Rye	2
Ender's Game	2
Hard Love	2
The Lost Boy	2
A Man Called Dave	2
Mick Harte Was Here	2
The Outsiders	2
Speak	2
A Tree Grows in Brooklyn	2
The Blue Day Book	1
The Contender	1
The Diary of Anne Frank	1
The Disappearance	1
Dr. Humor	1
The Face on the Milk Carton	1
Fatality	1
Girl's Life	1
Girls Speak Out	1
The Giver	1
The Godfather	1
Heartland series	1
Holes	1
Homecoming	1
Hush Little Baby	1
I Am Morgan Le Fey	1
If God Loves Me, Why Can't I Open My Locker?	1
Jacob Have I Loved	1
Life in the Fat Lane	1

(continues)

Table 2.4. Continued

Books	*Responses*
Life Strategies for Teens	1
Maggie Cassidy	1
Please Understand Me	1
The Poisonwood Bible	1
The Prayer of Jabez	1
Reviving Ophelia	1
Run for Your Life	1
A Runner's World	1
Safe Sex	1
Savage Nation	1
The Scarlet Letter	1
Shabanu	1
Sisterhood of the Traveling Pants	1
A Squire's Tale	1
Tiger Eyes	1
Where the Red Fern Grows	1

Table 2.5. Other Interests That Helped 14-Year-Olds

Interests	*Responses*
The Internet	17
Poetry	3
Movies	2
Magazines	1
College catalogues	1
Music	1

Males in all age groups recommended more books than they indicated having found helpful themselves; specifically they recommended both the Bible and books in the Chicken Soup series more often than they say they were helped by those books. It is significant that teen males have more books they'd recommend than they list as having read (or at least, that they say they were helped by) themselves. While the percentages are not much higher, it still is encouraging that they are higher. Males consistently recommended more books in the self-help category; except for 15-year-olds, the percentage in all other age groups doubles in the recommendations of self-help books. Fifteen-year-old males recommended more YA literature and classics than any other group.

Table 2.6. Books That Helped 15-Year-Olds (269 Responses)

Books	*Responses*
None	127
Chicken Soup books	27
Bible	23
Books from English classes	2
Caroline Cooney books	2
Cleopatra, Queen of Egypt	2
Don't Sweat the Small Stuff for Teens	2
Harry Potter books	2
The Outsiders	2
Speak	2
Atlas Shrugged	1
The Bean Trees	1
The Best Don't Rest	1
Biographies	1
The Blue Day Book	1
Books by Harwell K. Hamilton	1
Cat's Cradle	1
Chocolate for the Woman's Soul	1
Dear Abby	1
A Diary of a Teenage Girl	1
Eastbay	1
Fallen Angels	1
Forrest Gump	1
Freak the Mighty	1
Girl, Interrupted	1
He Chose the Nails	1
How to Be Cool in Third Grade	1
Kama Sutra	1
Let's Roll	1
Like Sisters on the Homefront	1
Lord of the Rings trilogy	1
Lyddie	1
Men Are from Mars, Women Are from Venus	1
My Name Is Davy	1
The Next Place	1
Night	1
The Perks of Being a Wallflower	1
The Pigman	1
Poems by Emily Dickinson	1
Pretense	1
The Princess Diaries	1
The Prophet	1

(continues)

Table 2.6. Continued

Books	*Responses*
Rachel's Tears	1
A Rooster Crows	1
See You at the Top	1
Shabanu	1
Skullcrack	1
Soccer Duel	1
Staying Fat for Sarah Byrnes	1
Story of Cassie Bernall	1
Ten Habits of Highly Effective Teens	1
That Was Then, This Is Now	1
Time to Let Go	1
Understanding Your Potential	1
A Walk in the Woods	1
Whale Talk	1
When the Last Leaf Falls	1
Where the Red Fern Grows	1
Winnie the Pooh	1

Table 2.7. Other Interests That Helped 15-Year-Olds

Interests	*Responses*
Magazines	14
Music	8
The Internet	2
Movies	2
Newspapers	1
Pamphlets from counselors	1
Poetry	1

Females also consistently recommended more books that they indicated having been helped by reading, including the Bible and the Chicken Soup books. Several age groups among females show a rise in recommendation of self-help books, though this observation fits human nature in general—we more easily recommend help to others than identify what we ourselves might need. In one age group, 17–21, the percentage of recommended YA literature doubles from what females said they'd read. That is an interesting distinction and one that fits with a purpose of this book overall—to help teens become more aware of the powerful resource in YA literature.

Table 2.8. Books That Helped 16-Year-Olds (190 Responses)

Books	*Responses*
None	96
Bible	24
Chicken Soup books	17
To Kill a Mockingbird	3
A Child Called It	2
Don't Sweat the Small Stuff	2
Jim the Boy	2
The Mists of Avalon	2
The Anarchist Cookbook	1
Angels Watching over Me	1
Athletic Shorts	1
Atlas Shrugged	1
Books by V. C. Andrews	1
Books by Beverly Cleary	1
Books and essays by Nietzsche	1
Books by Ayn Rand	1
Charlotte Doyle	1
Child of Prophecy series	1
The Corrections	1
Dangerous Angels	1
The Divine Secrets of the Ya-Ya Sisterhood	1
Dune	1
Ella Enchanted	1
E-mail from God for Teens	1
Ender's Game	1
Girl Interrupted	1
The Giver	1
Got Issues Man	1
The Hanged Man	1
Harry Potter books	1
Hatchet	1
Hitchhiker's Guide to the Galaxy	1
Holes	1
Howl	1
Icy Sparks	1
I Kissed Dating Goodbye	1
I Was a Teenage Fairy	1
Invisible Monster	1
Ironman	1
James and the Giant Peach	1
Japanese Manga	1
Juventud en extsis	1

(continues)

Table 2.8. Continued

Books	*Responses*
Leaves of Grass	1
Left Behind series	1
Lord of the Rings trilogy	1
Max Lucado books	1
Mustard	1
On the Road	1
One Day in the Life of Ivan Denisovitch	1
The Perks of Being a Wallflower	1
The Plague Tales	1
Prozac Nation	1
Rachel's Tears	1
Rainshadow	1
Siddhartha	1
Silent Honor	1
Soldier's Heart	1
Street Lawyer	1
Till Death Brings Us Apart	1
Transall Saga	1
Violet and Claire	1
Virgin Suicides	1
A Walk to Remember	1
The Way of the Samurai	1
The Wheel of Time series	1
World War II books	1

Table 2.9. Other Interests That Helped 16-Year-Olds

Interests	*Responses*
Magazines	4
Internet sites on colleges	2
Music	2
Online literature	1
Newspapers	1
Spiritual/philosophical books	1
All literature	1

Table 2.10. Books That Helped 17-Year-Olds (239 Responses)

Books	*Responses*
None	117
Bible	31
Chicken Soup books	16
Don't Sweat the Small Stuff	4
The Catcher in the Rye	3
Ironman	2
Left Behind series	2
A Man for All Seasons	2
Of Mice and Men	2
The Prophet	2
Allegory of the Cave	1
Atlas Shrugged	1
Black Like Me	1
Books by John Grisham	1
Books on coping skills and psychology	1
Catch 22	1
A Child Called It	1
Death of a Salesman	1
Divine Secrets of the Ya-Ya Sisterhood	1
Emerson's "Self Reliance"	1
Ender's Game	1
The Four Agreements	1
The Giver	1
Go Ask Alice	1
The Grapes of Wrath	1
The Great Gatsby	1
Guideposts for Teens (magazine)	1
Harry Potter books	1
How I Play Golf (by Tiger Woods)	1
Huckleberry Finn	1
I Kissed Dating Goodbye	1
Leap of Faith	1
Let the Circle Be Unbroken	1
Lord of the Flies	1
Love Is a Dog from Hell	1
Man's Search for Meaning	1
Mere Christianity	1
On Death and Dying	1
On the Road	1
Ophelia books	1
Ordinary People	1

(continues)

Table 2.10. Books That Helped 17-Year-Olds (239 Responses)

Books	*Responses*
The Others	1
The Perks of Being a Wallflower	1
The Power of One	1
Psycho Cybernetics	1
Roll of Thunder Hear My Cry	1
The Scarlet Letter	1
Self-Analysis (by L. Ron Hubbard)	1
Seven Habits of Highly Effective Teenagers	1
She's Come Undone	1
The Skin I'm In	1
The Sound and the Fury	1
The Sparrow	1
The Stranger	1
The Sun Also Rises	1
Tao Te Ching	1
The Teen Zone	1
Tess of the d'Urbervilles	1
Thus Spake Zarathustra	1
To Kill a Mockingbird	1
Tuesdays with Morrie	1
What to Say When You Talk to Yourself	1
Who Moved My Cheese?	1
Xenocide	1

Table 2.11. Other Interests That Helped 17-Year-Olds

Interests	*Responses*
Poetry (Robert Frost, etc.)	4
Quotes	2
College brochures	1
Books on mechanics	1
Literature in general	1
Movies	1
Music	1
Online reports	1
Pamphlets on the military	1
Short stories	1

Table 2.12. Books That Helped 18-Year-Olds (64 Responses)

Books	*Responses*
None	28
Bible	6
But What About Me?	2
Cyrano de Bergerac	2
The Alchemist	1
Book of Mormon	1
Catcher in the Rye	1
Chicken Soup for the Expecting Mother	1
Chicken Soup for the Teenage Soul	1
A Child Called It	1
The Coldest Winter Ever	1
Good in Bed	1
A Heartbreaking Work of Staggering Genius	1
Inferno	1
Lord of the Rings trilogy	1
The Nicomachean Ethics	1
The Once and Future King	1
The Poison Tree	1
The Screwtape Letters	1
Slaughterhouse Five	1
Still Following Christ in a Consumer Society	1
The Teenage Boy's Handbook	1
Ten Stupid Things Men Do to Mess Up Their Lives	1
Till We Have Faces	1
Why Me, Sunshine?	1
Xanth books	1

Table 2.13. Types of Books Recommended by Teens to Their Peers

Types of books	*Responses*	*Percent*
None	626	44.5%
Chicken Soup books	187	13%
Bible	167	12%
Self-help	132	9.4%
Young adult	131	9.3%
Classics	49	3.5%
Magazines, movies, music, newspaper, the Internet	72	5.2%
Poetry	1	0.07%
Bestsellers	29	2.1%
Couldn't remember the title	13	0.92%
Totals	1407	100%

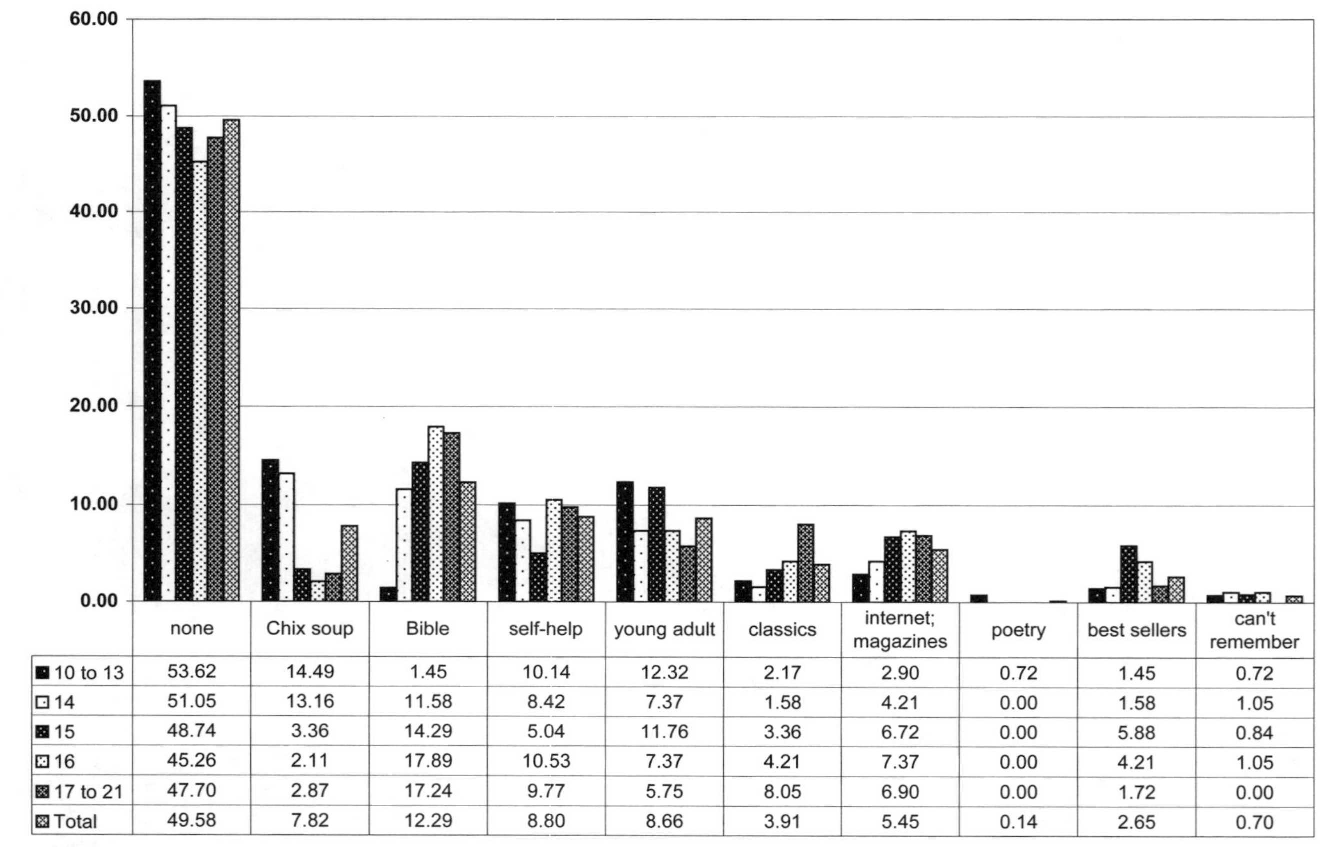

	none	Chix soup	Bible	self-help	young adult	classics	internet; magazines	poetry	best sellers	can't remember
10 to 13	53.62	14.49	1.45	10.14	12.32	2.17	2.90	0.72	1.45	0.72
14	51.05	13.16	11.58	8.42	7.37	1.58	4.21	0.00	1.58	1.05
15	48.74	3.36	14.29	5.04	11.76	3.36	6.72	0.00	5.88	0.84
16	45.26	2.11	17.89	10.53	7.37	4.21	7.37	0.00	4.21	1.05
17 to 21	47.70	2.87	17.24	9.77	5.75	8.05	6.90	0.00	1.72	0.00
Total	49.58	7.82	12.29	8.80	8.66	3.91	5.45	0.14	2.65	0.70

Figure 2.3. Books Recommended by Males (% of 726)

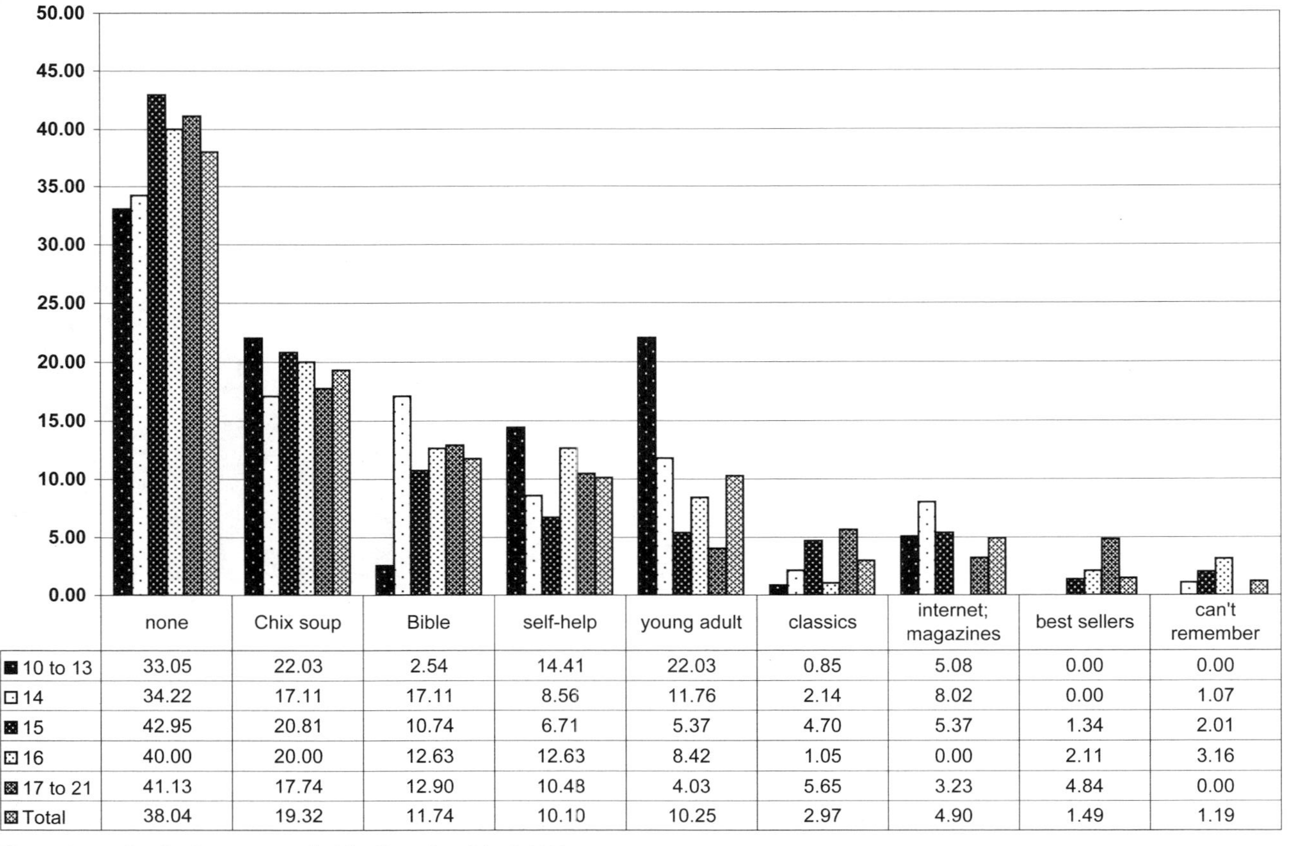

	none	Chix soup	Bible	self-help	young adult	classics	internet; magazines	best sellers	can't remember
10 to 13	33.05	22.03	2.54	14.41	22.03	0.85	5.08	0.00	0.00
14	34.22	17.11	17.11	8.56	11.76	2.14	8.02	0.00	1.07
15	42.95	20.81	10.74	6.71	5.37	4.70	5.37	1.34	2.01
16	40.00	20.00	12.63	12.63	8.42	1.05	0.00	2.11	3.16
17 to 21	41.13	17.74	12.90	10.48	4.03	5.65	3.23	4.84	0.00
Total	38.04	19.32	11.74	10.10	10.25	2.97	4.90	1.49	1.19

Figure 2.4. Books Recommended by Females (% of 680)

As mentioned earlier, 12-year-olds included magazine as a category they'd recommend. Interestingly, though, they listed fewer books they'd recommend than they included on the list of what they read. One example not included on this recommended list is the Harry Potter books (see table 2.14).

A number of the books that 13-year-olds recommended to their peers are not on the list of what they listed as being helped by reading (see tables 2.15 and 2.16). Some of these books include *Tuesdays with Morrie*, *A Wrinkle in Time*, and *A Wind in the Door*. Possibly what they choose to read for themselves, they don't see as necessarily helpful for others and maybe they had heard of these other books, whether or not they'd read them.

Fourteen-year-olds included many more books in their recommendations than they did in the lists of what they read that helped them, as shown in tables 2.17 and 2.18. Among the interesting additions in the recommended list are the writings of Dr. Phil—this clearly represents a popular culture trend—as well as books by Judy Blume, *Hard Love*, and *The Screwtape Letters*. Books on the recommended list also cover a sweep of ages with books like *Tuck Everlasting* and *The Wanderer*, which can be read by younger readers.

Fifteen-year-olds again have many more books they recommend than they included in the books they read (see tables 2.19 and 2.20). A number of the books recommended are frequently part of the English curriculum in grade

Table 2.14. Books Recommended by 12-Year-Olds (75 Responses)

Books	*Responses*
None	27
Chicken Soup books	13
Are You There God? It's Me Margaret	2
Cages	2
Mandy	2
Monster	2
The Other	2
Summer of My German Soldier	2
Beyond the Glory	1
DARE pamphlet	1
Hoops	1
The Lost Boy	1
Nancy Drew books	1
Slam	1
Strategies for Teens	1
A Walk to Remember	1

Table 2.15. Books Recommended by 13-Year-Olds (172 Responses)

Books	*Responses*
None	67
Chicken Soup books	31
Holes	7
Coming Clean	4
She Said Yes	4
Bible	3
Harry Potter books	3
Girl's Guide to Growing Up	2
Go Ask Alice	2
Look to the Stars	2
The Pit Dragon trilogy	2
Alice series	1
Annie's Baby	1
Artemis Fowl	1
Biography of Michael Jordan	1
Books by Lurlene McDaniel	1
Books by Phyllis Naylor	1
A Child Called It	1
Cooper Adventure Series books	1
The Diary of Anne Frank	1
Everything on a Waffle	1
Far Apart, Yet So Close	1
Georgia series	1
The Godfather	1
Hatchet	1
The Hobbit	1
I Know Why the Caged Bird Sings	1
Just Ella	1
Left Behind books	1
Life Guides	1
Life in the Fat Lane	1
The Lion, the Witch, and the Wardrobe	1
Make Lemonade	1
Merlin	1
Of Mice and Men	1
Peace Like a River	1
Please Help Me God	1
Sisterhood of the Traveling Pants	1
Stargirl	1
Sweet Valley High	1
Teen Heart	1
Tuesdays with Morrie	1
Where's My Horse Anyway?	1
A Wind in the Door	1
A Wrinkle in Time	1

Table 2.16. Types of Reading Material Recommended by 13-Year-Olds

Reading materials	*Responses*
Advantoon books	1
Biographies	1
Magazines (*Teen* and *People*)	1
The Internet	1
Newspapers	1
Garfield and Peanuts comics	1
Books from the REAP team meetings	1

10. Such titles included *All Quiet on the Western Front*, *Les Miserables*, and *Siddhartha*. Some surprising recommendations are *Hatchet* by Gary Paulsen and *Goosebumps*, which are frequently read by those in the 11–13 age group.

A title appearing in the 15-year-old list of recommendations which is also on the recommended list of the 16- and 17-year-olds is *Corazon a Corazon*. The lists of books read and recommended are more similar for the 16- and 17-year-olds than for any of the earlier groups (see tables 2.21 through 2.24).

The list of books recommended by those 18 and older (see table 2.25) is the one list of all those included which is nearly entirely different from the books the respondents in this age group said they were helped by reading. I am not sure I can identify any one reason for this. These teens closest to adulthood may simply have a sense that what they read may or may not help their peers.

Following the top twenty books listed in table 2.26, several books were named by four respondents, but these are too numerous to be significant.

Concluding Remarks

At first glance, starting with the books that 12-year-olds read and found helped them, some books seem more "adult" than might be expected—*The Divine Secrets of the Ya-Ya Sisterhood*, *Sisterhood of the Traveling Pants*, or *Monster*, for example. Yet these selections all deal with some universal themes and connect specifically to family life—healthy or unhealthy. As I noted earlier, family ranked high for sources of guidance, and "family issues" was listed as a significant issue, in the lives of many respondents 13 and younger.

Moving to the lists generated by 13-year-olds, a couple of surprising selections include *Coming Clean* and *A Child Called It*. When I read *A Child Called It*, I struggled in reading about the horrendous life David Peltzer experienced

Table 2.17. Books Recommended by 14-Year-Olds (377 Responses)

Books	*Responses*
None	154
Chicken Soup books	63
Bible	53
A Child Called It	8
Harry Potter books	7
The Outsiders	4
Be An Eleven	3
Ender's Game	3
Life in the Fat Lane	3
Lord of the Rings trilogy	3
Seven Habits of Highly Effective Teenagers	3
She Said Yes	3
A Walk to Remember	3
Biographies and autobiographies of role models	2
Books with prayers in them	2
Catcher in the Rye	2
Dr. Phil writings	2
The Giver	2
Hard Love	2
Holes	2
The Lost Boy	2
The Poisonwood Bible	2
Speak	2
Star Girl	2
To Kill a Mockingbird	2
The Adventure	1
All Quiet on the Western Front	1
Beach Music	1
The Blue Day Book	1
Blue Hole	1
Books by Judy Blume	1
Books by Isaac Asimov	1
Bud, Not Buddy	1
Cane River	1
Cannery Row	1
Captains Courageous	1
Catch Me If You Can	1
Charms for the Easy Life	1
Clan of the Cave Bear	1
Corazon a Corazon	1
Cut	1
Dr. Humor	1

(continues)

Table 2.17. Books Recommended by 14-Year-Olds (377 Responses)

Books	*Responses*
The Face on the Milk Carton	1
Freak the Mighty	1
Girl's Life	1
Girls Speak Out	1
Great Expectations	1
Heartland	1
Homecoming	1
Hoops	1
The House on Mango Street	1
Joy Luck Club	1
King of the Wind	1
Life Strategies for Teens	1
The Little Engine That Could	1
The Little Prince	1
Lottery Rose	1
Love You Like a Sister	1
A Man to Watch the Mountain	1
The Maze	1
Northwest Passage	1
The Odyssey	1
Of Mice and Men	1
The Oldest Rookie	1
Outside Shot	1
Pay It Forward	1
The Phantom Tollbooth	1
Please Understand Me	1
The Prayer of Jabez	1
The Princess Diaries	1
Reviving Ophelia	1
Savage Nation	1
The Scarlet Letter	1
The Screwtape Letters	1
Seven Habits of Highly Effective People	1
Sisterhood of the Traveling Pants	1
Slam	1
Sports stories	1
Sweet Valley High	1
Tiger Eyes	1
Tuck Everlasting	1
The Wanderer	1
Where the Red Fern Grows	1
You Don't Know Me	1

Table 2.18. Types of Reading Material and Pursuits Recommended by 14-Year-Olds

Reading Materials and Pursuits	*Responses*
Music	2
Poetry	2
College catalogues/magazines	1
The Internet	1
Writing a book	1
Movies	1
Newspapers	1

from the time he was five. It seemed nearly impossible that a parent or parents could treat any child this way. When I considered the issues listed—the responses in the original database indicating abuse by parents or stepparents or a parent's friend—I noted that the number of young people who are abused by parents is sadly high. The national news recently presented a story about a couple in New Jersey who did foster care; among the story's shocking details were that four of the boys in this foster home had been starved. All four weighed only 50 pounds, even a 19-year-old. Remembering how David Peltzer had also been starved, I saw how, for any young person affected by such cruelty and unable to talk about the treatment for fear of retribution, the David Peltzer series might indeed "save lives."

Given the high percentage of respondents indicating peer pressure as a major issue in their lives, *Coming Clean* also made sense as a selection. Similar to the DARE pamphlet or other motivational books, no doubt this title is helpful. The question for teachers or others guiding teens may be whether these books are the best that adolescents could be reading. In chapter 4, I provide a number of titles that address peer pressure or show teens in the struggle to do what they know is best despite what the "crowd" is doing. My goal is to get more of these books into the hands of young adults.

The frequency on all the lists of the various Chicken Soup books, primarily *Chicken Soup for the Teenage Soul*, again indicates that these are helpful for advice and provide stories that teens want to read. The number of books fitting the self-help category is also fairly high. Once more, the wording of Question 3 on the survey (about books that have "helped you with the issues that challenge you") may have led teens to respond with works that literally address issues like pressure, stress, self-esteem, and the like. The question of quality arises again—how do we help adolescent readers find the books that can take these readers into the realm of more complex literary styles and

Table 2.19. Books Recommended by 15-Year-Olds (269 Responses)

Books	*Responses*
None	112
Bible	34
Chicken Soup books	34
Les Miserables	4
Speak	4
The Outsiders	3
Books by Clive Cussler	2
Cleopatra, Queen of Egypt	2
Ender's Game	2
Freak, the Mighty	2
Hatchet	2
Lord of the Rings trilogy	2
Of Mice and Men	2
All Quiet on the Western Front	1
Animal Farm	1
Atlas Shrugged	1
Baby Help	1
Books by Agatha Christie	1
Books by Matt Christopher	1
Call of the Chetulu	1
Call of the Wild	1
A Child Called It	1
A Doll's House	1
Don't Sweat the Small Stuff	1
Dracula	1
Eastbay	1
Fallen Angels	1
Fear and Loathing in Las Vegas	1
Goosebumps books	1
The Green Mile	1
Guts	1
I Want to Live	1
Left Behind books	1
Let's Roll	1
Lisa Bright and Dark	1
The Lone Hunt	1
1984	1
The Pearl	1
The Prophet	1
Red Rabbit	1
Roll of Thunder, Hear My Cry	1
Siddhartha	1
Slander	1

SSN (Tom Clancy)	1
Stories for the Teen Heart	1
"Thanatopsis"	1
Though None Go with Me	1
Time to Let Go	1
To Kill a Mockingbird	1
Whale Talk	1
When the Last Leaf Falls	1
Where the Heart Is	1
Winnie the Pooh	1

Table 2.20. Types of Reading Material and Pursuits Recommended by 15-Year-Olds

Reading materials and pursuits	*Responses*
Teen magazines	12
Journaling	2
Movies	2
Music	2
Autobiographies for teens	1
Pamphlets	1
Religious books	1

help them find the richness in so many of the YA titles? How do we connect the teens with works from the authors interviewed in chapter 3 of this book, as well as the many other writers who address the very same issues written about in the Chicken Soup series or in books like *Don't Sweat the Small Stuff* and who write much more powerful fiction?

The other work cited frequently is the Bible. It is not clear from any of the respondents what part or parts of the Bible they are indicating. I venture that they have selected portions, possibly books or chapters emphasized by clergy or youth ministers. There is little dispute that the Bible is a major work of Western civilization. From my experience teaching a course in The Bible as Literature on the university level, I hope to propose a curriculum guide for teaching the Bible in high school. This work is still in the planning stage.

In any of the age groups above there are also books that seem "younger" that the age group listing the book. *The Giver* is cited by 17-year-olds as are the Harry Potter books; the fact that these books are cited by older teens is a good sign of the range of the books and of the potential for such works to

Table 2.21. Books Recommended by 16-Year-Olds (190 Responses)

Books	*Responses*
None	75
Bible	33
Chicken Soup books	21
Corazon a Corazon	3
Street Lawyer	3
Ender's Game	2
Harry Potter books	2
Left Behind books	2
Lord of the Rings trilogy	2
The Mists of Avalon	2
The Outsiders	2
Athletic Shorts	1
Books by V. C. Andrews	1
Books by William Faulkner	1
Books by Jerry Jenkins	1
Books by Tim LaHaye	1
Books by Max Lucado	1
Books and poems by Edgar Allan Poe	1
Books by Danielle Steele	1
Books by John Steinbeck	1
Books by Jacqueline Wilson	1
Child of Prophecy series	1
Christianity	1
Dictionary	1
The Divine Secrets of the Ya-Ya Sisterhood	1
Don't Sweat the Small Stuff	1
Dragon Dawn	1
Dune	1
Edge of Heaven	1
Gerald's Game	1
The Gift	1
The Giver	1
The Hitchhiker's Guide to the Galaxy	1
The Hobbit	1
Holes	1
Howl	1
I Kissed Dating Goodbye	1
I Was a Teenage Fairy	1
Ironman	1
James and the Giant Peach	1
Jim the Boy	1
Leaves of Grass	1
Let the Circle Be Unbroken	1

Maxim (magazine)	1
Mustard	1
On the Road	1
One Day in the Life of Ivan Denisovitch	1
The Perks of Being a Wallflower	1
Places I Never Intended to Be	1
The Plague Tales	1
Rachel's Tears	1
Siddhartha	1
Sultan of Swat	1
Thus Spake Zarathustra	1
Virgin Suicides	1
The Way of the Clans	1
Way of the Samurai	1
The Wheels of Time	1

Table 2.22. Types of Reading Material and Pursuits Recommended by 16-Year-Olds

Reading materials and pursuits	*Responses*
Magazines	3
All literature	1
Books on how drugs affect life	1
College catalogs	1
Internet	1
Movies	1
Music	1
Newspapers	1
Poetry	1
Quotes	1
Radio	1
Spiritual books	1
Writing your own diary	1
Writings about teens	1

be read on many levels. *The Giver* holds many levels of meaning—many that can't be grasped by students in grades 5–8. The lists share what the youth in "the audience" said, and that is their power. I have attempted to include as many of these "teen recommended" works as possible in the annotations given in chapters 4 through 8. Maybe the works cited on the lists above are more familiar to teachers and parents than I think, but I hope seeing the selections provides you with some insight into the adolescents you teach and/or parent.

Table 2.23. Books Recommended by 17-Year-Olds (239 Responses)

Books	*Responses*
None	109
Bible	36
Chicken Soup books	27
Don't Sweat the Small Stuff	3
George Washington's Rules of Civility	2
The Great Gatsby	2
Left Behind books	2
Man's Search for Meaning	2
Slouching toward Gomorrah	2
Allegory of the Cave	1
Angels Watching over the Earth	1
Anger Is My Choice	1
Animal Farm	1
Black Like Me	1
The Bluest Eye	1
Books by Piers Anthony	1
Books by Joyce Brothers	1
Books by Patricia Cornwell	1
Books by Stephen King	1
Books by Anne Rice	1
Books by Dr. Seuss	1
Catch 22	1
Cheaper by the Dozen	1
The Chosen	1
Corazon a Corazon	1
The Crucible	1
Divine Secrets of the Ya-Ya Sisterhood	1
The Fifth Elephant	1
The Forgiven	1
The Four Agreements	1
Girl Talk	1
The Giver	1
God's Little Devotional for Teens	1
Go Dog Go	1
The Grapes of Wrath	1
The Great Divorce	1
Green Eggs and Ham	1
Harry Potter books	1
Hockey Enforcers	1
I Kissed Dating Goodbye	1
Interpretation of Dreams	1
Joy Luck Club	1
The Jungle	1

Les Miserables	1
Let the Circle Be Unbroken	1
Like Water for Chocolate	1
Mere Christianity	1
A Midsummer Night's Dream	1
Native Son	1
Nigger	1
Night	1
1984	1
Of Mice and Men	1
On the Road	1
The Other Side of the Mountain	1
Pride and Prejudice	1
The Prophet	1
Psycho Cybernetics	1
Roll of Thunder, Hear My Cry	1
The Scarlet Letter	1
The Screwtape Letters	1
Self-Analysis (L. Ron Hubbard)	1
Seven Habits of Highly Effective Teens	1
The Skin I'm In	1
Socratic dialogues	1
Starship Troopers	1
The Stranger	1
A Tale of Two Cities	1
Tao Te Ching	1
The Traveler's Gift	1
The Trial	1
What to Say When You Talk to Yourself	1
When God Writes Your Love Life	1
Who Moved My Cheese?	1
Wild at Heart	1
Wooden (autobiography)	1
The Worthing Saga	1

While the days of "reading for pleasure" may be gone, I believe that teens can be captured by many of the authors and books in the continually expanding field of YA literature. Parents, teachers, and librarians need to be better "salespeople" for the books, and teens themselves need to share what they like with their peers.

Table 2.24. Types of Reading Material and Pursuits Recommended by 17-Year-Olds

Reading material and pursuits	*Responses*
Magazines	9
Books that inspire	1
Books about emotional issues	1
College brochures	1
Essays by Aquinas, Emerson, Thoreau, Voltaire	1
Newspapers	1
A philosophy class	1
Writing from peers	1

Table 2.25. Books Recommended by 18- to 21-Year-Olds (64 Responses)

Books	*Responses*
None	8
Bible	3
Other	3
Catholic Youth Bible	2
Chronicles of Narnia	2
The Bluest Eye	1
Catcher in the Rye	1
Chicken Soup books	1
Clan of the Cave Bear	1
Gates of Fire	1
Go Ask Alice	1
Harley Like a Person	1
I Know Why the Caged Bird Sings	1
Night	1
Plain Song	1
Poetry	1
Riding in Cars with Boys	1
Skin I'm In	1
Star Girl	1
When I Was Puerto Rican	1

Table 2.26. Top 20 Books Read and/or Recommended

Books	*Responses*
Chicken Soup books	357
Bible	291
Harry Potter books	23
A Child Called It	21
Holes	16
The Outsiders	13
Lord of the Rings trilogy	12
Ender's Game	11
She Said Yes	11
Speak	11
Don't Sweat the Small Stuff	10
Go Ask Alice and Alice series	10
Seven Habits of Highly Successful Teenagers (or *of Highly Effective People*)	9
Catcher in the Rye	8
Left Behind books	8
Of Mice and Men	8
To Kill a Mockingbird	7
A Walk to Remember	7
Corazon a Corazon	5
Life in the Fat Lane	5

CHAPTER THREE

Young Adult Authors Describe Their Commitment to Adolescents

This chapter begins with brief introductions, in alphabetical order, of the YA authors who responded to a questionnaire I created. Similar to the survey of young adults, the questionnaire for authors also had four questions:

1. Why is it important to write for young adults?
2. How did you start writing for young adults?
3. What books did you read as a young adult?
4. What would you suggest that young adults read?

Following the introductions of the YA authors, I have grouped their responses to each question, aligning similar views. Overall, this chapter gives a sample, from the authors' perspectives, of their commitment to adolescents and of the wide range of writers creating stories for young adults.

Obviously, not every author writing books, short stories, or other literature for adolescents can be included in this chapter, but these authors represent a range of those writing for young adults, from some of the pioneers in YA literature to some of the newer authors. They are authors that teachers and librarians in particular should know about since many of their books are ones that the teen survey respondents recommended. Additional resources for background on these and other YA authors are found at the end of the chapter.

Laurie Halse Anderson

After writing several picture books for children, Laurie Halse Anderson launched herself into the young adult field with *Speak*, a gut-wrenching story about a ninth-grade girl who cannot talk about a horrifying incident she experienced at a party during the summer. Her actions make her an outcast in her new high school, until she can develop the strength to speak out. This brilliant first novel has earned Anderson a long list of awards, including a Printz Honor Book Award, a National Book Award nomination, and a Golden Kite Award. *Fever 1793*, Anderson's second book for teens, shows her versatility as well as her ability to create an engaging story from historical details. Her newest work is *Catalyst* (2002). (From authors4teens.com)

Ann Angel

One of the newer writers to the young adult literature field, Ann Angel is a teacher and writer of YA literature who lives in Brookfield, Wisconsin. She has written several articles for *The ALAN Review*, including "The Voices of Cultural Assimilation in Current Young Adult Novels," which appeared in the Winter 2003 issue. She is currently editing a collection of short stories by new and known authors called *Defining Beauty*. Angel is donating profits from the book to the Vermont College for Writing for Children and Young Adults program for a YA scholarship. (From the author biography following her essay in the *ALAN Review*, Winter 2003)

Jan Cheripko

Among Cheripko's publications is *Imitate the Tiger*, winner of the Joan Fassler Memorial Book Award, named a New York Public Library Best Book for the Teen Age, an IRA Young Adults' Choice, a Society of School Librarians International Honor Book, and an *American Bookseller* "Pick of the Lists." He is also the author of *Rat* and *Voices of the River: Adventures on the Delaware*, a photo essay that chronicles his ten-day, two hundred-and fifteen-mile canoe journey from Hancock, New York, to Philadelphia, Pennsylvania, with a fourteen-year-old boy. Cheripko teaches at The Family School, a private school for at-risk young adults and speaks at conferences throughout the country about heroes, literature, and at-risk teenagers. (From the book jacket of *Rat*)

Chris Crutcher

One of a select few to receive the Margaret A. Edwards Award for lifetime achievement in writing for teenagers, Chris Crutcher has been a leading author of books for young adults since his first novel, *Running Loose*, was published in 1983. Since then, every one of his novels and short stories has been a hit with teens, teachers, and librarians. In fact, the American Library Association lists five of his books among the one hundred Best of the Best Books for Young Adults published during the last four decades of the twentieth century. Informed by his background as a child and family therapist, Crutcher's portrayals of teenagers dealing with very painful personal conflicts are handled with humor, sensitivity, and insights that few adults ever achieve. His writing has the power to change lives. Other titles by Crutcher include *Athletic Shorts: Six Short Stories*, *Crazy Horse Electric Game*, *Ironman*, *Staying Fat for Sarah Byrnes*, *Stotan*, and *Whale Talk*. Crutcher is from Cascade, Idaho and sets most of his novels in the Idaho-eastern Washington area. (From authors4teens.com)

Karen Cushman

Karen Cushman has no trouble coming up with ideas for books and no trouble sharing them with her husband. But one day, as she started to tell him about a new idea she had, he handed her paper and pencil and told her this time he wanted her to write it down. What she wrote was the outline for her first book *Catherine, Called Birdy* (Clarion 1994), a Newbery Honor Award-winner. Cushman calls herself a "late bloomer." Growing up in a working-class family in Chicago, she never put much thought into becoming a writer. Though she wrote poetry and plays as a child, Cushman didn't begin writing professionally for young adults until she was fifty.

Cushman had always been interested in history. Her research into medieval England and its culture led to both *Catherine, Called Birdy* and *The Midwife's Apprentice* (Clarion 1995), her second book and winner of the prestigious Newbery Award in 1996. Cushman says, "I grew tired of hearing about kings, princesses, generals, presidents. I wanted to know what life was like for ordinary young people in other times." In her book *The Ballad of Lucy Whipple* (Clarion 1996), she strikes a balance between rich historical detail and the engaging voice of the storyteller. Cushman's books address many of the "issues a young person is interested in—issues of identity, responsibility, limitation, and what it means to be human in this world." She holds an MA in both Human Behavior and Museum Studies and lives on Vashon Island in Seattle, Washington with her husband Philip. (From www.eduplace.com/rdg/author/index.html)

Don Gallo

Don Gallo, with the assistance and guidance of Lynn Malloy and Beth Dufford, is the originator of the website Authors4Teens.com. In the education world, Gallo is known as an authority on books for teenagers and a trainer of English teachers. But he is also known as the editor of a number of award-winning collections of short stories for teen readers, chief among them *Sixteen*, which is considered by the American Library Association as one of the one hundred Best of the Best Books for Young Adults published during the last four decades of the twentieth century. Educator and reviewer Chris Crowe calls Gallo "the godfather of young adult short stories." Among Gallo's edited short story collections are *Connections: Short Stories by Outstanding Writers for Young Adults* (1989), *Short Circuits: Thirteen Shocking Stories by Outstanding Writers for Young Adults* (1992), *Join In: Multiethnic Short Stories by Outstanding Writers for Young Adults* (1993), *Ultimate Sports: Short Stories by Outstanding Writers for Young Adults* (1995), *No Easy Answers: Short Stories About Teenagers Making Tough Choices* (1997), *Time Capsule: Short Stories About Teenagers Throughout the Twentieth Century* (1999), *On the Fringe* (2001), and *Destination Unexpected* (2003). (From authors4teens.com)

Karen Hesse

Hesse presents herself this way in her biography included on Scholastics Authors Studies Homepage (www2.scholastic.com/teachers/authorsandbooks/authorstudies/authorhome.jhtml?authorID=45&collateralID=5183&display Name=Biography):

> While growing up in Baltimore, Maryland, I dreamed of becoming many things: an archaeologist, an ambassador, an actor, an author. In 1969, I attended Towson State College as a theater major, but transferred after two semesters to the University of Maryland, where I eventually earned a B.A. in English with double minors in Psychology and Anthropology. From the time I was ten I thought of myself as "good with words," thanks to a perceptive and supportive fifth grade teacher, Mrs. Datnoff. Though I gave up all my other career dreams, I never gave up dreaming of publication. It took more than thirty years to see that fifth grade dream come true.
>
> I have earned wages as a waitress, a nanny, a librarian, a personnel officer, an agricultural laborer, an advertising secretary, a typesetter, a proofreader, a mental-health-care provider, a substitute teacher, and a book reviewer. In and around the edges of all those jobs, I have written poems, stories, and books, books, books. The seed for *Out of the Dust* grew out of a picture-book idea. Presented with an early draft of the forthcoming picture book, *Come On, Rain* (1999), my writers group insisted I elaborate on why my characters wanted rain so badly. I began researching times when people desperately wanted rain and *Out of the Dust* blossomed into existence. National Public Radio is a frequent companion . . . the inspiration for *The Music of Dolphins* came from an interview I heard on "Fresh Air."

Karen Hesse lives in Vermont with her husband and two teenage daughters. Her book *Out of the Dust* (Scholastic) was awarded the Newbery Medal for 1998; other books by Hesse include *Letters from Rifka* and *Witness*. (From www.indiana.edu/~reading/ieo/bibs/hesse.html)

Norma Fox Mazer

One of the top writers of books for young adults for the past thirty years, Norma Fox Mazer has published more than 25 novels (three of them co-authored with her husband Harry), a large number of short stories including two books of her own, edited two collections of poetry and prose, and written several articles for professional journals. Nine of her books have been designated Best Books for Young Adults by the American Library Association, two of them among the 100 Best of the Best Books for Young Adults published between 1967 and 1992. In addition, her books have won two Lewis Carroll Shelf Awards, an Edgar Award for Best Juvenile Mystery, a Newbery Honor Book award, and a nomination for the National Book Award. Mazer continues to provide teen readers with realistic, thought-provoking stories about such topics as friendship, love and sex, sexual harassment, emotional abuse, physical survival, and inter-generational relationships. Her most recent novels include *Silver* (1988), *Babyface* (1990), *Out of Control* (1993), *Missing Pieces* (1994), *When She Was Good* (1997), and *Girlhearts* (2001). (From authors4teens.com)

Shelley Fraser Mickle

Shelley Fraser Mickle grew up in Arkansas and Tennessee and graduated from the University of Mississippi in 1966. She studied writing at the University of Mississippi, the Harvard Extension School, and Wellesley College. She lives in Alachua County, Florida, with her three horses, Skip, Mullet, and Precious, and her dog, Stella. She is married and the mother of two children.

For five years, Shelley Fraser Mickle has been a regular commentator for Mid-Florida Public Radio, reading humorous essays. Some of these received a Special Achievement Award by Associated Press in 1997. These essays now frequently are heard state-wide on Public Radio's Capital Report, broadcast out of Tallahassee, and she has been the guest commentator for the University of Florida football team for the last two years.

Her humorous essays have also recently become a part of the public radio program *Recess*. In August 2000 she began reading her humorous essays on NPR's "Morning Edition." Her novels include *The Queen of October*, *Replac-*

ing Dad, and *The Turning Hour*. (From www.shelleymickle.com/biography.htm)

Han Nolan

The novels of Han Nolan are complex as well as compelling and thought-provoking, peopled with well-drawn offbeat characters who, like so many real-life teenagers, are longing to be loved, understood, and accepted. In recognition of her writing talent, each of her novels has received several awards, among them a National Book Award for *Dancing on the Edge* and a National Book Award nomination for *Send Me Down a Miracle*. There will surely be more to come. Nolan's novels include *If I Should Die Before I Wake* (1994), *Send Me Down A Miracle* (1996), *Dancing on the Edge* (1997), *A Face in Every Window* (1999), *Born Blue* (2001), and *When We Were Saints* (2003). (From authors4teens.com)

Katherine Paterson

Katherine Womeldorf Paterson was born in Qing Jiang, Jiangsu, China in 1932. Her parents were Christian missionaries there and helped develop her deep religious faith. While living in China, she not only learned the Chinese language but also respect for people's differences, humility, and patience during times of difficulty. By the time she was fifteen, the family had moved fifteen times. Because they moved so frequently, the young Katherine sometimes felt lonely and different from the other young people her own age. She loved to read and wrote stories as a way of overcoming her loneliness, yet she also made friends whom she could not bear to leave when the time came to move again. In an interview in *Bookpage* in March of 1993, she said, "I always knew I was worth something because I had many wonderful friends who knew all my faults and failings and they still cared for me." Katherine Paterson went to Kings College in Bristol, Tennessee and graduate school in Richmond, Virginia. Her teachers encouraged her to write seriously. It took nine years before for her first book, *Sign of the Chrysanthemum*, was published in 1991. During this period, Paterson was also balancing the roles of being a busy wife and the mother of four children and recovering from an operable cancer. Her family was touched by tragedy when her son's best friend was killed by lightning. In dealing with this tragedy and her personal grief, she wrote *Bridge to Terabithia*, her first Newbery Medal winner. She credits her experiences in China and Japan and her strong biblical heritage for adding deeper dimensions to her books and for making her the person she is today.

Katherine Paterson has won many prestigious awards for her books, recently receiving the Scott O'Dell Award. Among her other awards are the Newbery Medal, the National Book Award for Children's Literature, the American Book Award, the American Library Association's Best Books for Young Adults Award, the *New York Times* Outstanding Books of the Year Award, the *School Library Journal* Best Books Award, the Children's Book Council's Children's Choice Award, the Edgar Allan Poe Award runner-up from the Mystery Writers of America, and numerous others. She was honored with the Hans Christian Anderson Award, which is given every two years, in recognition of her lifetime contributions to children's literature. (From Catherine Morris and Inez Ramsey on www.falcon.jmu.edu/~ramsey il/index.html; site now inactive)

Gary Paulsen

Born on May 17, 1939 in Minneapolis, Minnesota, Gary Paulsen is the prolific author of more than 40 books, 200 magazine articles and short stories, and several plays, primarily for young adults. Paulsen's interests in books and reading came when he was a teenager and walked into a library to escape the cold of a Minnesota winter. Once inside, and much to his surprise, the librarian offered him a library card and a book to read (Something About the Author, 1995 [Vol. 79, Detroit: Gale Research, 159–165]). Reading helped Paulsen cope with a difficult family situation then and remains a constant in his life today.

Since the age of 15, Paulsen has worked at many jobs in an effort to support himself: migrant worker, soldier, field engineer, truck driver, and magazine editor (Handy, 1991 ["An interview with Gary Paulsen," *The Book Report* 10, no. 1, 28–31]). Paulsen used his work as a magazine editor to learn the craft of writing. In 1966, his first book was published, *The Special War*. Using his varied life experiences, but especially those of an outdoorsman—a hunter, trapper, and two-time competitor in the Iditarod, a 1,200-mile Alaskan dogsled race—Paulsen writes about what he knows best. This knowledge comes through clearly in the descriptive details he uses, making the reader feel part of the narrative.

Much of Paulsen's work features outdoor settings showing the importance of water and woods to the harmony of nature. He often uses a coming of age theme, where a character masters the art of survival in isolation as a rite of passage to manhood (From "Learning about Gary Paulsen," www.scils.rut gers.edu/~kvander/paulsen.html)

Rodman Philbrick

Most teen readers associate Rodman Philbrick with *Freak the Mighty* and the popular feature film, *The Mighty*, based on the book. But Philbrick has also written an impressive number of other novels for adults as well as young people, most of them mysteries, suspense, horror, fantasy, and science fiction. In Philbrick's books, you'll be as likely to find a vampire, a werewolf, or an alien as you will a normal human character. He's also written a graphic novel—a novel available only on the Web—and recently, a historical novel in diary form for young people. Other Philbrick novels include *The Fire Pony* (1996), *Max the Mighty* (1998), *REM World* (2000), *The Last Book in the Universe* (2000), *The Journal of Douglas Allen Deeds* (2001), and *The Young Man and the Sea* (2004). (From authors4teens.com)

Marilyn Reynolds

Marilyn Reynolds is the author of seven young adult novels and a collection of short stories, all part of the "True-to-Life" from Hamilton High series. Her titles appear on a variety of American Library Association's "Best Books" lists and are also found on the New York Public Library's lists of "Best Books for the Teen Age."

Drawing on decades of experience working with at-risk students in California alternative schools, Reynolds takes on tough issues that permeate the lives of many of today's teens: abuse, teen pregnancy, racism, acquaintance rape, gay/lesbian harassment and bullying, school failure, sexual abstinence, and a myriad of other sub-issues.

Reynolds's personal opinion essays have appeared in the *Los Angeles Times* and other national newspapers, such as the *Dallas Morning News*, *San Francisco Chronicle*, and the *Chicago Tribune*. Her work has also appeared in small literary magazines, professional journals, and anthologies.

In an attempt to broaden her students' reading possibilities, Reynolds wrote *Telling*, the story of a twelve-year-old girl who was being molested by a neighbor. Seeing the responses of her students to this book encouraged Reynolds to write *Detour for Emmy*, the story of a girl who gets pregnant at the age of fifteen. Thus the "True-to-Life from Hamilton High" series was launched—other books in the series include *If You Loved Me*, *Love Rules*, and *Too Soon for Jeff*.

After a lifetime in southern California, Reynolds and her husband, Michael, now live in northern California, near Sacramento. She continues to work with at-risk students and to solicit their help in keeping her stories realistic and believable. (From www.morningglo-rypress.com/pages/fictrite.html)

Jerry Spinelli

Jerry Spinelli is probably the only author in history whose writing career began because of a lunch bag full of chicken bones. Since the publication of the hilarious *Space Station Seventh Grade*, Jerry Spinelli has brought laughter and tears to readers of all ages with his memorable characters, chief among which are *Maniac Magee*, *Crash Coogan*, and *Stargirl*. In 1991 he received the prestigious Newbery Medal for *Maniac Magee*, and *Wringer* was a Newbery Honor Book in 1997. Spinelli's most recent books are *Loser* (2002) and *Milkweed* (2003). (From authors4teens.com)

Ruth White

Ruth White was born and raised in the 1940s and 1950s in and around the coal-mining town of Whitewood, Virginia. She has many fond memories from her childhood of the hills, creeks, and of family read-alouds. Before she even started school, she knew she would be a writer, but it took years before she realized that the Appalachian region would be the best source for her books. For White, attending college was a rare opportunity; a turning point in her life was attending Montreat College in North Carolina. White holds Bachelor of Arts degrees in English and Library Science. She has worked in schools in North Carolina, South Carolina, and Georgia both as a teacher and a librarian. She currently resides in Virginia Beach, where she works as technical services librarian for the Association of Research and Enlightenment. Among her novels are *Sweet Creek Holler* (1988), *Weeping Willow* (1992), and *Belle Prater's Boy* (1996)—all of which are award winners as ALA Notable Books. (From a Farrar, Straus and Giroux author pamphlet)

Jane Yolen

She has been called America's Hans Christian Andersen as well as a Twentieth Century Aesop. But comparisons don't do justice to Jane Yolen, whose creative output and subsequent honors are enormous. Since her first book in 1963, she has published more than 250 others. Her creativity is not restricted to just one or two genres; she has produced children's picture books, novels for middle grade readers, young adult novels, nonfiction, short stories, books for adults, and even a comic book. She can re-tell fairy tales, imagining fantastical creatures such as werewolves, vampires, witches, ghosts, unicorns, and dragons; compile and edit anthologies of stories written by colleagues;

and collaborate successfully with other writers and illustrators, especially her own three children, Heidi, Jason, and Adam. She has written biographies, mysteries, adventures, songbooks, essays, and poems.

Her work has garnered innumerable awards and honors, including two Christopher Medals, two Nebula Awards, a Caldecott Medal, a World Fantasy Award, a Golden Kite Award, a Lewis Carroll Shelf Award, several Best Book of the Year awards, a California Young Reader Medal, and the Kerlan Award. And there is more coming from this amazing author. Yolen's YA novels include *The Devil's Arithmetic* (1988), *Sister Light, Sister Dark* (1988), *White Jenna* (1989), *Dragon's Boy* (1990), *Briar Rose* (1992), *The Books of Great Alta* (1997), *One-Armed Queen* (1998), *Armageddon Summer* (1998), *Sword of the Rightful King: A Novel of King Arthur* (2003), *Dragon's Blood* (1982), *Heart's Blood* (1984), *A Sending of Dragons* (1987), *Queen's Own Fool* (2000), and *Girl in a Cage* (2002). (From authors4.teens.com)

Author Responses to Four Questions

In response to the following four questions, these outstanding writers share insights to their writings as well as reveal their commitment to young adults.

1. How did you begin writing for young adults? (In their responses to this question, many of the authors talk about how they began writing specific novels.)
2. What kind of writing do you do and how are these works helpful to adolescents?
3. Why is writing for young adults important?
4. What books would you suggest to young adult readers? Why? What books have influenced you most in life? Why?

Response to Question 1: "How Did You Begin Writing for Young Adults?"

Laurie Halse Anderson, the author of *Speak*, a book that many teens recommend, explains that the book started as a bad dream. "Literally, I had a nightmare about a weeping young girl and I wrote about her to find out why she was crying." Anderson didn't plan to write about date rape, being an outcast, or the hostile forces that can be part of the high school culture, but *Speak* addresses all of these, and Melinda is someone to whom teens can relate. Readers have told Anderson that *Speak* is "honest," and for Anderson, this is "the greatest thing anyone can tell an author."

In her second book, *Fever 1793*, Anderson researched the Yellow Fever epidemic of 1793 that ravaged Philadelphia. In researching the book, she read diaries and letters by teenage girls of the Federalist period and discovered that they had conflicts similar to what young women today experience: strife with parents and the desire to become an adult, but not too quickly. She provides a good reason for today's young adults to read historical fiction: the conflicts have not changed even though other cultural factors have.

Anderson wrote *Catalyst* from what she considered a "foreign point of view"—that of a teen who loves science and math. She focused on this subject after seeing so many teens "sacrifice their high school years on the altar of ambition," taking advanced courses and participating in multiple extracurricular activities to get into "the right school." So often these teens "burn out" in the mistaken hope they have to be successful and see themselves as failures for years after. "It's criminal and it made me angry. And when I get angry, I write" (e-mail to Mary Warner).

Karen Hesse (*Out of the Dust*, *Witness*, and others) remembers *A Time of Angels* because this book relates to the themes of healing and support. In 1994 when a good friend of Hesse's was diagnosed with a brain tumor, Hesse asked how she could help. The friend asked to be surrounded by angels, and Hesse began writing one angel piece after another: poems, vignettes, character studies, short stories—"all the while keeping my friend at the center of my thoughts." Her friend recovered, and Hesse completely forgot about her file of angel writings. Her daughters found the file and convinced their mother to publish; one particular piece, "A Gift for the Angel," eventually became a longer work, *A Time of Angels* (e-mail to Mary Warner).

For several authors, writing for adolescents came from teaching or working with teens. Jan Cheripko knew in ninth grade, when his teacher at Valley Central High School in Montgomery, New York, told him that he had talent as a writer, that he would write. In 1990, after several years of working on newspapers, Cheripko began as an assistant editor for the magazine *Highlights for Children*. *Highlights* magazine was launching Boyds Mills Press, a children's book publishing company. While working with Boyds Mills, Cheripko began teaching at the Family Foundation School, a private institution for kids in trouble. That experience and his connections in the publishing world led to his first novel, *Voices of the River: Adventures on the Delaware*. He has since written *Imitate the Tiger*, a semiautobiographical story about a high school football player who has a drinking problem, and *Rat*, about a basketball manager who has to choose between telling the truth and keeping a friend.

Marilyn Reynolds (True-to-Life from Hamilton High series) worked for over 25 years with at-risk high school students and, because she was with teens all day, did not really want to spend weekends and evenings writing about them. The nagging of Gloria Miklowitz, a prolific YA writer who taught Reynolds in a "writing for publication" course, eventually convinced Reynolds to try a novel. Over time, Reynolds had realized the best gift she could give her students at Century High School was the "gift of a reading habit." She also knew that students need the "right book for them"—other than works like *The Outsiders*, *Go Ask Alice*, *Down These Mean Streets*, and *The Cross and the Switchblade*, where were student readers to go to find books with which at-risk teens could connect? Reynolds acknowledges it was "more out of desperation than ambition" that she tried her hand at writing (e-mail to Mary Warner).

In 1989, after more publisher rejections than she might have tolerated, Reynolds published *Telling*, the story of a 12-year-old girl who is being molested by a neighbor. While waiting for a publisher to accept the book, she had a manuscript copy in her classroom and watched her students actually coming to school early so they could get their turn at reading the manuscript. Their interest was her motivation; Reynolds went on to address the need for realistic novels about teen pregnancy. *Detour for Emmy* and *Too Soon for Jeff* address the challenges of teen pregnancy from female and male perspectives, respectively.

Another author who began writing for adolescents while she was teaching high school is Ann Angel. Angel, like many other writers who come to be associated with YA literature, didn't begin writing for publication with this age group in mind until a few years ago. She began writing for teens, though, when she realized that this was the age of characters to whom she was most drawn: "I love the irony, the idealism and the immediacy of the young adult perspective" (e-mail to Mary Warner).

Author Jerry Spinelli (*Stargirl*, *Wringer*, *Maniac Magee*, and other books) maintains, "I don't write for kids; I write about kids." (Spinelli's distinction is well taken; after all, the best answer I can give to what I do is that I teach young adults, not just that I teach English.) Spinelli, like a number of other writers, has been caught in the publishers' quandary about where to "put" certain books. He continues to simply write his stories, "not with kid readers in mind, or adults for that matter." He likes to "interview [my] idea and ask it how it wants to be written and [I] go ahead and do it and let all that stuff about reading levels take care of itself" (e-mail to Mary Warner). *Space Station Seventh Grade*, originally titled *Stuff*, was "shopped around to adult publishers by my agent, who was told adults wouldn't read this book about a 13-

year-old kid." When the agent showed the manuscript to those working with juvenile books, "that's where it—and I—landed." Spinelli believes though, that possibly because he did not have kid readers in mind as he wrote, the book is "a fairly honest portrayal of adolescents (some of them, anyway); and the fact that it's still in print over 20 years later suggests that this remains a story in which they can see something of themselves" (e-mail to Mary Warner).

Another author who began writing, as he says, "for kids" is Gary Paulsen. Paulsen writes, "I began writing for young people because I believe it is artistically fruitless to write for adults. They have car payments and divorces and other worries, all of which takes them away from art. Kids are different—they're open to new experiences and they throw themselves wholeheartedly into the act of reading a book if you capture their attention quickly. Young people take the books so personally—I've gotten letters chewing me out for things my characters did or situations I put them in. The letter writers wanted—needed—to let me know that, as far as they were concerned, I'd blown it. 'You don't know shit about football, Mr. Paulsen,' was one deeply felt letter I received years ago when I was writing a series of sports books" (e-mail to Mary Warner).

For Rodman Philbrick (*Freak the Mighty*, *Max the Mighty*, and others), writing for young readers began very much by accident. After publishing more than dozen adult mysteries and suspense novels, he stumbled on a story "close to home." A friend of the Philbricks had a boy with Morquio syndrome; he was a very bright, imaginative kid with an immense vocabulary. A year or so after the boy died in a tragic accident, Philbrick realized he could use parts of the boy's personality, as well as his physical self, to inspire a fictional character. The real boy had a large friend who sometimes carried him around on his shoulders. Though Philbrick didn't meet the friend until after he wrote the book, he used the image of the large boy to create Max, the shy, lumbering boy who narrates the story. At first, Philbrick wasn't sure who the audience would be for this story, but as he wrote, he felt comfortable with having Max talk to kids his own age. Because the voice of Max came so naturally for Philbrick, he continues to write for younger readers as well as for adults (e-mail to Mary Warner).

Norma Fox Mazer (*When She Was Good*; *Girlhearts*; *Good Night, Maman*; and others) also did not set out to write for young adults. One of the first short stories she wrote (and subsequently sold to a teen magazine) arose from a painful adolescent memory, so when Mazer came to the point of writing a novel, doing so from the viewpoint of a young person seemed natural. "It *was* natural. I had an open channel to and vivid memory of my own adolescence" (e-mail to Mary Warner).

Like Mazer, who began writing short stories, Don Gallo (*Sixteen* and other short story anthologies) had worked primarily on nonfiction for young adults in the form of reading and literature textbooks and workbook lessons. In the early 1980s, Gallo realized that teens were reading novels by people like Richard Peck, M. E. Kerr, Robert Lipsyte, Norma Fox Mazer, Robert Cormier, and Walter Dean Myers, but that only a handful of YA authors had written short stories. He talked to a publisher about the need for short stories featuring teenagers and collaborated with authors about compiling an anthology. The result was *Sixteen*; Gallo has truly pioneered the genre of short stories for adolescents. Given the number of teens who are not open to reading novels or other full-length works, Gallo's contribution is significant.

Chris Crutcher (*The Crazy Horse Electric Game*, *Ironman*, *Staying Fat for Sarah Byrnes*, and numerous other novels) had been working with "hard-time kids" for ten years in an Oakland, California, dropout school, and he was involved with "hard-time families" as a therapist in child abuse and neglect when he began to write novels. Crutcher didn't know he was writing for "young adults," a term he explains bothers him. "If I am an adult and I am young I'm at least eighteen years old, by definition. Also it [young adult] is a limiting term." He did know that stories about teenagers came fast and furious to him; most of his books include stories that were inspired by the stories he heard, though he had to change names and mix-and-match for purposes of confidentiality and the storytelling art. Crutcher also remembers his own adolescence well and finds "it's an easy place to go for stories" (e-mail to Mary Warner).

Like Chris Crutcher, Ruth White (*Belle Prater's Boy*, *Weeping Willow*, and others) remembered her own adolescence. "I think I chose to write young adult literature because adolescence was a very difficult time for me." White feels her writing has always been catharsis. She also learned to know this age group when she taught seventh- and eighth-grade language arts. These students are her favorite age group because they are so lively and interested in everything. "They have not yet become skeptical, but they are old enough to think for themselves. And they have such a wonderful sense of humor" (e-mail to Mary Warner).

For Han Nolan (*If I Should Die Before I Wake*, *Dancing on the Edge*, *A Face in the Window*, and others), writing for young adults just happened naturally. When she began writing *If I Should Die Before I Wake*, she saw a teenager as her protagonist. "I guess that [a teenage protagonist] is because part of the reason I wrote the book was in response to an article I had read about young Neo-Nazis" (e-mail to Mary Warner). She felt that telling the story through the eyes of Hilary and Chana was the best way to tell it.

Katherine Paterson (*Jacob Have I Loved*, *Bridge to Terabithia*, *The Great Gilly Hopkins*) was asked by the Presbyterian Church to write a book for fifth and sixth graders as part of a special curriculum. After she wrote this book, she decided to try writing other things. Seven years and many rejections later, her first novel, *The Sign of the Chrysanthemum* was published. Paterson had written the first version of this novel chapter by chapter in a county adult education class, Writing for Children.

Another author who began writing for younger readers first is Jane Yolen (*The Devil's Arithmetic*, *Briar Rose*, *Children of the Wolf*). Yolen wrote a dozen or so books for younger children, and claims she began writing for young adults "when I finally had something I wanted to write about for teens" (e-mail to Mary Warner).

Shelley Fraser Mickle's (*Queen of October*, *The Turning Hour*, and others) four published books are adult novels that have also found an audience with young adults. She chooses young adults or children as her protagonists because of her childhood. At age six, Mickle contracted polio, and she spent much of her childhood in braces, wheelchairs, and hospitals. "Such an event quickly makes a young child old," Mickle commented, "There is something in me that was frozen at that point of time." Mickle is fascinated with children's minds discovering that they exist in a world they cannot control. She sees this happening to children frequently as families break up in divorce and is drawn to trying to express for children and young adults this baffling and disconcerting experience of "being in a world that seems to be spinning off into directions where no maps exist" (e-mail to Mary Warner).

Karen Cushman (*Catherine, Called Birdy*; *The Midwife's Apprentice*; *Matilda Bone*; and others) wrote all the time as a child, but never thought about being a writer since she knew no one who wrote and "certainly no adult who wrote for a living." For forty years she made up stories in her head but didn't write them down. She'd frequently tell these stories to her husband; finally, when she told him in the late 1980s that she had a great idea for a book, he refused to listen and told her, "Don't tell me. Write it down and I will read it." Cushman's books often build on history. She explains that *Catherine, Called Birdy* grew from her long-standing interest in children and history. She had often thought about what life might have been like for children in the past when they had no power and little value, especially girl children. Cushman wanted to tell the story of a girl from long ago who was at odds with her family and her times, who didn't want to do what was expected of her, who thought she had no choices and no options. "I wanted to know what happened to that girl and the only way I could find out was to make it up. Three years later the story turned into *Catherine, Called Birdy*" (e-mail to Mary Warner).

Madeleine L'Engle (*A Wind in the Door, The Swiftly Tilting Planet, A Wrinkle in Time*, and others), whose health prohibited her from answering the author survey, still provides some good answers as to why writing for young adults is important. In a special introduction by the author to the commemorative edition of *An Acceptable Time*, L'Engle explains that she writes books because she's still asking big questions about time, the future, and the mysteries of the universe. She understands that these questions and others have no finite answers, but "the questions themselves are important" (L'Engle 1997). L'Engle advises readers, "Don't stop asking, and don't let anybody tell you the questions aren't worth it. They are" (L'Engle 1997, L'Engle 2000). She also affirms why books and other literature can be a source of meaning: "Story always tells us more than the mere words, and that is why we love to write it, and to read it" (L'Engle 2000).

Another seminal author for young adults is the late Robert Cormier (*The Chocolate War, After the First Death, I am the Cheese*, and numerous others). Cormier shared several ideas about writing for teenagers in an interview with Judith Bugniazet, which was first published in the *ALAN Review* in winter 1985. Bugniazet told Cormier that his books were cathartic for her and that she couldn't read them without crying; she wondered how boys responded to Cormier's books.

> Boys won't admit to me that they cried, but when I go out to speak to them, they will say things like, "That's exactly the way we feel." The things that upset some adults are not the things that upset kids. They're very sophisticated, today's youth, but they're still kids. They have questions about things, like masturbation, and one boy told me that when he read about that in *The Chocolate War*, and it was so casually referred to, it helped him because he had worried about what was wrong with him. It made him feel that he wasn't strange. (Bugniazet 1999, 9)

Cormier and the other writers express similar ideas; they write for young adults because adolescence is a time of multiple levels of experience and because young adults need the reassurance of those who have gone through what these teens are experiencing.

Response to Question 2: "What Kind of Writing Do You Do?"

Several of the authors have similar perspectives about why their works are helpful for young adults. Han Nolan, like many of the other writers, doesn't set out to write a story thinking what lessons she can teach adolescents of today. Nolan wrote, "I just have a story to tell and because I enjoy writing about young people and exploring their inner lives, my books end up being about various young people and their struggles to be noticed, loved and accepted by the people who are supposed to care for them as well as other people in their lives" (e-mail to Mary Warner). Among the themes of Nolan's works are love, religion, tolerance, the search for self, and self-acceptance. She admits that her books don't always have the happiest endings, but believes her stories can give readers hope as they either recognize they are not alone in their feelings, or read about the lives of people quite different from themselves and realize that they have it pretty good. Nolan has received "some wonderful letters from young people and adults as well who tell me that this is true for them" (e-mail to Mary Warner).

Some young people have told Nolan that they have changed the way they treat people in their schools. "One young person was so connected to one of my characters he felt he just had to meet her and talk to her because he knew she would understand what he had been through in his life" (e-mail to Mary Warner). Nolan's books have been used in schools and also by psychologists, though Nolan is not sure how psychologists have used the books. "I think my books, like many YA books, give young people a place and a time to think about their lives" (e-mail to Mary Warner). The books give teens a safe place to explore their beliefs about God, their thoughts about their relationships with their families and friends, and to question who they are and who they are becoming.

Like Han Nolan, Marilyn Reynolds wants teens to know that they are not alone. She writes books that deal with difficult issues that teens often are faced with—teen pregnancy, acquaintance rape, partner abuse, school failure, abstinence, gender identification. She believes her books offer a perspective that is sometimes hard to come by in the midst of crises. "They offer hope" (e-mail to Mary Warner).

"I take a universal issue, such as child abuse or the loss of a parent, and set it a time and place which is most familiar to me, which, of course, is the 1950s in Virginia, when I was an adolescent myself," says Ruth White. White asserts that a story is more believable if the setting is authentic; if the themes are universal, then the reader can relate to any setting. She aims for authenticity and believability as the two basic characteristics of her books and hopes "young people of the [twenty-first] century can find themselves somewhere in [my] books" (e-mail to Mary Warner).

Shelley Fraser Mickle follows on the same themes as Ruth White. "We all seek at early ages, beliefs or theories that we can hold onto in the face of diversity. Characters in my books come to an acceptance of the unexpected events in their lives and learn to persevere" (e-mail to Mary Warner). In *The Queen of October*, Mickle's main character, a 13-year-old girl, learns that her parents' divorce is not something she is responsible for and that love between parent and child does not die, though the love between parents may no longer exist. In *Replacing Dad*, Drew, a 15-year-old boy, learns that his mother's happiness affects his life but that he is not responsible for her happiness. He develops strengths and his own serenity apart from his family and their needs, even as he realizes that his father can never be replaced and that his family is a source of strength for him; he grows from these experiences of adversity.

Mickle's *The Turning Hour* offers direct coping skills for young adults to handle despair. She sees *The Turning Hour* as her most important book in that it deals with a 17-year-old young woman's recovery from a suicide attempt. It also expresses her mother's anguish and concerns through her own viewpoint. Mickle asserts, "The consequences to the drastic decision to commit suicide cannot be too graphic; we must as members of a nation that frequently suffers from media intoxication, never romanticize the act of teen suicide. And we must, through our opportunities to discuss the issue, prevent it from ever being seen as an act of honor" (e-mail to Mary Warner).

Norma Fox Mazer writes, as does Shelley Fraser Mickle, fiction that is almost always family centered, almost always about relationships, almost always set in our present world with characters she hopes are both readily identifiable and deep enough to engage readers on more than a superficial level. Mazer is another author who affirms that she does not write with the intention of being helpful to adolescents. "I write because writing is like breath to me—it's something I must do to feel wholly alive, so the basic impulse to write is selfish. It's for me" (e-mail to Mary Warner). When she writes a novel, she's consumed by the challenge and joy and difficulty and thrill of creating a world and the characters that inhabit that world.

Mazer is completely attached, as both writer and reader, to narrative, to story, to answering the question "And then what happened?" Inevitably, she explains, story or events alone cannot sustain a novel; rather the novel must have meaning and must answer questions: Why this story? Why these characters? In answering those questions during the writing and through the actions of the characters, ideas, values, and moral precepts are conveyed. "If my novels provide more than entertainment to young readers, if they open windows into other lives, if they provoke readers to think, if they deliver an emotional experience—if they do any of the above, then I'm well rewarded" (e-mail to Mary Warner).

Most of Jerry Spinelli's work is contemporary fiction. "To the extent that readers can see themselves in the stories, is, I think, a good thing in and of itself. To find their lives portrayed, dramatized—heck, enshrined—in *books* is to give them a legitimacy, an affirmation to the quotidian in their days that might not be available elsewhere" (e-mail to Mary Warner). Spinelli goes on to explain that beyond the simple, self-contained value of seeing one's life reflected in fiction, there are, of course, "lessons." He admits he tries not to think of a lesson that way, though, "lest they trump the story and the thing becomes tract or sermon instead of book" (e-mail to Mary Warner). So readers of *Wringer* or *Stargirl* might find encouragement to be true to themselves. They might learn in *Maniac Magee* to keep color a matter of skin, not heart; in *Crash*, about the perils of bullying; or in *Loser*, to take the real measure of winning and losing.

Gary Paulsen found that all of the sequels to *Hatchet*—*The River*, *Brian's Winter*, *Brian's Return*, and *Brian's Hunt*—were written as direct responses to letters kids had written to him about Brian. "I was done with his story after *Hatchet* and never thought I'd revisit that character. But kids wanted to know what happened to him after he came back from such a life-altering experience—so I wrote *The River*. Then I got letters chiding me for getting Brian out of the brush before as they put it, 'the going got really rough in the winter,' so I had to amend the ending of the original story to set up *Brian's Winter*. Then the letters came asking how after having learned so much about the wilderness and being self-sufficient, he could ever 'fit back in' to regular life. Since this has been a problem I have in my own life—I'm never comfortable when I'm not in the woods or on a dogsled or at sea—I wrote *Brian's Return*. And yet still more letters about Brian—did he have any friends, did he miss talking to anyone, was he ever lonely—and so I gave him the best friend anyone could ever have, a dog in *Brian's Hunt*" (e-mail to Mary Warner).

Don Gallo comments that although anyone can enjoy and benefit from discussing short stories, it's the reluctant readers—mainly boys—who seem to like them most. He knows that if you ask most avid female readers about short stories, they are less than enthusiastic because these readers want the work to last, to extend the pleasure. But ask a reluctant male teenager the same question and the answer will more likely be that they like the short stories because they're short!

Good short stories though, Gallo explains, are no different from good novels in that their value is in the quality of the story and the realness of the characters. Among the advantages of short stories are the time in which they can be read; they take far less time than novels and that is helpful for readers with short attention spans. Short stories give readers enough of the writing style of an author, and, as opposed to novels which don't allow readers to skip sections if they are going to comprehend the total work, a short story can be skipped and readers can go on to another one that interests them more. "It's a buffet of choices as opposed to a single entrée. And in anthologies like mine that include a variety of authors, the choices are even more varied than if the stories were all written by the same author" (e-mail to Mary Warner).

Several authors write historical fiction and see that it offers some particular gifts to young adult readers. Jane Yolen writes four kinds of books for teens—historical novels, fantasy/science fiction, short story collections, and realistic novels, though she writes fewer of the last kind. "Since I write to tell a story, not to be helpful for kids, I leave the understanding of that [how the books are helpful to young adults] to the critics and social workers" (e-mail to Mary Warner).

Katherine Paterson started out writing historical fiction and has written seven volumes in this genre. Three of them are set in feudal Japan (written probably out of her homesickness for Japan) and one is set in nineteenth-century China (the country of her birth); these books explore what happens when in the pursuit of a righteous cause, people use unrighteous means. The remaining three of her historical novels are set in nineteenth-century Vermont—a way for Paterson to learn about her adopted home. Her seven contemporary novels each have their own history, but "I think all of them are searches for an answer to a question that troubled me" (e-mail to Mary Warner).

"I write historical fiction and I love to write historical fiction" is Karen Cushman's answer to what kind of writing she does. For Cushman, a historical novel is a realistic story set in the past; a story in which imagination comes to the aid of facts; a story that answers not only "what happened," but also "what were they like." She believes the most important attribute of a historical novel is that it tells a story that could not have possibly happened in any other place or time, a story that results from the combination of character and circumstances.

Cushman believes that young readers benefit from historical fiction because it can give them a feeling for the living past by illustrating the continuity of life; it also gives readers a sense of history and their place in it. Historical fiction allows a glimpse of the lives of ordinary people who are like us in many ways, and thus it increases our sensitivity and understanding. "I'd hope my novels, although historical, speak to today's young people who may not be suffering from the feudal system or arranged marriages, but who still feel like Birdy, that they have few options, few choices, and little power" (e-mail to Mary Warner).

Some issues cross time and place—issues of identity, responsibility, change and becoming, and what it means to be human in this world. Again, though, Cushman, like other authors, doesn't write "issue books" or books that impart specific ideas. She tells stories and hopes that readers will see themselves in the books and situations and get their own ideas. "Still I must admit I would like my readers to come away believing in the value of being yourself, against all odds; of independence, compassion, and compromise; of the necessity and possibility of remaking the world" (e-mail to Mary Warner).

Quoting historical novelist Leon Garfield, Cushman comments, "If the young discover that in the past we have been governed, led, abused, and slaughtered by fools and knaves, then perhaps they will look about them and see that matters have not greatly changed, and possibly they will do so before they vote." This is why historical fiction is helpful for adolescents.

Laurie Halse Anderson wants her readers to stay up late in order to find out what happens next in her books. Readers have told Anderson that *Speak* encouraged them to speak out about sexual assaults. Some have been raped by boyfriends; others have been sexually harassed for years. One girl was gang-raped at a party by classmates she had to sit next to every day. Boys have written about being sexually abused by neighbors, or an uncle, or a babysitter. "There is so much hidden sexual assault and abuse in our country. Some kids say the book helped them find the courage to speak up about other issues in their life. Boys tell me it helped them understand the impact of rape, which many of them never took seriously before. Some of my favorite letters are the ones in which the writer reports she now looks at the outcasts in her school differently, and now she says hello and sits with them at lunch" (e-mail to Mary Warner).

Catalyst, Anderson's book about the stress in academics, has not been out that long, but the early mail Anderson has received has been from high-achieving kids who are exhausted by the effort of appearing perfect all the time. "I guess that for some readers, my books provide a lens through which [they] can look at themselves a little differently. I have enormous respect for these readers. They have the courage to grow and change" (e-mail to Mary Warner).

Chris Crutcher describes his works as novels and short stories about coming of age in America. Crutcher sees these books and works like these by many other wonderful authors as helpful in that they supply characters with whom readers can find intimacy, as well as information about responding to hard times that many readers might not have imagined on their own.

Ann Angel writes about themes of faith and hope, though she explains this isn't in a religious sense so much as in a sense of transcending daily existence and believing in a power beyond humanity. In "Pink Gun," she wrote about relationship abuse; in *Beauty*, a collection of short stories by new and known writers, she wrote about the topic of beauty; in "Bella's Spirit Guide," she has ghosts who come back to help their siblings; and in "Moon Daughter," she writes of a reluctant healer who isn't sure where his ability came from. Angel is currently writing a novel about a girl who leaves her baby in the garbage, thinking it's dead. She is also editing a collection of short stories that deal with nontraditional perspectives of beauty in order to give young adults a starting place to consider that beauty isn't necessarily what our culture defines as beautiful. "All of these stories I hope transcend daily lives and help teens think through their own choices and beliefs" (e-mail to Mary Warner).

Regarding how her books can be helpful to young adults, Karen Hesse comments that this is difficult to answer since each reader takes what he or she is ready to take from a book. Her sense is that adolescents might read her books and have a range of possible responses. For some, truth will resonate; for others, the book may be a vehicle to help them navigate through troubled times; for still others, the book may lead them to a path for working through life's challenges; or perhaps for some readers, there will be no immediate response, but in a year the reader may be ready to embrace the book and grow with the protagonist.

Hesse suggests that it's possible to read *The Music of Dolphins* on a superficial level, but "it takes a maturing individual to comprehend the questions about humanity raised in the story" (e-mail to Mary Warner). A 10-year-old reader might enjoy *The Music of Dolphins* as a fast-paced story about a girl who lives with dolphins; five years later, the reader will be able to use his or her emerging understanding of alienation to explore identity issues.

As far as the type of books Karen Hesse writes, she explains that she enjoys experimenting with form and content. Finding the perfect way to express the story through an organic form challenges and excites her. "I don't set out to write a novel in an unconventional fashion. I simply try to tell the story as it might best be told, resulting at times, in an unusual form" (e-mail to Mary Warner).

Jan Cheripko's primary writing arena is young adult fiction, though he also enjoys nonfiction writing, such as biography. Like many other authors, he doesn't think about writing to a specific audience; he is simply writing a story. His protagonists tend to be teens because they are the focus of his work as a high school teacher. Cheripko doesn't know to what degree his writings are useful. He does know it's rewarding to have young people tell him his books have meant a great deal to them. "I recall one boy in Queens, New York, telling me that he had never read a book in his life, but he read mine and it was his story" (e-mail to Mary Warner).

Response to Question 3: "Why Is Writing for Young Adults Important?"

Having shared how they began writing for young adults, the writers get to the essentials when they respond to why writing for young adults is important. Katherine Paterson thinks that young people are searching for answers in a very troubling world. "I seem to be asking some of those same questions—I'm not so much giving answers as presenting a story which is my own search." Society, Paterson goes on to say, is happy to give youth answers; in fact, "our culture is terrified that kids might think for themselves and not buy what's being packaged" (e-mail to Mary Warner). Stories allow readers to find their own answers or lessons.

Jane Yolen's comments follow the theme of Paterson's. Yolen thinks reading helps kids of all ages come to terms with the chaos that is the world. "It gives them some control over the pacing with which they take in that information; it gives them time to 'take the cup of borrowed courage' on whatever journeys they find themselves" (e-mail to Mary Warner). Building on the journey motif, Ann Angel suggests, "Young adults are at a point in their lives where they've often secretly crossed into adult behaviors, but have no map to maturity in dealing with some of the adult choices they've made" (e-mail to Mary Warner).

"Because young adults are important, extremely important," is Laurie Halse Anderson's answer to Question 3. She points out that we value children in our culture, but it seems the only thing teenagers are valued for is their money. They are viewed as an "important demographic" (e-mail to Mary Warner). At the age when they most need adult patience and understanding, teenagers are more often the object of greed or fear or disgust. Adolescence is marked by the loss of innocence. Teenagers need books, stories that will help them understand what they are leaving and what they are walking toward. They are filled with confusion and looking for understanding and (though loath to admit it) guidance. Books can provide this understanding and guidance.

"I don't know that I ever write with the idea of being 'helpful' to adolescents," Gary Paulsen comments. "At least in my case, reading saved my life. I was a terrible student, hated school, failed the ninth grade, and a librarian I didn't even know gave me a library card and then handed me a book. That one woman helped me to find a place where it didn't hurt, a place where I fit in, a place where I belonged—the pages of a book. She saved me, she really did. Everything I am and everything I've become, I owe to her. I know what books can do for young people firsthand—and maybe that's why I write for them—to help them find the same safe place that I discovered" (e-mail to Mary Warner).

Paulsen suggests, "Writing for young adults is vitally important because they have to be told the truth. I will never understand why anyone would want to keep a book from a child. Young people can learn how to deal with ugly or dangerous situations or controversial subjects or rough language or ideas and values that differ from the ones they're being raised with at home through the pages of a book. Books can provide a safe harbor for kids to begin learning about the world, about people and situations they may never face or will have to deal with eventually. Books and the discussions they raise can serve as sort of a dress rehearsal, if you will—a place to begin to experiment with new ideas and look at life from a different point of view. I believe that exposure equals education. We can't protect our kids from harsh realities forever and books provide a forum for discussion and debate and learning and tolerance and understanding" (e-mail to Mary Warner).

Jan Cheripko sees his ability to write as a gift that he must use to the best of his ability. "Much has been given to me freely in my life. If my words can help young people realize that they, too, have been given much and that they have an obligation to give back, then I will have been successful" (e-mail to Mary Warner). Ironically, as Cheripko has worked closely with hundreds of troubled teens for almost two decades, he knows that the very happiness many teens seek in drugs, alcohol, sex, violence, or food can only be found in giving of themselves to their universe around them.

"Writing for young adults is important because they themselves are important," Han Nolan responds. Adolescence is the time in people's lives when they're especially open to new ideas, to exploring who they are and who they want to become. "It's a time when so many of us wake up to the world around us for the first time and we're so greatly influenced by what we see in that world, and what we think about the things we see" (e-mail to Mary Warner). For Nolan the question is "what do we want to fill young people's heads with because whatever it is, it will greatly impact the rest of their lives." That means for her that she has a responsibility to her audience to treat them with respect, not talk down to them or try to imitate them, but try to understand them and speak to them from this place of understanding.

Norma Fox Mazer affirms Nolan's view. Mazer comments, "Writing for any group of people is important, but young adults are so vulnerable, so swept by emotional and physical change, so suffused with emotion and questions and doubts that writing for them does seem to carry an extra weight of responsibility and meaning" (e-mail to Mary Warner). Ruth White concurs: "Adults often forget how hard it was to be part child and part grown-up. As writers, we need to make an effort to remember those years, and to write about them, in order to show the adolescent he/she is not alone, the confusion will end, and there is much to laugh about." White also hopes that teens will learn to laugh at themselves, as we all should (e-mail to Mary Warner).

Karen Cushman simply believes in the value of writing for young people. She notes that she isn't a children's author until she "gets good enough or old enough to write for adults." She's committed to writing for adolescents because "young people are not only what they eat and hear and experience; they are also what they read. Books inform and shape our adolescents." Books expand their horizons, give a sense of life's possibilities, and help determine what kind of people they will become. Cushman cites Herbert Kohl who said that what is read "can help young people get beyond family troubles, neighborhood violence, stereotyping and prejudice . . . and set their imaginations free." And Cushman says to this, "What could be more important than that?" (e-mail to Mary Warner).

Marilyn Reynolds points out that realistic representations of the teen years are not often available in mainstream books. Teens need books that reflect their lives and that offer insight into the lives of others. Jerry Spinelli's simple comment affirms Reynolds's viewpoint. Spinelli sees the importance of writing for young adults because "young adults become old adults" (e-mail to Mary Warner). And Don Gallo echoes a similar message: "Kids need (and want) literature that deals with people and issues important to them, written by authors who understand their needs and interests and respect how they think and feel. Kids want to know that someone understands them" (e-mail to Mary Warner). This is precisely why Gallo works on short stories that, in contrast to many typically anthologized ones like "To Build a Fire," "The Most Dangerous Game," "The Bride Comes to Yellow Sky," "The Gift of the Magi," "The Window," or "The Necklace"—all of which have adult protagonists and are written for adults—feature teens like the readers themselves, with teen problems.

"I believe strongly in giving young adults voices, especially related to reading literary novels and discussing them," says Shelley Fraser Mickle (e-mail to Mary Warner). Mickle has a weekly newspaper column, "Novel Conversations," with an open invitation to readers of all ages to respond in the format of a newspaper-based book club. Communication is done through "snail mail" and e-mail. The blend of young readers' voices with older ones is enlightening and valuable. A link to the column is located at Mickle's web site (www.shelleymickle.com).

Several authors spoke directly to the importance of reading and writing for any human being. Karen Hesse maintains that "reading gives us the opportunity to sample life, to experiment, to survive and transcend difficulties in a sort of dress rehearsal fashion, so that when we are called upon to confront the complexities of life in reality, we have models upon which to draw for support, comfort, and example." Rod Philbrick sees that writing for young adults is important because it gives the author a chance to help instill a lifelong "need to read." All human beings, he asserts, use stories and legends to help shape a sense of who they are in the world, but with so many other story sources available—TV, film, video games—young people do not necessarily turn to books for stories that give them meaning or purpose. That's why Philbrick believes "it's so important to make a story compelling, to *keep them reading*. I happen to believe that of all the story sources, the written word is best because it requires the most complete act of imagination from the reader. A book forces you to think, to use, if you will, the muscles of your brain" (e-mail to Mary Warner).

For Chris Crutcher, all storytelling is important. It provides something to relate to, other perspectives, and stimulation to the imagination. "I think [writing for young adults] is no different from any other writing" (e-mail to Mary Warner).

Response to Question 4: "What Books Would You Suggest to Young Adult Readers?"

What books do the authors encourage young adult readers to read and what influenced the authors themselves? Some of the responses can be neatly "charted"; others include comments that add insight to their selections (see table 3.1).

Don Gallo's answer to the books he'd suggest to young adult readers and the books that have influenced him is more descriptive and more conveniently cited in paragraph format than in a table. Gallo asserts that because everyone has different needs and different interests, it's foolish to recommend only a handful of titles that are good reads for teens. On the other hand, "hundreds of first-rate books have been published for teens during the last 35 years, and the quality is getting better and better, especially for high school students" (e-mail to Mary Warner). He could list 50 YA titles published just in 2003 that are excellent reads for teenagers—including fantasy, historical fiction, poetry, short stories, mysteries, and realistic fiction. Some of the writings are better for seventh graders, while he'd recommend others for eleventh- and twelfth-graders; some are just for girls and others just for guys; a few are better for fantasy lovers and others would work best for high school reluctant readers. "Variety is the rule, and readers need to be allowed to choose."

As a teenager, Gallo was not a reader, and "absolutely nothing I was required to read for school had any effect on me. The only book I valued was the *Boy Scout Handbook* because I was an outdoors kind of kid and wanted to know all about trees, birds, outdoor cooking, surviving in the woods, etc." Halfway through college, he realized books did have an impact on him, and since then everything he has read has influenced his life in some way—"as in I am a part of all that I have met." He doesn't have a favorite book or author, though at the top of his favorites list are Robert Cormier, Chris Crutcher, and Laurie Halse Anderson.

Han Nolan's responses are also more discursive. She suggests that young adults read books that entertain them, delight them, make them think, make them laugh and cry and feel every other emotion, but most importantly she suggests that they read books that turn on the lights for them. She always believed that she'd let her children read any book they wanted to read, but then she had one child who started reading books that just "brought such darkness to her world." This child started the whole routine of dressing in black clothes, keeping her shades drawn, and writing poems about death and dying. Nolan knew that these behaviors were connected to what her daughter's new friends were recommending that she read. "I didn't discourage her from those books, but we went to the book store and I helped her pick out some other books that I wanted her to have especially, because they had meant so much to me and I thought they would mean a lot to her as well."

Table 3.1. Author Suggestions and Influences

Name of Author	*Books They Suggest to Teen Readers*	*Books That Influenced Them*
Laurie Halse Anderson	"Some of my personal favorites include the works of Francesa Lia Block and Chris Crutcher."	"James Joyce has had a profound influence on me . . . his use of language leaves me stunned. He takes language to another level, no, to several other levels."
Ann Angel	"*The Shadowboxer*, *Slot Machine*, and *Freewill* by Chris Lynch; *After the Rain* and *When She Was Good* by Norma Fox Mazer; *When You Come Softly*, *I Hadn't Meant to Tell You*, and *Locomotion* by Jackie Woodson; *Speak* by Laurie Halse Anderson; *To Kill a Mockingbird* by Harper Lee; *Dinky Hocker Shoots Smack* by M. E. Kerr; *A Step from Heaven* by An Na; *The Buffalo Tree* by Adam Rapp; and so many others I can't recall the names right now."	
Jan Cheripko	These are the types of books Cheripko suggests teens *don't read*: those that are violent for violence's sake; those that pander to cheap sensuality; those that are nihilistic in tone and meaning; those that offer no hope or offer misguided hope; those that offer easy answers; those that are deceptive; those in which the authors have not discovered any real answers themselves.	His list starts with the Bible and includes many plays of Shakespeare; the Hindu Bhagavad-Gita; Tolkien's Ring trilogy; many books by C. S. Lewis; a somewhat unknown book called *The Way of the Pilgrim*; *The Big Book of Alcoholics Anonymous*; Goethe's *Faust* and Dante's *Inferno*; the works of Ernest Hemingway, Samuel Beckett, Jean Paul Sartre, and St. Augustine; biographies of John Adams, George Washington, Abraham Lincoln, Winston Churchill, and Carl Jung; *A Study in History* and *An Historian's Approach to Religion* by Arnold Toynbee. He also recommends the poetry of

		e.e. cummings; William Wordsworth; Francis Thompson; Wilfred Owen; Dame Edith Sitwell; the Rosettis; Alfred, Lord Tennyson; and a host of others.
Chris Crutcher	Other than suggesting his own books for "narcissistic reasons," Crutcher says, "find the books you want to read. Check them out. Read the flap . . . look at the first chapter. If I were to mention titles, I would leave out as many good ones as I named."	Works of Kurt Vonnegut, Pat Conroy, and Alice Walker; *To Kill a Mockingbird, The Things They Carried* . . . "Again, I leave out scores more than I name."
Karen Cushman	"*Slave Dancer, A Chance Child, The Diary of Anne Frank, The Great Gilly Hopkins, Joey Pigza Swallowed the Key, Night* by Elie Wiesel; anything by Rosemary Sutcliffe or Mary Renault; early Kurt Vonnegut; *Mad* magazine; the graphic novel *Maus;* Russell Hoban's *How Tom Beat Captain Najork and His Hired Sportsmen*. Katherine Paterson said it better than I can when she wrote, 'It is not enough to simply teach children to read; we have to give them something worth reading, something that will stretch their imaginations—something that will help them make sense of their own lives and encourage them to reach out to people whose lives are quite different from their own.'"	These are books Cushman read in her adolescent years: *Forever Amber, Strawberry Girl, Cotton in My* Sack—these were the first works of historical fiction she read, and they resulted in the passion that remains to this day. She also recommends *Microbe Hunters* and *Triumph over Pain* (about medical matters—some of which appear in her books today); *Missing May*; and *Sarah, Plain and Tall*.
Karen Hesse	"I would not suggest individual titles. What I would suggest is a well-read mentor, for example, a dedicated librarian who is familiar with a wide range of literature who can hand pick a bibliography of must-reads, tailored for individual readers."	"The book that most profoundly influenced my young adult years is *Hiroshima* by John Hersey."

(continues)

Table 3.1. Continued

Name of Author	*Books They Suggest to Teen Readers*	*Books That Influenced Them*
Norma Fox Mazer	"Some of the most wonderful novels for young adults are being written today. Recent favorites include *Many Stones* by Carolyn Coman; *One Step to Heaven* by An Na; *Feed* by Tobin Anderson; *Miracle's Boys* by Jackie Woodson; *Kissing Kate* by Lauren Myracle; and *French Kiss* by Adam Bagdasarian."	"No particular book, but reading itself has influenced me deeply. Reading remains one of my greatest pleasures. I cannot pass a day without reading. And I am eternally grateful that I can do for readers what other writers have done for me for so many years—provide me with stories, with insight, with entrée to worlds and people and lives I would otherwise never know."
Shelley F. Mickle	"James Agee's *A Death in the Family* is one of the most beautiful classics written in America; *Jim the Boy* by Tony Earley is suitable for anyone age 11 to 97."	"I am particularly fond of *An American Childhood* by Annie Dillard; books that influenced me while I was growing up were some of the childhood standards, mainly *Little Women; A Member of the Wedding* and *The Heart Is a Lonely Hunter* by Carson McCullers are as true and magnificent today as in the years when they were published."
Katherine Paterson	"There are so many good books; there have to be. Readers are very different and the same book will not fit every reader. I suggest readers ask their librarians as well as their friends for titles. Someone who knows you is much more likely to know what book would be great for you. I am a product of all I have read and I have read a lot."	"Two books I read as a young adult continue to matter to me: *The Yearling* and *Cry the Beloved Country*; I love Endo's *Silence*; I also love Dickens—what a great storyteller; Tolstoy, Undset, Jane Austen, and George Eliot among the classics. Robertson Davies, Anita Desai, Ann Pachett are contemporary novelists I especially like. As for poets, my favorite is Gerard Manley Hopkins. I also love Emily Dickinson and modern poets David Whyte, Mary Oliver, and A. R. Ammons. I was raised on and still get my sustenance from the Bible."

Gary Paulsen	"I always tell kids to read like a wolf eats. Read anything, read everything, read all the time. Read what they tell you to read, read what they tell you not to read. Just read. Comic books and graphic novels, newspapers and magazines, nonfiction and fiction, cereal boxes and sweepstakes entry forms—everything, anything. I read every night before I go to sleep. I'm always reading new things and I'll reread old books, too."	"I think I've read some of Dickens' books 12 times and I learn something new each time."
Rod Philbrick		"The book that probably has made the most lasting impression on me is *Huckleberry Finn*. By the time I was 15, I'd read everything Twain had written—at least what was readily available, including some of his posthumously published stuff."
Marilyn Reynolds	"I suggest books that hold their interest, that connect in one way or another, the book they can barely put down because that book will reach them on a deep level."	"It's impossible to choose a few books that have influenced me; there are so many. I love the work of Robertson Davies, Anne Tyler, William Styron, Alice Walker, Margaret Atwood, early Rita Mae Brown (forget the cat detectives!), Kazuo Ishiguro, Jane Hamilton, Gail Godwin, Virginia Woolf, Charles Dickens, etc., etc. In YA, I particularly admire Chris Crutcher, M. E. Kerr, Judy Blume (early), Gloria Miklowitz, Richard Peck, etc."
Jerry Spinelli	"I am a believer in reading the best of contemporary literature as opposed to stilted 'classics.' In place of *Silas Marner*, which I had to read, I would suggest to any kid to read *The Chocolate*	

(continues)

Table 3.1. Continued

Name of Author	*Books They Suggest to Teen Readers*	*Books That Influenced Them*
	War or *A Wrinkle in Time* or *A Summer to Die* or *The Greatest Christmas Pageant Ever* or *The True Confessions of Charlotte Doyle*."	
Ruth White	"I recommend *Up the Road Slowly* by Irene Hunt, *The Giver* by Lois Lowry, and *Jacob Have I Loved* by Katherine Paterson. There are many, of course, but those stand out. For older teens I recommend *To Kill a Mockingbird* by Harper Lee, and a lesser known but remarkable book called *The Education of Little Tree* by Forrest Carter."	"At this late stage in my life I am discovering and devouring the Jane Austen novels. I can't believe I missed out on them all these years simply because I didn't understand *Pride and Prejudice* in high school. The books that have had the greatest influence on me in my life are definitely the *Little House* books. First, my mother read them to me, and later I read them for myself. I believe they are the reason I decided to be a writer."
Jane Yolen	"It depends on the individual reader. The books my three kids read as teens differed enormously. The books I read as a teen were not the ones my brother read."	"The King Arthur stories, which spoke about honor and truth and loyalty and working to better the world for all humans. The fairy tales, which led me to believe that there was a structure for the universe encoded deep in the bones of earth and sun and stars, and in the human bones as well."

Nolan and her daughter also discussed the types of books she thought she might like that were outside the darker category she had been reading.

Nolan realized that her daughter, like so many young people, had outgrown her young childhood books and didn't really know where to turn next. She had no direction and didn't know what she would really like. So "we got a variety of books and eventually, she found new genres that appealed to her. Soon, the shades were up in her room and she began to wear more than black and her writing was more upbeat." Books can have such a great influence on young people.

"The books that have influenced me most in my life could fill a library," Nolan commented. Naming a few though, she began with the Nancy Drew mysteries because they got her excited about reading. Then there was *Harriet the Spy*; Nolan thought she would become a spy, too, so she dressed like Harriet, had a spy route, and carried a notebook. When she got caught spying, she quickly gave up her spying but not her notebook. Then she read *A Wrinkle in Time*, which got her excited about traveling through time and the tesseract. Next she read *David Copperfield*, and "loved living in this strange world of his, day after day." She tried writing just like Dickens after she'd read *David Copperfield*, and she "went through [her] days for a while talking, in [her] head, like the characters in that book" (e-mail to Mary Warner).

The description of Nolan's investment in her daughter's reading exemplifies the commitment of these authors and many other adults who believe in the world of reading and story and the ways this world can be a source of meaning, particularly for young adults. Since not all young people have such adults in their immediate situation, the ideas and the commitment of authors, librarians, and teachers is particularly crucial for young adults.

Many writers hesitate to suggest specific titles since they realize there is such a wide variety of writing to appeal to a wide variety of teen tastes and interests. Ann Angel cautions that many of her suggestions contain controversial subject matter, but all of the books she recommends tell stories of young adults who have overcome adversity in order to see the world in a redeemable light. Among the websites the authors suggest is that of the American Library Association (www.ala.org), which has great booklists. There is a commonly quoted adage that "it takes a village to raise a child." This adage could be aptly adapted for the many teenagers of our world, "it takes a library and caring adult readers and writers to mentor a young adult."

Works Cited

"About Shelly Mickle." www.shelleymickle.com/biography.htm.

Anderson, Laurie Halse. "My Responses." E-mail to Mary Warner. 24 July 2003.

(Angel, Ann biography) *ALAN Review*, Winter 2003.

Angel, Ann. E-mail to Mary Warner. 30 August 2003.

Authors4teens.com. www.authors4teens.com. (YA author biographies.)

Bugniazet, Judith. "A Telephone Interview with Robert Cormier." *ALAN Review* 12, no. 2 (Winter 1985): 14–18. Reprinted in *Two Decades of "The ALAN Review,"* edited by

Patricia P. Kelly and Robert C. Small Jr. Urbana, IL: NCTE, 1999. Page references are to the reprinted version.
Cheripko, Jan. E-mail to Mary Warner. 29 September 2003.
Cheripko, Jan. *Rat*. Honesdale, PA: Boyds Mills Press, 2002.
Crutcher, Chris. "Books that Can Save Lives . . . Author Response." E-mail to Mary Warner. 20 June 2003.
Cushman, Karen. E-mail to Mary Warner. 19 September 2003.
Flannery, Jennifer, for Gary Paulsen. E-mail to Mary Warner. 30 January 2004.
Gallo, Don. "YA Lit Project." E-mail to Mary Warner. 3 September 2003.
Hesse, Karen. Personal Letter to Mary Warner. 7 July 2003.
"Karen Cushman." Education Place. www.eduplace.com/rdg/author/index.html.
"Karen Hesse." www.indiana.edu/~reading/ieo/bibs/hesse.html.
"Karen Hesse's Biography." Scholastic. www2.scholastic.com/teachers/authorsandbooks/authorstudies/authorhome.jhtml?authorID=45&collateralID=5183&displayName=Biography.
"Learning about Gary Paulsen." www.scils.rutgers.edu/~kvander/paulsen.html.
L'Engle, Madeleine. *An Acceptable Time*. Commemorative Edition. New York: Bantam Doubleday Dell, 1997.
———. "Is It Good Enough for Children?" *The Writer*, July 2000, 8–10.
Mazer, Norma Fox. E-mail to Mary Warner. 1 September 2003.
Mickle, Shelley Fraser. E-mail to Mary Warner.
Morris, Catherine, and Inez Ramsey. "Katherine Paterson Teacher Resource File." www.falcon.jmu.edu/~ramseyil/index.html (site now discontinued).
Nolan, Han. "From Han Nolan." E-mail to Mary Warner. 2 June 2003.
Paterson, Katherine. "Questionnaire." E-mail to Mary Warner. 9 April 2003.
Philbrick, Rodman. "Rodman Philbrick." E-mail to Mary Warner. 9 April 2003.
Reynolds, Marilyn. "Author Questions." E-mail to Mary Warner. 16 June 2003.
(Reynolds, Marilyn biography.) www.morninggloryp ress.com/pages/fictrite.html.
Spinelli, Jerry. E-mail to Mary Warner. 14 June 2003.
White, Ruth. "From Ruth White." E-mail to Mary Warner. 12 June 2003.
Yolen, Jane. "Author Response." E-mail to Mary Warner. 17 March 2003.

Resources for YA Authors and Readers

authors4teens.com.
www.eduplace.com/rdg/author/index.html.
www.indiana.edu/~reading/ieo/bibs/paterson.html. (Fill in the author name right before "html.")
ca.dir.yahoo.com/arts/humanities/literature/authors/Young_Adult/.
www.lajuene.com/ginny/yaauthors.html.
www.millnthps.sa.edu.au/websites/english/authors_and_books.htm.
Bantam Doubleday Dell—Teacher Resource Center. www.bdd.com/teachers.

Clarion Books, a Houghton Mifflin Company. www.houghtonmifflinbooks.com.

Farrar, Straus and Giroux—publishing company. 19 Union Square West, New York, NY 10003.

Gallo, Don, ed. *Author Insights: Turning Teenagers into Readers and Writers*. Portsmouth, NH: Boynton/Cook Heinemann, 1992.

Hipple, Ted, ed. *Writers for Young Adults*. Suppl. 1. Scribners, 1999.

Scarecrow Studies in Young Adult Literature series. This series continues the body of critical writing established in Twayne's Young Adult Author's Series and expands beyond single-author studies to exploration of genres, multicultural writing, and controversial issues in YA reading. Patty Campbell is the series editor.

PART TWO

RECOMMENDATIONS

In chapters 4 through 8, a selection of books is presented that contain stories of young adults experiencing the pressures that teens have indicated are most significant in their lives. These pressures include peer pressure (concerning drugs, alcohol, sex, and use of weapons as well as moral and ethical choices); school-related pressure (academic achievement, grades, homework, extracurriculars, sports and the pressure to win, and holding a job while attending school); and divorce or separation of parents. Young adults found these books meaningful and worth the read and suggested their peers read them. Again, valuing what the teens themselves have to say about their lives, half of the books included in the following chapters were recommended by teens in response to the survey—these books are signaled with "**Teen Recommended**." In addition, many of these books are simply good reads.

I also built on the issues that survey respondents said are the biggest in their lives, and selected books that supplement the teens' recommendations. My choices are based on eight years of extensive reading and research in young adult literature; on books about YA literature, specifically publications like the *Books for You* series from NCTE; on numerous recommendations from the *ALAN Review*; on the other works of YA authors I've enjoyed; on presentations by authors at National Council of Teachers of English and ALAN (Assembly on Literature of Adolescents of NCTE) conferences; on the recommendations of colleagues in the field of YA literature (Joan Kaywell, Pamela Sissi Carroll, Sue Ellen Bridgers, and Virginia Monseau, in particular); and on the recommendations of many authors of YA literature. An essay, "What's Good about the Best?" by Ted Hipple and Amy B. Maupin in *The English Journal* of January 2001, an issue devoted to the "Lure of YA Literature," reinforces many of my reasons for including the books I have.

Not every book listed below is appropriate for teaching to an entire class; in addition, teachers frequently face tight curricular demands that do not allow them to expand the literary canon. But many of the teaching ideas indicate ways the books could be paired with more "canonical" works. Teachers and librarians should specifically examine the "Why You Should Give This Book to Teens" section included in each of the book annotations for reasons to support their use or suggestion of the book. Further, many of the books would work particularly well in thematic units related to character education.

Obviously not every book that the teen respondents recommended or every book you as teachers, librarians, and parents might include is among those annotated below. However, I hope that the books included provide a useful introduction to the "powerful resource of story" that we can tap in guiding adolescents to meaning. In providing these (over 120) book summaries and teaching resources, I have aimed to give teachers and librarians a wealth of information that they may not have time to search out on their own. The books included in this part are prioritized according to the issues that teens responding to the survey (described in chapter 1) signaled as most important, and they are organized in the following five chapters:

Chapter 4: Books about Real-Life Experiences
Chapter 5: Books about Facing Death and Loss
Chapter 6: Books about Identity, Discrimination, and Struggles with Decisions
Chapter 7: Books about Courage and Survival
Chapter 8: Books on Allegory, Fantasy, Myth, and Parable

The first category (found in chapter 4) includes books related to peer pressure and making life choices, the number one issue of survey respondents; to violence, which is often related to peer pressure and the desire to belong and be accepted; and to the struggles adolescents meet in relationships with friends and family.

The second category of books (chapter 5) relates to death and loss. Suicide is a leading cause of death for adolescents; in addition, suicide deaths of peers or classmates create huge voids, affect the survivors on numerous levels, and in unique ways, raise questions about the meaning of life. The books suggested here offer powerful stories for adolescents, not only about suicide, but also about continuing with life after the death of a parent, grandparent, sibling, or friend, or in a larger context, the death of ideals and hopes.

The third category (chapter 6) presents books related to identity, struggles with decisions, and discrimination. Again, in direct correlation to the highly ranked issue of peer pressure identified in the survey, these books speak to those teens who are often "outsiders" because of difference—gender, ethnicity, race, physical or mental exceptionalities, religious preference, or socioeconomic status—and to those who need to understand difference. Books in this section, with the poignant stories they present, could be effectively used for character education; so often humans fear what they don't know, and these novels help readers to step into the worlds of the characters, worlds which mirror our own worlds.

Courage and survival is the title of the fourth category of books (chapter 7). Here, adolescents can meet characters that have faced seemingly insurmountable difficulties yet have overcome them. A source of hope for anyone in a tough situation is the story of someone else who has made it through a similar struggle. Many books in this set present characters who are immigrant Americans or who have firsthand experience of war, genocide, or oppression. These characters' stories show how the human spirit can find meaning, without bitterness or without continuing the cycle of violence.

Finally, the category of allegory, fantasy, myth, and parable (chapter 8) connects with the many survey respondents who suggested that various books in the Chicken Soup series or the Bible are the books that helped them with issues in their lives or were ones they would recommend to other teens. The books included in this section are those that call readers to go beyond literal worlds to worlds that may be utopias or dystopias: to examine the real struggles of good versus evil, of leadership that is service versus a quest for power, of knowledge and rationality versus wisdom and understanding. These books are filled with wisdom figures like Dumbledore and Aslan, and of heroes like Jonas in *The Giver*, Charles Wallace and Meg in *A Wrinkle in Time*, and Frodo and Gandalf in *The Lord of the Rings* trilogy.

Some books address themes that cross categories; possibly some of the books will be in categories different from those you as teachers or librarians might put them in, but the fact that these books address multiple issues speaks of their depth and potential to appeal to young adults. Within the categories, each book entry provides:

- complete publication information, including author and title
- a brief summary, which emphasizes those aspects of the book that cause it to be placed in this category
- teaching ideas and resources, both print and electronic

- a list of reasons for giving the book to teens
- other books by the same author (for many entries, though not all)

Lists of print and electronic resources follow the book annotations. While no list can be exhaustive, my goal has been to be as inclusive as possible of the titles, authors, and scholars related to the rich resource of YA literature.

CHAPTER FOUR

~

Books about Real-Life Experiences

Making Life Choices, Facing Violence or Abuse, and Living through Family and Relationship Issues

Anderson, Laurie Halse: *Speak*
Reprint edition 1 April 2001, ISBN 014131088X
****Teen Recommended****

Melinda has been at an end-of-summer party—the party that precedes her first year in high school. She and her friends are flattered to be invited and Andy, a popular senior guy, is there. When those at the party start drinking, Melinda, who has had a couple beers, wanders out into the woods and meets Andy, who looks at that point like a Greek god. He wants more than kisses though; Melinda can't fight back because she's drunk. She knows enough to call 911 and get help, but everyone at the party thinks she's ratting. Her life becomes solitary and silent. The book is her inner monologue.

Teaching Ideas and Resources

1. Writing can be therapeutic; this book demonstrates the power of inner monologues. Use selections of the book to help your students write memoirs, diaries, or dramatic monologues.
2. Melinda hangs a poster of Maya Angelou in her "sanctuary," actually an empty closet previously used by custodians. Maya Angelou was also raped and stayed silent—discuss with your students the symbolism of the poster and the struggle that Melinda and Maya Angelou faced in deciding whether to reveal the names of their assailants.

3. Art class becomes a healing place for Melinda; discuss with your students how art can be used to heal. Ask your students what kind of artwork would represent their life at this point. Have your students do an artistic or creative representation—one that voices their sense of themselves.
4. "Between Voice and Voicelessness: Transacting Silence in Laurie Halse Anderson's *Speak*" by Elaine J. O'Quinn (*ALAN Review* 29, no. 1 [2001]: 54–58) is a resource for background on the novel.
5. "Speaking Out," by Laurie Halse Anderson (*ALAN Review* 27, no. 3 [Spring 2000]) shares Anderson's insights on the novel.
6. For background on Laurie Halse Anderson, check the following websites:

   www.authors4teens.com
   greenwood.scbbs.com/servlet/A4TStart?authorid=landerson&source=
   www.writerlady.com
   www.viterbo.edu/personalpages/faculty/GSmith/LessonPlanforSpeak.htm

Why Give This Book to Teens?

- Because many teens have been "rejected" when others thought they "ratted" on them, and because rejection often leads to violent actions. This novel shows how one young woman survived the rejection of her peers.
- Because they may have "fallen" for someone who looked handsome and was popular, but have had a terrible experience like Melinda and are now dealing with the shame and guilt of rape or sexual assault.
- Because they might be misunderstood by parents and teachers, as Melinda is, and they need to learn from her story how to handle the difficult position of peer pressure. They can decide whether Melinda's silence and all she faces because of her silence is the best way to respond.

Other books by Laurie Halse Anderson to consider reading: *Yellow Fever 1793* and *Catalyst*.

Angelou, Maya: *I Know Why the Caged Bird Sings*
Published by Bantam, reissue edition 1 April 1983,
ISBN 0553279378
Teen Recommended

The book presents a series of memoirs of Maya Angelou's life from the time she was three and her beloved brother Bailey was four. Much of their childhood was spent under the care of their paternal grandmother, known to them as Momma. They lived in Stamps, Arkansas, in the years before and during the Depression. Stamps was rigidly segregated and Maya, then known as Marguerite, experienced the results of segregation and fear of Blacks.

Bailey and Marguerite are first sent to Stamps because their parents divorced. Eventually they are taken back to live with their mother in St. Louis. During this time, their mother, Vivian Baxter, is living with Mr. Freeman. Freeman begins sexually abusing Marguerite and eventually rapes her. Eight-year-old Marguerite is threatened with Bailey's death if she reveals anything about the assault. Because she is so ill after the rape, her mother does find out and Freeman is brought to trial. He is later found murdered, and Marguerite believes that her "words" caused his death. She becomes silent for many months following the assault.

The memoirs also chronicle Marguerite (Maya's) and Bailey's adolescence, poignantly describing what it meant to be Black in the pre–Civil Rights era.

Teaching Ideas and Resources

1. Mrs. Bertha Flowers is Angelou's first "lifeline" after the terrifying experience of the rape and her silence after Mr. Freeman's death. Mrs. Flowers gives Angelou books and tells her to read them aloud. She also offers this wise advice: "Now no one is going to make you talk—possibly no one can. But bear in mind, language is man's way of communicating with his fellow man and it is language alone which separates him from the lower animals" (*I Know* . . . , 95). Have your students write a response to Mrs. Flowers's words.
2. Should Angelou have spoken out? What is the witness's responsibility, particularly if the witness is a child or young adult? Discuss these questions with your students and relate Angelou's decision to current situations in your students' lives and school setting.
3. Maya Angelou was chosen by President-elect Bill Clinton to write a poem for his first inauguration. Her poem is "On the Pulse of Morn-

ing"—locate a copy of the poem and have students analyze Angelou's use of language in light of what they know of Angelou from reading the book.

4. Oprah Winfrey did a conversation with Maya Angelou—an extended interview. The video is excellent for accompanying a lesson on Angelou and it gives your students the opportunity to "see" Angelou.
5. *Borrowed Finery* by Paula Fox is a memoir—nonfiction—that traces a life of a white girl from 1923 onward. It would make a good comparison work for study with Angelou's novel. Paula Fox has also experienced loss of parents, particularly her mother, and the memoir traces that theme of loss throughout Fox's childhood and adolescence. Use both novels to teach your students about the genre of memoir.
6. "Seeking *Cuentos*, Developing Narrative Voices" by Louise Garcia Harrison, an essay in *United in Diversity* edited by Jean E. Brown and Elaine C. Stephens (NCTE, 1998), presents ways to teach Angelou's novel in tandem with *The House on Mango Street* and *Woman Hollering Creek* by Sandra Cisneros; *Blue Skin of the Sea* by Graham Salisbury; and *Living Up the Street* by Gary Soto. Using these novels, you can incorporate a number of multicultural perspectives.
7. "*The Awakening* and Young Adult Literature: Seeking Self-Identity in Many Ways and Many Cultures" by Pamela Sissi Carroll (chapter 4 in Kaywell, *Adolescent Literature as a Complement to the Classics*, vol. 2, 1995) uses *I Know Why the Caged Bird Sings* as one of the autobiographical pieces to complement *The Awakening*, a text frequently taught in American literature courses.
8. The following are websites with lesson plan ideas:

   www.westga.edu/~kidreach/lessonplans/cagedbirdlesson.html
   www.pinkmonkey.com/booknotes/monkeynotes/pmCagedBird01.asp
   www.webenglishteacher.com/angelou.html
   www.planetbookclub.com/teachers/civil.html
   www.beyondbooks.com/bbteacher/lessons/indexlam12.asp
   www.yale.edu/ynhti/curriculum/units/1985/3/85.03.03.x.html

Why Give This Book to Teens?

- Because many more teens today are raised by grandparents or relatives if the teen's parents have separated or divorced, so teens can relate to Maya's and Bailey's experiences; Black American students frequently live with grandparents.

- Because they might have to live with a stepparent or with a live-in male or female friend of their parents and find this stepparent is abusive, so Angelou's story can be a guide for them in the lonely position of not being believed by the parent who has remarried.
- Because they might be a victim of prejudice or harassment, and Maya Angelou is both a role model and a spokeswoman for Black Americans and tolerance.

Blume, Judy: *Are You There God? It's Me, Margaret*
Published by Laurel Leaf; Reissue edition 1 October 1991, ISBN 0440904196
Teen Recommended

Margaret is nearly 12 and she and the "Pre-Teen Sensations" are filled with questions about what it will be like to start maturing, have their menstrual periods, and date. At the same time, Margaret has a much larger issue—she is "no religion" since her mother was baptized a Christian and her father is Jewish. When her parents marry, neither set of in-laws is happy about the mix of religions. Thus Margaret's parents do not participate in any organized religion and decide they will let Margaret choose for herself.

Ironically, Margaret, without any formal religion, has a great sense of God—enough to write to God about everything that's happening in her life. And Margaret lets God know that she finds God in these times when she talks to God alone—not when she visits the temple with her Jewish grandmother, or goes to the First Presbyterian Church with Janie or to the First Methodist Church with Nancy. Although Margaret is only going on 12, she has some wisdom that many adults never achieve.

Teaching Ideas and Resources

1. This book would work well for a unit on Images of God—fitting with a study of *The Odyssey* or *Siddhartha*. Have your students research the religion their family practices, if they do practice any particular one; if the family doesn't practice any particular religion, your students could explore the approaches of Native Americans, Jews, Muslims, or any group that the students want to explore; and present their findings to the class. A unit exploring world religions would also fit with character education in promoting understanding and appreciation of other cultures' religions. The following website lists books for teaching children about religion: www.chicagoforum.org/books.htm

2. You might consider inviting ministers or representatives of various religions to come and make presentations about the basic beliefs of the groups they represent.
3. "An Overlooked Characteristic of a Good Literary Choice: Discussability" by Robert C. Small Jr., in "Adolescent Literature: Making Connections with Teens" (special issue, *Virginia English Bulletin* 44, no. 2 [Fall 1994]), focuses on this novel and presents teaching ideas.
4. The following websites have background on Judy Blume and teaching resources:

   falcon.jmu.edu/~ramseyil/blume.htm
   www.ashland.edu/library/irc/blume03.pdf

5. This site is for girls and women, and parents and daughters:

   www.celebrategirls.com/readings.html

Why Give This Book to Teens?

- Because teens are often searching for a religion, wanting to know more about religion, or wondering about God, but they rarely want to talk with their parents about religion. By reading this novel, they can see how Margaret handles some of the questions that they may have and learn ways to find out about religion.
- Because they might not be able to participate in the same religious practices their parents or others participate in and want to do some exploring like Margaret does.
- Because they might have the same feeling as Margaret—God might seem more "real" to them when they talk to God alone and not in any particular church service or ritual; Margaret's story and her questions demonstrate a "real" relationship with a higher being.

Other books by Judy Blume to consider reading: *Tiger Eyes*, *Forever*, and *Places I Never Meant to Be*.

Bridgers, Sue Ellen: *All Together Now*
Published by Banks Channel Books, December 2001, ISBN 1889199060

Casey is 12; she's gone to stay with her grandparents, Ben and Jane, in the small town that was Casey's dad's home. Casey's dad is in the Air Force in

Korea; Casey's mom is working two jobs and isn't available to be with Casey much. Casey learns to love and care for a man, Dwayne Pickens, who is nearly Casey's dad's age—Dwayne is mentally retarded. Dwayne's brother, Alva, finds Dwayne an embarrassment and is constantly trying to get him committed to a mental institution. Casey discovers the gentleness of Dwayne; how Dwayne loves baseball, watching Casey's Uncle Taylor race, and going to movies. Pansy, a lifelong friend of Jane, goes through her own struggles—marrying Hazard Whitaker, a man of 52 who feels like much of his life has been a disaster.

This caring family circle saves Dwayne. The book is set during the polio epidemic, and Casey nearly dies of it. At the same time, Casey is loved back into life by her grandparents as well as Pansy and Hazard, Taylor and Gwen, and Dwayne. Dwayne learns that Casey is really a girl but is okay with that; for a long time, Casey had been hiding that fact from Dwayne, afraid he wouldn't like her if he knew she was a girl.

Teaching Ideas and Resources

1. This is a good book for teaching respect for and acceptance of mental handicaps. There are also a number of central themes: friendship, family relationships, and the importance of extended families. Consider having your students do a "Take a Stand" game following reading of the book. "Take a Stand" is played by first creating a list of value statements (for example: "the best parenting is done by two parents with the mother staying at home"). Once you have a list of such statements, direct students to indicate how they feel about each statement by moving to various locations along an imaginary line on the floor. On one end of the line is the spot for "I strongly agree," the middle signifies "I'm neutral," and the other end is the spot meaning "I strongly disagree." Ask your students to explain their positions and comment further on their perspectives. This activity allows them to clarify values and can work to help foster character education goals.
2. You can also have students create value statements to be used; this allows them to see how important wording of statements can be and also helps them put some of their values into words.
3. A newer novel to teach or read in tandem with *All Together Now* is *The Silent Boy* by Lois Lowry (2003). This novel, set in the early years of the twentieth century, is a first-person narrative of Katy Thatcher and how she learns about what it means for a young person to be described as "touched" and comes to understand what an "asylum" is. This is a

relatively brief novel, which could be read to your students as part of a larger unit on differences. These two novels would connect well with teaching *Of Mice and Men* and with focus on the mentally challenged.

4. "Introducing *To Kill a Mockingbird* with Collaborative Group Reading of Related Young Adult Novels" by Bonnie O. Ericson (in Kaywell, *Adolescent Literature as a Complement to the Classics*, vol. 1, 1993) uses *All Together Now* as one of the core YA novels in this unit.
5. For further background on Sue Ellen Bridgers, see *ALAN Review* 13, no. 2 (Winter 1986) for several articles.
6. "Creating a Bond between Writer and Reader" by Sue Ellen Bridgers in *Reading Their World: The Young Adult Novel in the Classroom*, 2nd ed. (Monseau and Salvner 2000) gives author's insights to this novel and others by Bridgers.
7. Lynne Alvine and Devon Duffy, in "Friendship and Tensions in *A Separate Peace* and *Staying Fat for Sarah Byrnes*" (chapter 8 in Kaywell, *Adolescent Literature as a Complement to the Classics*, vol. 2, 1995) use *All Together Now* as one of five YA novels to complete the unit.
8. Also check the following websites:

    www.sueellenbridgers.com/works.htm
    www.scils.rutgers.edu/~kvander/bridgers.html
    scholar.lib.vt.edu/ejournals/ALAN/fall96/f96-11-Research.html

Why Give This Book to Teens?

- Because they might have a sibling or a friend who has mental or physical exceptionalities and find themselves having to protect that person from intolerance or hurtful comments. In a larger scenario, they might be called to make some difficult decisions as do the protagonists in *Of Mice and Men* and *The Silent Boy*.
- Because teens, facing peer pressure, are often fearful of differences they have never thought about or encountered before.
- Because, like Casey, they might be teens who are separated from parents and living with grandparents or other extended family and who, by reading Casey's story, can learn about how to live through their situation.

Other books by Sue Ellen Bridgers to consider reading: *Home before Dark*, *Permanent Connections*, *Notes for Another Life*, and *Keeping Christina*.

Bridgers, Sue Ellen: *All We Know of Heaven*
Published by Banks Channel Books, July 1999, ISBN 188919901X

When Bethany first sees Joel, she is helping the women prepare a meal for the men doing the hog slaughtering. He's a loner type who been away at a military academy and has the reputation for needing the discipline of such a school. Bethany lives with her Aunt Charlotte because Bethany's mother has died and Warren, her father, is a hopeless alcoholic. Though she's only 15, Bethany falls in love with Joel and will not wait to go on to school before she gets married. The marriage is doomed from its start, but Bethany is blinded by love.

Teaching Ideas and Resources

1. "Why Sue Ellen Bridgers' *All We Know of Heaven* Should Be Taught in Our High Schools," by Susanne M. Miller (*ALAN Review* 27, no. 1 [Fall 1999]) is a helpful essay for teaching this novel, particularly in providing rationale for teaching the book.
2. The title of the book relates to a poem by Emily Dickinson; find the poem and discuss it with your students. This will be especially appropriate as part of American Literature studies. Why is "parting all we know of heaven / and all we need of Hell"? What do your students know about "partings"?
3. Bridgers' novel comes from a family story about a relative she knew. Have your students interview an older relative to learn of family stories that may be important to the students' maturing and understanding of their family heritage.
4. The novel is set in the rural South; it is a good novel to use in a rural setting since so many teenagers marry young and do not get to experience much of the broader world. A good journal prompt to use with this novel would be: "How old should you be to get married? Why?"
5. Bridgers uses multiple characters to convey the story. Her book is an excellent example of point-of-view. Consider having your students select their favorite character and write additional entries in that character's voice.
6. "Time and Tradition Transforming the Secondary English Class with Young Adult Novels," by Gary Salvner in *Reading Their World: The Young Adult Novel in the Classroom*, 2nd ed. (Monseau and Salvner 2000) talks about characters in this novel and a number of Bridgers' other novels.

Why Give This Book to Teens?

- Because they may be in an abusive relationship and need guidance on how to help themselves, and reading Bethany's story could help them to make wiser choices. In addition, it is frequently easier for a teen to "hear" from another teen what action to take rather than to be told by a parent or another adult.
- Because it is easy for a female to be in a relationship for love, but the male in the relationship may be at another stage that doesn't value emotional attachments.
- Because they may be a friend of someone who is in an abusive relationship, and reading this novel could help them be of help to their friend.
- Because reading Bethany's story and realizing her personal tragedies may help teens who are in abusive situations realize they need to leave the relationship.

Cormier, Robert: *After the First Death*
Published by Laurel Leaf, reissue edition 1 February 1991, ISBN 0440208351

Three teenagers experience the hijacking of a busload of preschool children by terrorists. Kate is the substitute driver, who the terrorists have tapped as the first to die. Miro is a hijacker appointed to execute her. Ben is the messenger; he has been sent by his father, the general of the secret military organization that is being blackmailed. Ben and Miro are tormented by questions of loyalty and failure, while Kate struggles with what it means to be brave. The book deals with many topics related to terrorism, especially the involvement of young adults on suicide missions.

Teaching Ideas and Resources

1. Before your students read the text, have them brainstorm possible implications of the book's epigram by Dylan Thomas: "After the first death there is no other." Post the possibilities and pause during the reading to see how the book explores many of these meanings.
2. *After the First Death* plays with names, aliases, and ideas of hidden and concealed identity. Have your students chart the passages concerning names; have them journal possible meanings of the final dialogue between Ben and his father. Finally, some say these themes of names suggest Cormier's examination of the hiddenness of God and the mys-

terious name "I am" that God gives to Moses. What evidence in the text can you find to support this?

3. Cormier wrote that this book was the result of his own struggle with the biblical story of Abraham and the sacrifice of Isaac. Read the story from Genesis, and have your students discuss under what circumstances fathers might sacrifice or send sons to potential death and for what causes. What questions about God does Cormier's book raise for the reader?
4. Lois Stover and Connie Zitlow, in "Using Young Adult Literature as a Companion to World Literature: A Model Thematic Unit on the 'Clash of Cultures' Centered on *Things Fall Apart*" (chapter 5 in Kaywell, *Adolescent Literature as a Complement to the Classics*, vol. 2, 1995), use *After the First Death* for character connections with *Things Fall Apart*.
5. *The ALAN Review* (vol. 12, no. 2 [Winter 1985]) had several essays on Robert Cormier; all offer good resources for teaching his works.
6. An excellent website with numerous resources is available at:

   www.west.asu.edu/library/research/awareness/educational.html

7. A good site for other resources on Robert Cormier and his works:

   www.carr.org/mae/cormier/corm-web.htm

Why Give This Book to Teens?

- Because we live in a world with terrorists, and we don't understand their actions, so reading Cormier's novel could help teens better understand tendencies of terrorists. Also, many suicide bombers in contemporary situations are teens.
- Because the hijackers in this novel are teenagers—teen readers need to know why these teens take these actions and what leads to the violence that some of their peers commit.
- Because the bus driver is a teenager who has to make incredible decisions and show courage beyond her years. Maybe some teens have faced situations where they've needed courage they didn't feel they had and reading Kate's story will affirm their decisions.

Other books by Robert Cormier to consider reading: *Heroes* and *The Rag and Bone Shop*.

Covey, Sean: *Seven Habits of Highly Effective Teens*
Published by Simon & Schuster, 9 October 1998, ISBN 0684856093
Teen Recommended

Sean Covey, son of the well-known author and motivator Stephen Covey, offers principles from his father's book *The Seven Habits of Highly Effective People* and encourages teens to apply them to issues they face. *Seven Habits/Teens* asks teens to picture how they want their lives to be and then make the choices needed to get there. Using the tools of self-awareness, conscience, imagination, and willpower, Covey encourages teens to select solid core values and then to be proactive ("those who make things happen") rather than reactive ("those who get happened to"). Covey advises:

1. Be proactive: Take responsibility for your life.
2. Begin with the end in mind: Define your roles and goals in life.
3. Put first things first: Do the most important things first.
4. Think win-win: Have the attitude that everyone can win.
5. Seek first to understand and then to be understood: Listen first. Talk later.
6. Synergize: Working together achieves more.
7. Sharpen the saw: Maintain physical, emotional, and mental balance.

Teaching Ideas and Resources

1. For each of the seven habits, ask students to choose and mark the anecdote or illustration from the book that made the concept clearest for them. They can share the anecdote and its meaning for them in a talking circle.
2. Go to the Seven Habits of Highly Effective Teens website at www.educationcentral.org/tlam/7Habits.htm. Check the website for examples, but encourage your students to use their own writing voice. After reading each chapter, ask your students to write their own journals about a specific issue or situation they wish to affirm or to change. Include a personalized "I am" paraphrase of the habit as a journal title.

Master Teacher's Guide

- Stephen Covey [Contemporary Authors Online, Gale, 2003] was quoted in *Fortune*: "Remember, we are not human beings having a spiritual experience. We are spiritual beings having a human experience."
- Using examples from other biographies or fiction, ask your students to

describe characters who illustrate ways in which their spiritual values and priorities shape experiences.

Why Give This Book to Teens?

- Because Sean Covey's book is more teen-friendly, funny, and readable than his father's classic *The Seven Habits of Highly Effective People*.
- Because cartoons, quotes, and stories keep teens interested in reading.
- Because teens will get ideas on improving self-image, building friendships, resisting peer pressure, and achieving goals.

Crutcher, Chris: *Staying Fat for Sarah Byrnes*
Published by HarperCollins Juvenile Books, 18 March 2003, ISBN 0060094893
Teen Recommended

This novel is filled with characters—adolescents in particular—who face lack of acceptance because of difference. Eric Calhoune is fat; his nickname is "Moby." Sarah Byrnes has a physical disfigurement and hides the story of the horrible abuse she's experienced. Mark Brittain is a young man set on upholding the highest moral values, but he has a story hidden behind his self-righteous facade. Jody Mueller looks like the "all together" young woman, but she too holds a painful difference inside. A good read for students who are willing to question some of the status quo.

Teaching Ideas and Resources

1. The characters in this novel are all facing some kind of struggle with identity: Eric Calhoune, the main character, is heavy, called "Moby"—he's the one who stays fat for Sarah after he begins to lose weight by being on the swim team. Sarah Byrnes has been scarred—when she was three, her father pushed her face against the wood stove; her mother has deserted the family. Sarah is feigning silence and is catatonic to protect herself from her dad. Mark Brittain is a very self-righteous person/Christian who, though he preaches a "good line," is rigid in his thinking; he has forced his girlfriend Jody to have an abortion. Steve Ellerby, son of an Episcopalian minister, is a good questioner who is a supporter of Eric. Dale Thornton is a young man who has been held back in school; he acts the part of a bully or tough to antagonize others but he becomes an ally for Sarah.

   Ask your students to do writing and thinking about these characters and about what these characters represent, particularly since the characters face so many issues that teenagers experience.

2. Ms. Lemry is a teacher who is vital in helping these students think and creates the CAT—Contemporary American Thought course. Have students identify which topics should be discussed as contemporary American issues. Students can research and present their stances on the issues.
3. "Introducing My Students to My Friends in Young Adult Literature" by Patricia L. Daniel in the *ALAN Review* (Winter 2002) focuses on *Staying Fat for Sarah Byrnes* and other novels, giving teaching ideas.
4. Lynne Alvine and Devon Duffy in "Friendship and Tensions in *A Separate Peace* and *Staying Fat for Sarah Byrnes*," (chapter 8 in Kaywell, *Adolescent Literature as a Complement to the Classics*, vol. 2, 1995) offer a unit plan for using this novel.
5. "Playing the Game: Young Adult Sports Novels" by Chris Crowe, chapter 11 in *Reading Their World: The Young Adult Novel in the Classroom*, 2nd ed. (Monseau and Salvner 2000) has insights on this and several other of Chris Crutcher's novels.
6. The following websites are helpful for teaching the novel:

   www.webenglishteacher.com/crutcher.html
   www.sonoma.edu/users/l/lord/343/Links.htm
   scholar.lib.vt.edu/ejournals/ALAN/spring97/s97-10-Sheffer.html
   scholar.lib.vt.edu/ejournals/ALAN/fall98/wilder.html
   www.jsonline.com/enter/books/jun03/148761.asp?format=print
   www.Authors4Teens.com
   www.aboutcrutcher.com

Why Give This Book to Teens?

- Because they might be the only source of support for a peer who has confided in them.
- Because they might have experienced or be experiencing abuse and need to learn through this book how to manage some of the pain they've known.
- Because the teens in this book are real and experience many of the things other teens experience, especially isolation and the challenge to "fit in."
- Because participation in sports and athletic activities can do more than build physical strength.

Other books by Chris Crutcher to consider reading: *Ironman* (one of the many Crutcher books that are **Teen Recommended**), *The Crazy Horse Electric Game*, *Chinese Handcuffs*, and *Stotan*.

Crutcher, Chris: *Whale Talk*

Published by Laurel Leaf, reprint edition 10 December 2002, ISBN 0440229383

****Teen Recommended****

T. J. Jones is Black, White, Japanese, and adopted. He's a good athlete, but he doesn't necessarily go for the "all jock" sports of football and basketball. T. J. befriends some of the school's outcasts, organizes them into a swim team, and confronts some of the school's and the community's most bigoted people. This novel presents the real world of high school athletics, of small town communities where "winning" is everything, and it tells the story of some terrible human suffering and wonderful human triumphs.

Teaching Ideas and Resources

1. This novel presents a number of teachable moments—experiences of diversity and the intolerance of diversity—to discuss with your students, especially in the context of character education. One of the issues tackled in this book is *race*. T. J.'s biological father was Black and Japanese, so T. J. is a multiracial adolescent in a town where there are very few people of color. Georgia is a child therapist who is also mixed race. Heidi is an abused child; she's also Black and hated by her stepfather. Another issue is *abuse and special needs*. Chris Coughlin is a teen with severe brain damage, resulting jointly from a mother who was a crack cocaine user and her boyfriend who put saran wrap over Chris' head when Chris was one year old—the boyfriend said he only wanted to stop Chris from crying. Discussion of the characters in the book and their various aspects of diversity could provide a rich classroom experience, though you and your students need to be mature enough to talk about these sensitive issues. A quote from the book could be an excellent lead-in: "For this moment, high atop my shoulders, Heidi [a child who is biracial] squeals, visible and proud. I know she'll come crashing down the moment she is degraded again. I know—just because I know—that despair moves in like a flash flood when she is diminished. It isn't even about a race, really. It's about nothingness." (Crutcher 2002, *Whale Talk*, 70–71)

2. "A Teacher of High School Language Arts Speaks with Chris Crutcher," an interview by Debbie Erenberger in the *ALAN Review* (vol. 28, no. 3 [Spring/Summer 2001]) presents good insights on the author and on how to present the novel.
3. For additional resources, consult www.aboutcrutcher.com.

Why Give This Book to Teens?

- Because they may be tired of those who bully them for being "different."
- Because sometime during the high school years, they may tire of seeing certain athletes "get away with everything," including degrading remarks.
- Because they may have had parents who didn't know a lot about parenting and who made mistakes that these teens can avoid in their own lives.
- Because they may be young males who do not want to follow the crowd and the pressures of being a "jock."

Cushman, Karen: *Matilda Bone*
Published by Yearling Books, reprint edition 12 March 2002, ISBN 0440418224

Fourteen-year-old Matilda has been raised on a manor by Father Leufredus, with the religious emphasis of medieval England. She has been taught reading, writing, Latin, and Greek, and "to seek the higher things." She is not eager to be in the guardianship of Red Peg, the bonesetter in "Blood and Bone Alley," who is eager for someone to tend fires, prepare meals, brew lotions, boil tonics, soothe and restrain patients, and help in the setting of bones. The book conveys much of the medieval world, the role of women in medicine, and the challenges they faced, but most central is Matilda's coming of age in life and in her faith, coming to think for herself, and coming to realize she is not alone.

Teaching Ideas and Resources

1. Guide your students to consider the ways Matilda learns of life or refuses to learn from life. Have them respond to the following quotations:

> "You are so priest-ridden that one might think you have nothing of your own to say." (Peg to Matilda, in *Matilda Bone*, 39)

"Why I was tied by my feet to a team of horses and dragged through thistles and thorns. That was torture! This is healing. Watch and learn." (Words Matilda "hears" as she calls on St. Hippolytus, complaining about Peg's method of healing, in *Matilda Bone*, 35)

"I myself think laughing is mighty like praying," said Tildy, "as if saying, 'Listen, God, how much I enjoy this world You have made.'" (The "other Matilda" speaking to Matilda, who has just commented she should be praying, in *Matilda Bone*, 59)

"Bah. Enough of what Father Leufredus thinks. Let us talk more about this when you know what Matilda thinks." (Peg to Matilda who has spoken aloud what she thought was only in her mind about Tom, Peg's husband—Matilda is not impressed with the kind of learning Tom has, in *Matilda Bone*, 70)

Matilda says she's been taught of Hell and to fear demons; her friend Walter asks, "What about God's love?" Matilda thinks, "God's love? Walter must know a different God than she did." (*Matilda Bone*, 137)

2. If you are teaching Chaucer and *The Canterbury Tales* or are studying medieval England, use this book or others by Karen Cushman: *Catherine, Called Birdy* and *The Midwife's Apprentice* to give your students a more personal approach to the period.
3. "The Girls' Story: Adolescent Novels Set in the Middle Ages," by Mary H. McNulty in the *ALAN Review* (vol. 28, no. 2 [Winter 2001]) provides good background on *Matilda Bone*, *Catherine, Called Birdy*, and *The Midwife's Apprentice*.
4. "Historical Fiction or Fictionalized History?" by Joanne Brown in the *ALAN Review* (vol. 26, no. 1 [Fall 1998]) is a good place to begin teaching Karen Cushman's novels.
5. For more information on Karen Cushman and teaching guides check the following websites:

   www.neiu.edu/~gspackar/INDEX.html
   www.indiana.edu/~reading/ieo/bibs/cushman.html
   www.harperchildrens.com/schoolhouse/TeachersGuides/cushmanindex.htm
   www.eduplace.com/author/cushman/activities.html

Why Give This Book to Teens?

- Because they might be confused, as Matilda is, by the adults in their life and can see in her story how she learns who to trust and why.

- Because teens often wonder, is knowledge everything? How does life experience come into play?
- Because they might have lost parents or have to live in a situation where they feel isolated, lonely, and misunderstood.
- Because keeping the law and following strict guidelines might not always be possible.

Other books by Karen Cushman to consider reading: *The Ballad of Lucy Whipple*; *The Midwife's Apprentice*; and *Catherine, Called Birdy*.

Dorris, Michael: A *Yellow Raft in Blue Water*
Published by Picador USA, 5 March 2003, ISBN 0312421850

Starting in the present and moving backward, three Native American women narrate this story of love and sacrifice, twined with secrets and kinship. Rayona, 15, "the half-African American, half-Indian girl," is brought by her mother, Christine, back to the Montana reservation, where Christine appears to abandon her during the 1980s. Christine herself adds 1960s history including the death of her "brother" Lee in Vietnam. Finally, "grandmother" Aunt Ida reveals choices she made in the 1940s—rescuing another woman, Clara, from the shame of bearing the baby Christine.

Teaching Ideas and Resources

1. One reviewer said, "The shifting POV [points of view] was also a good reminder that each episode of a family's history has many versions, many perspectives—each flawed, each true." Guide your students with the following question: What pieces of "truth" are added to the story at each level and what questions emerge? Use the various points of view to review the perspectives of narration.
2. Help your students compare Rayona and Christine as daughters, and compare Christine and Ida as mothers. What qualities of the child and the parent do your students like as good models of children or mothers?
3. "Using Multicultural Literature to Expand the Canon in 11th and 12th Grade English Classes," by Jim Cope in "Adolescent Literature: Making Connections with Teens" (special issue, *Virginia English Bulletin* 44, no. 2 [Fall 1994]), uses this novel as one of the focus novels in the unit, giving a model for how to teach *Yellow Raft*.
4. Bonnie O. Ericson, in "Heroes and Journeys in *The Odyssey* and Several Works in Young Adult Literature" (chapter 1 in Kaywell, *Adoles-*

cent Literature as a Complement to the Classics, vol. 2, 1995), describes how to teach *A Yellow Raft in Blue Water* in conjunction with *The Odyssey*.
5. "Character Education + Young Adult Literature = Critical Thinking Skills" by Mary Ann Tighe in the *ALAN Review* (vol 26, no. 1 [Fall 1998]) focuses on this novel.

Master Teacher's Guide

- In the final pages of Rayona's story, Christine tells her about a letter from the Pope which was to reveal the end of the world in 1960. Direct students to reread the passage when they finish the book and have them reflect about how perceptions about one's future may influence present choices.
- Look for teaching ideas in Elizabeth Belden and Judith M. Beckman's review of *A Yellow Raft in Blue Water* (*English Journal* 77, no 4 [April 1988]: 81).
- Look for more discussion of the novel in the article by Anatolia Board, "Eccentricity was all they could afford" (*New York Times*, June 7, 1987, late city final edition, sec. 7, p. 7, col. 1).
- Locate author information in *Contemporary Authors Online* (see www.gale.com).
- Use the following for further resources: "Family Photographs: Relationships among the Generations." Wyoming Council for the Humanities. Resources for Book Discussion Program Scholars and Project Directors: BDTalk-Ed Archives, www.uwyo.edu/wch/arcfamily.htm.

Why Give This Book to Teens?

- Because the ability to see different points of view is an important skill for young adults.
- Because *Yellow Raft* takes readers to a place that is so different, yet so familiar, and can give readers new perspectives.
- Because the novel shows that love is stronger than pain, deception, and loss.

Enger, Lief: *Peace Like a River*
Published by Grove Press, 20 August 2002, ISBN 0802139256
Teen Recommended

A family's journey begins in a Minnesota town in the early 1960s. Reuben Land, a shy asthmatic boy born with "swampy lungs," loves to hear his favorite story: how his father's first miracle was getting him to breathe although a doctor had already pronounced the newborn dead. Neighbors view the father Jeremiah, a religious, poetry-loving school janitor, as well meaning but dreamy. Little sister Swede writes about a cowboy hero named Sundown but can't make the ending come out right. Only 16-year-old Davy seems anchored in reality. When teenage thugs invade his home and attack his family, Davy shoots them. Briefly he is a local hero, but when the media frenzy turns ugly, he gets arrested, breaks jail, and runs. His family tracks him to the North Dakota badlands where he has taken refuge with Jape Waltzer, a menacing survivalist rancher and his "captive" daughter Sarah. The Lands wait for contact from Davy. Jeremiah finds love for himself and a mother figure for his children in Roxanne, only months before Waltzer cuts him down.

Teaching Ideas and Resources

1. Using a Bible dictionary, ask your students to offer rationales for choices of biblical names: Jeremiah, Reuben (describing himself as an asthmatic Lazarus), Davy/David, and Sarah.
2. Is the heroic Davy a fugitive from justice, a bringer of justice, or a person whom justice has deserted? Students can use this question for written responses and then for discussion.
3. "We all hold history differently inside us," says narrator Reuben. After your students finish the last chapter, have them reread the opening sequences and discuss how the dreams/fate of Swede, Reuben, and Davy might have been foreshadowed there.

Master Teacher's Guide

- "No miracle happens without a witness. Someone has to declare 'Here's what I saw. Here's how it went. Make of it what you will'" (*Peace Like a River*, 3).
- "Once touched by truth, Swede wrote years later, a little thing like faith is easy" (*Peace Like a River*, 33).
- "One person's chance incident is another person's miracle," Enger suggests. Have your students select one of these three quotations to write about and connect with an experience in their own life.
- Michael Pearson, in an *Atlanta Journal-Constitution* review, said Enger's novel "has the power to convince that, despite sorrow, human experience is a miracle of ordinary truth and extraordinary love." Ask students to journal about something in their own experience that either

they or someone else might consider miraculous. Sometimes the most profound "miracles" rise from the beauty of family and land. Many students may have "miracles" they would like to list.
- Explore more about Leif Enger at *Contemporary Authors Online*: infotrac.galegroup.com.

Why Give This Book to Teens?
- Because the novel is a good fugitive escape story and a good read.
- Because the Land family has been turned upside down by an event and readers can relate to the Land family's story.
- Because teens like to explore ideas about fate vs. miracles.

Greene, Bette: *Summer of My German Soldier*
Published by Penguin USA, reissue edition September 1999, ISBN 014130636X
Teen Recommended

Patty Bergen is a young Jewish girl in Jenkinsville, Arkansas, in the years of World War II. Her unlikely small town becomes the site of a prisoner of war camp for Germans, who the townspeople see only as "Nazis." Patty is also the victim who suffers from an abusive, controlling father and a mother who can't seem to love her. In her precociousness, Patty sees herself as a constant irritation and wonders why she is the way she is. A German prisoner, Frederick Anton Reiker, and the Black nanny, Ruth, teach Patty to see herself as a talented and potentially beautiful young woman. Is it any wonder that Patty is willing to risk all to hide Reiker when he escapes?

Teaching Ideas and Resources
1. Consider pairing this novel with *Farewell to Manzanar* to explore the Japanese Americans who were interned during World War II as well as for further study of the hysteria that fostered anti-German sentiments in the 1940s.
2. "Beyond the Holocaust: Exploring Jewish Themes through Contemporary Young Adult Literature" by Jeffrey S. Kaplan, an essay in *United in Diversity: Using Multicultural Young Adult Literature in the Classroom* edited by Jean E. Brown and Elaine C. Stephens (NCTE, 1998) includes a brief discussion of the novel and provides teaching ideas.
3. "Using Young Adult Literature to Modernize the Teaching of *Romeo and Juliet*" by Arthea J. S. Reed (chapter 6 in Kaywell, *Adolescent Litera-*

ture as a Complement to the Classics, vol. 1, 1993) uses this novel as one of the books in the unit.

4. Websites directed specifically at the historical context are:

   theliterarylink.com/yaauthors.html
   www.cfep.uci.edu/ProDevel/uci-sati/faculty/rodebaugh_unit.html
   www.cis.yale.edu/ynhti/curriculum/units/1997/2/97.02.03.x.html

5. Lesson plan ideas are available at:

   falcon.jmu.edu/~ramseyil/greene.htm
   www.amazon.com/exec/obidos/tg/detail/-/B00006G3LL/002-9576977-6113636?v=g lan ce
   www.geocities.com/Athens/Troy/9122

6. *Bette Greene's "Summer of My German Soldier": A Study Guide*, from Gale's *Novels for Students*, vol. 10 (Gale, 2000) offers additional teaching ideas.

Why Give This Book to Teens?

- Because, like Patty, they might have felt unloved by parents, particularly if the parents are strict disciplinarians or controlling.
- Because their actions on behalf of someone who is shunned might be misunderstood.
- Because they need to learn, as the people of Jenkinsville, Arkansas, did, that not every member of a nationality or group can be judged according to the negative actions of a single person in that group or nationality.

Other books by Bette Greene to consider reading are *Philip Hall Likes Me, I Reckon Maybe*; *Morning Is a Long Time Coming*; *Get on Out of Here, Philip Hall*; and *Them That Glitter and Them That Don't*.

Haruf, Kent: *Plainsong*

Published by Vintage, 22 August 2000, ISBN 0375705856

****Teen Recommended****

Ike and Bobby Guthrie don't understand why their mentally fragile mother has left their father, a middle-aged history teacher. They discover that many people in their little Colorado town feel lots of pain: lonely old people, abused teens, even their dad. Maggie Jones, another teacher, builds unlikely links between many of the characters, even though her senile elderly father makes her own life difficult. When she invites two bachelor ranchers to take a pregnant girl into their home, even she calls the situation improbable.

Teaching Ideas and Resources

1. Motherless children fill Haruf's story: Bobby and Ike, Tom Guthrie's kids who have been abandoned by their mother; Victoria Roubideaux, the pregnant Indian girl; and the bachelor McPheron brothers, orphaned 50 years ago. Discuss with your students how these characters are "mothered" by others and how they return that goodness to others. Are these positive or negative actions?
2. The deaths of their horse Elko and the old lady who has befriended them terrify Ike and Bobby; the situations also give them opportunity to seek shelter and receive support. Lead students to consider the following question: What situations do other characters encounter that show a similar rhythm of death and life?

Master Teacher's Guide

- In plainsong, a single voice may initiate a melodic line to set in motion a call-and-response pattern. Have students read in Postlethwaite's review about how Haruf uses literary "plainsong" as characters seem to call and respond to each other. Ask your students to find examples from the story.
- Look at the essay by Diane Postlethwaite, "A Healing Melody," in which she writes: "Kent Haruf's unadorned yet elegant novel makes extraordinary music out of the ordinary rhythms of daily life in a small Colorado town" (*World and I* 15, no. 2 [Feb. 2000]: 258).

Why Give This Book to Teens?

- Because the small-town, open-plains setting is so accurately described, they'll feel as if they've lived there too.
- Because broken families, problems of aging, and abuse touch people they know, possibly even their own families.
- Because the novel shows that love and caring make a difference.

Hinton, S. E.: *The Outsiders*

Published by Prentice Hall (K–12), reprint edition November 1997, ISBN 014038572X

****Teen Recommended****

Ponyboy, an orphaned 14-year-old who loves reading and movies, lives with brothers Darry and Sodapop. Looking back on a tragic round of events, Ponyboy describes the rivalry between two gangs, the lower-middle-class greasers and the upper class Socs (for Socials). When rumbles lead to violence, one of the Socs is killed. When an abandoned church/hideout catches fire, some children are trapped. Greasers Johnny, Dallas, and Ponyboy run back into the fire to save them. Loss unites the brothers who agree that Ponyboy can escape the life of an "outsider" if he chooses.

Teaching Ideas and Resources

1. Have your students make lists of situations/words of others that contribute to Ponyboy's sense of being an outsider in a dead-end situation and lists of situations/words of others that offer hints of hope for a better future. Which will be his future? Can we make the best of situations when many aspects seem to be "against" us?
2. When Cherry, a Soc, tells Ponyboy about the upcoming rumble, he seems to catch a glimpse of what the young people from two gangs have in common. He asks, "Can you see the sunset real good from the West side?" and then adds, "You can see it real good from the East side, too." Discuss with your students what feelings and dreams of these teen characters from a sixties' gang seem to transfer to our time.
3. "*The Outsiders* Is Still 'In': Why This Old Novel Is So Popular with Teens, and Some Activities Students Enjoy" by Lauren Groot with Martha Story in the *ALAN Review* (Winter 2002) gives a current perspective on this older novel.
4. "The 'I' of the Beholder: Whose 'Truth'?" by Joanne Brown in "*Adolescent Literature: Making Connections with Teens*" (special issue, *Virginia English Bulletin* 44, no. 2 [Fall 1994]), uses *The Outsiders* as one of the novels in the unit.

Master Teacher's Guide

- During their hideout in the abandoned church, Johnny and Ponyboy discuss *Gone with the Wind* and the Robert Frost poem "Nothing Gold Can Stay." With his dying words, Johnny tells Ponyboy to "stay gold." Ask your students: what are things in our lives that may be "gone with the wind" and what things do we want to "stay gold"?
- Author background may be found on *Contemporary Authors* Online (see www.gale.com).
- Jay Daly, *Presenting S. E. Hinton* (Twayne, 1987) is another good resource for author background.
- Read Michael Pearlman's essay "The role of socioeconomic status in

adolescent literature" in *Adolescence* (vol. 30, no. 117 [Spring 1995]: 223) for further teaching ideas.

Why Give This Book to Teens?

- Because this novel is much more than a quick-read about teen violence.
- Because teens may feel like outsiders sometimes, and Ponyboy's story might be helpful.
- Because they'll find out about the teen world of their parents or grandparents.

Kingsolver, Barbara: *The Bean Trees*
Published by HarperTorch, reissue edition 1 October 1998, ISBN 0061097314
Teen Recommended

Taylor Greer leaves Kentucky when she graduates from high school, determined not to get tied down by a family or tangled up by love. When an abused and abandoned child is pushed into her arms, Taylor begins a series of adventures in discovery and commitment. Central American refugees Esperanza and Estevan, their protector Mattie, and neighbor LouAnn intertwine their lives with Taylor's like the fruitful growing of the bean trees.

Teaching Ideas and Resources

1. Ask your students to draw a bean tree to illustrate the themes of this book. Around what central character would their vine grow? What are the problems and situations that prune the vines of family and trust or encourage new growth? What products does the vine/story produce as the characters grow?
2. Have your students write in response to the following quotation by Barbara Kingsolver, discussing how this quotation relates to the novel: "Living in the middle of an alfalfa field was an important influence, I grew up noticing where things come from and where they go—in the sense of seed and compost rather than heaven and hell. I think the whole way I look at the world was formed on a farm" (from www.unm.edu/~wrtgsw/kingsolver.html).
3. Bonnie O. Ericson, "Heroes and Journeys in *The Odyssey* and Several Works in Young Adult Literature" (chapter 1 in Kaywell, *Adolescent Literature as a Complement to the Classics*, vol. 2, 1995) describes how to teach *The Bean Trees* in conjunction with *The Odyssey*.

4. Rebecca Luce-Kaple and Sylvia Pantaleo have an essay on *The Bean Trees* in *Rationales for Teaching Young Adult Literature* (Reid and Neufeld 1999).
5. *Master Teacher's Guide: A Collection of Forty Guides for Middle and High School Teachers* includes a guide for teaching *The Bean Trees*. The guide is available from Harper Collins Publishers, www.HarperAcademic.com.
6. Another resource on *The Bean Trees* is "Barbara Kingsolver's *The Bean Trees*: A New Classroom Classic" by Karen M. and Philip H. Kelly (*English Journal* 86, no. 8 [1997]: 61–64).
7. Some online teaching guides are available at:

   www.pinkmonkey.com/booknotes/monkeynotes/pmBeanTrees37.asp
   www.kingsolver.com/guides/bean_trees.asp

Why Give This Book to Teens?

- Because like Taylor, they are making choices about their future and can learn from her story.
- Because there are many immigrants in the United States and not many of these people face an easy life in our country; some teen readers will be immigrants themselves and others might be friends of immigrants.
- Because if they've never met someone who had to leave his or her homeland because of violence, oppression, war, or poverty, they might learn to be more accepting of people from different cultures.

Kingsolver, Barbara: *The Poisonwood Bible*
Published by Perennial, 1 October 1999, ISBN 0060930535
Teen Recommended

Nathan Price's rigid understanding about being a missionary radically and sometimes violently affects his wife, Orleana; his four daughters, Leah, Adah, Rachel, and Ruth May; and the Congolese. He tries to convert the natives over a year and a half period of hunger, disease, drought, witchcraft, political wars, pestilential rains, and political upheaval. In Kilanga, Leah's sisters help their mother, while Leah chooses to work in her father's garden. The garden, which he stubbornly plants and cultivates by Western methods, is as barren as his cultivation of souls. The education and eventual liberation of the five women from Nathan's arrogant tyranny suggest Africa's resistance to destructive colonialism. Leah falls in love with and eventually marries Anatole, an African teacher. Adah suffers from a language disorder and chooses silence; she knows that saying words wrong creates disrespect and disaster. When she finally chooses to speak, she becomes a researcher on AIDS and Ebola.

Teaching Ideas and Resources

1. Each Price daughter comes to terms with Africa's complexities in her own way. Have your students make a circle for each daughter and describe what happens to her. What events or actions lead to her liberation from her abusive father? Discuss each daughter's response to the father and why the response is or is not justified.
2. When Reverend Price shouts "TATA JESUS IS BANGALA!" he thinks "bangala" means precious and dear. But with his incorrect inflection (balanga), it means the poisonwood tree which causes itching and misery. Ironically, the culturally insensitive message he gives makes his sentence true. Direct your students to find examples of "miseries" he imposes on the Congolese. Follow up with a discussion about Reverend Price's ministry. What problems arise when we impose a religion on another culture? How might the situations in this novel connect with other attempts at liberating a culture (for example, trying to liberate Iraq)?
3. Clueless and self-centered Rachel best represents America's material culture. Make a list of some of Rachel's goofy expressions and her focus on possessions. Are her possessions appropriate for the culture she's in? Have students consider their own possessions and what they need or don't need.
4. Teaching ideas are also located at the following sites:

   www.uua.org/re/reach/fall00/adult/poisonwood_bible.html
   www.readinggroupguides.com/guides/poisonwood_bible.asp

5. *Master Teacher's Guide: A Collection of Forty Guides for Middle and High School Teachers* includes a guide for teaching *The Poisonwood Bible*. The guide is available from Harper Collins Publishers, www.HarperAcademic.com.

Master Teacher's Guide

- In all her fiction, Kingsolver grapples with clashing cultural values, social justice issues, ecological awareness, and the intersection of private and public concerns. Direct your students to identify some of the issues that are clashing.

- Review the following essay by Elaine R. Ognibene for insights on the novel: "The Missionary Position: Barbara Kingsolver's *The Poisonwood Bible*" (*College Literature* 30, no. 3 [Summer 2003]: 19).
- Secondary students will probably read Kingsolver's novel mainly to discover what happens to each of the four daughters. Like five-year-old Ruth May, they may also experience the complexity and mystery without fully understanding some of the deeper issues, but that's okay!

Why Give This Book to Teens?

- Because maybe their parents have "forced" them to accept religious beliefs that they need to claim as their own.
- Because they might want to learn about living in another culture, particularly one that is much more primitive as far as comforts of life that many American youth are used to having.
- Because loyalty to family may be a challenge for them, as it is for the Price daughters.
- Because Kingsolver transports readers to Africa in ways that are almost physical.
- Because words can hurt and heal as Reverend Price shows, and readers can learn from his experiences.
- Because in reading the story of the Price family, they can discover how to use the experiences of their lives.

Other books by Barbara Kingsolver to consider reading: *Animal Dreams*, *Pigs in Heaven*, and *Prodigal Summer*.

Lamb, Wally: *She's Come Undone*
Published by Pocket Books, 1 June 1998, ISBN 0671021001
Teen Recommended

Does this sound like a comic novel? Dolores's parents' troubled marriage lands her mother in a mental hospital and sends Dolores to live with her grandmother. Loneliness and even rape by a neighbor characterize her childhood. Fat and sullen, Dolores dreams about her college roommate's boyfriend Dante, a hopeless prospect. After a suicide attempt and a spell in a mental ward herself, she reinvents herself, then catches and marries Dante. Her happy ending turns sour. Hilarious and oh-so-sad, she finally meets Thayer who offers "happily-maybe-sometimes-ever-after."

(Although funny and filled with contemporary social color, *She's Come Undone* may be inappropriate for immature readers because of some explicit sexual content and profanity.)

Teaching Ideas and Resources

1. One reviewer compares people like Dolores to barnacles on a ship's bottom—we want to scrape them out of our consciousness, but we also find ourselves "laughing, crying, hoping and praying for them as they stumble through life." Have your students list several situations where they were disgusted by yet cheering for Dolores. Have them relate Dolores and her experiences to other characters they've read about.
2. Discuss with your students when and where Dolores uses food to appease her hunger for love and self-worth and even for God. Are Dolores's actions common among your students' experiences? In what ways?

Master Teacher's Guide

- Susan Bauer writes: "Stories of suffering, to be honest, must end with one of two truths: the presence of God, or a void where he should be . . . not all sufferers will come face to face with the person of God. Those who do, like Job, will bow their heads and admit a riddle that cannot be solved. Those who do not will live in a world without God." (Bauer, see below.) Talk with students about Dolores—Does Dolores fit either of these categories or is there another source of meaning for her?
- For further insights on the topic of stories of suffering, read "Oprah's Misery Index" by Susan Wise Bauer (*Christianity Today* 42, no.14 [Dec 7, 1998]: 70). It describes the Jobian suffering in the books Oprah Winfrey recommends on her talk show.
- For additional author information, see *Contemporary Authors Online*, Gale, 2003 (see www.gale.com).
- Additional guides for *She's Come Undone* can be located at www.readinggroupguides.com/guides/shes_come_undone.asp.
- "Author Profile: Wally Lamb" on Teenreads (www.teenreads.com/authors) offers further information for you and your students.
- Also consider reading Hilma Wolitzer, "It's a Miserable Life" (*New York Times Book Review*, Aug. 23, 1992, 78).

Why Give This Book to Teens?

- Because sometimes we all feel "fat and ugly" and like Dolores, we can change that outlook.
- Because of the many cultural references in the novel, teens can make a research game of identifying and relating these references.
- Because the novel will cause readers to both cry and laugh out loud.

Lee, Harper: *To Kill a Mockingbird*
Published by Little Brown & Company,
reissue edition 11 October 1988, ISBN 0446310786
****Teen Recommended****

Told from the perspective of Scout Finch, *To Kill a Mockingbird* is a classic of the American South during the height of the Depression. Scout, her brother Jem, and their summertime friend Dill Harris are fascinated by their mysterious and hermit-like neighbor, Boo Radley. Atticus Finch, Scout and Jem's father, defends a Black man, Tom Robinson, who has been falsely accused of raping a white woman, Mayella Ewell. The racism of Maycomb, Alabama, erupts and Scout, Jem, and Dill are thrown into the adult world of racial prejudice, sexual assault, deceit, narrow-mindedness, ignorance, and hatred.

Teaching Ideas and Resources

1. This novel, with its tension-filled court case, is a good one for a debate or mock trial. After your students read the novel, they can hold a debate on the justice or lack of justice in Tom Robinson's trial.
2. "Introducing *To Kill a Mockingbird* with Collaborative Group Reading of Related Young Adult Novels" (in Kaywell, *Adolescent Literature as a Complement to the Classics*, vol. 1, 1993) provides excellent ways to teach this novel—locate this essay for the teaching ideas.
3. For a more complete study of racism, consider teaching this novel along with novels by Mildred Taylor; *Roll of Thunder, Hear My Cry* is a direct parallel to *To Kill a Mockingbird*. Students can make Venn diagrams to compare the novels; they could do a compare/contrast essay discussing the novel that is most relevant to them and their experience.
4. This site is helpful if you are using the film version of the novel as part of your teaching: www.teachwithmovies.org/samples/to-kill-a-mocking-bird.html.
5. One of the many teaching guides is available in *Master Teacher's Guide:*

A *Collection of Forty Guides for Middle and High School Teachers* (HarperCollins Publishers: www.HarperAcademic.com).

6. In "John Wayne, Where Are You? Everyday Heroes and Courage" by Pamela S. Carroll (chapter 2 in Gregg and Carroll, *Books and Beyond*, 1998), the novel is used as one of the "canonical" novels in the unit.
7. For more about the author and the novel, see the following websites:

   wilmette.nttc.org/wjhs/staff/byrne/resources/tkam.html
   www.educeth.ch/english/readinglist/leeh/index.html
   www.lausd.k12.ca.us/Belmont_HS/tkm/teacher.html
   www.lausd.k12.ca.us/Belmont_HS/tkm
   www.duluth.lib.mn.us/Programs/Mockingbird/Resources.html
   www.freebooknotes.com/guides/tokillamockingbird.htm
   www.planetbookclub.com/teachers/civil.html

Why Give This Book to Teens?

- Because they, like Jem and Scout, may have parents who take unpopular stands and have to suffer harassment or ridicule because of their positions.
- Because they may be falsely accused and need the courage to challenge their accusers.
- Because they may need to read stories like this one about people who are courageous enough to defend those who are oppressed.
- Because they may need to identify prejudice and intolerance in their school situation.

Mazer, Norma Fox: *When She Was Good*

Published by Scholastic, reprint edition February 2003,
ISBN 0590319906
****Teen Recommended****

This is a complex novel told in the voice of Em, who is 13 when her mother dies and who lives in a completely dysfunctional family. Most problematic is Em's older sister Pamela, who is plagued by emotional illness that is never treated. Em's dad is alcoholic and abused his wife, who sometimes told Em and Pamela to hide from their dad's alcoholic rages. When his wife dies, he cannot cope with life, and the family plunges deeper into problems.

When their father suddenly remarries, life only gets worse for Em and Pamela. Particularly for Em, who was closer to her mother, Sally, the new wife, drives any memories of Em's mom away. Sally eventually demands that Pamela and Em get jobs—even though Em is only 14 then and still in school—and pay for room and board. At this point, Pamela and Em run away and Pamela secures an apartment for them in the city. Pamela's illness precludes her ever holding a job or really being functional in normal society; she is also physically abusive of Em. The novel is dark, but it portrays Em's ability to survive in her search for love and acceptance.

Teaching Ideas and Resources

1. Em learns, when she is out at a lake campground, about the beauty of nature. She describes the experience of seeing a "double moon"—the actual moon and the reflection of the moon in the water. Em expresses this insight saying, "I felt that I had stumbled on a truth . . . if I had it—'it' being not the moon and the lake, as such, not its stark and startling beauty, but the 'itness' of it—if I had that, I could finally be happy and like other people." Have your students write about a place or time when and where they have learned a similar insight through nature.
2. "Creating Imaginative Worlds: Unique Detail and Structure in Norma Fox Mazer's Young Adult Fiction" by Ann Angel in the *ALAN Review* (Fall 2001) (the same issue includes an interview with Norma Fox Mazer) provides insights on *When She Was Good.*
3. "To Tell the Truth: What Names Mean to Female Characters in Young Adult Novels" by Caroline S. McKinney in the *ALAN Review* (vol. 26, no. 1 [Fall 1998]) has insights to this novel and a number of others. Consider reading it for further ideas on teaching the novel.
4. Websites for topics related to this novel, especially about abusive relationships:

   www.Authors4Teens.com
   www.apa.org/pi/pii/teen
   www2.scholastic.com/teachers/authorsandbooks/authorstudies/authorhome.jhtml?authorID=1390&collateralID=5229&displayName=Biography

Why Give This Book to Teens?

- Because they might have lost a parent and have to deal with the issue of second marriages and how to relate to these new adults in their lives.
- Because they might have lived with the urging of a parent that they

have to "be good" and then face guilt and remorse for all they think they haven't done well.
- Because they might have a sibling, a friend, or a classmate who is plagued by emotional illness, and they can learn from Em's story.
- Because despite anything that happens in their family, they have a right to be happy, to be free, and to feel safe.

Other books by Norma Fox Mazer to consider reading: *Girlhearts*; *Good Night, Maman*; *After the Rain*; *Silver*; and *Out of Control*

Mikaelsen, Ben: *Touching Spirit Bear*
Published by HarperTrophy, 30 April 2002, ISBN 038080560X

Cole Matthews is 15, an angry and increasingly violent young man. When he smashes Peter Driscal's skull into the sidewalk, Cole has reached a point of no return. The options are jail and serious juvenile detention. Cole's parole officer is a "never-give-up" kind of man who has been through some difficult experiences in his own life; he also knows about an alternative called "Circle Justice" designed to heal both perpetrator and victim. Cole's "punishment" takes him to an isolated Alaskan island and to encounters with a mysterious white bear.

Teaching Ideas and Resources

1. This book offers a venue for discussing youth violence. In working with the book, you might consider inviting parole officers, juvenile court personnel, or others involved with youth crime and detention to come to your class. Have your students prepare questions in advance and allow them to interview your guests.
2. Is anyone ever completely "totally a lost cause"? Students could have a debate on this topic as well as on the question, are all actions forgivable? Why or why not? Have students prepare their responses to these questions building on evidence from the novel and then give two- to three-minute oral presentations on their position.
3. Some websites related to the book include:

   www.somerset.lib.nj.us/teens/gstba20036-8.htm (this site suggests the book for grades 5–8; I'd suggest grades 8–11)

   www.teenspoint.org/reading_matters/display_key.asp?sort=101&key=515

www.wildernessdrum.com/html/adventure_fiction.html
www.BenMikaelsen.com

Why Give This Book to Teens?

- Because they might be someone everyone else is ready to give up on.
- Because they might be angry at the abuse they've experienced and not have a way to channel that anger.
- Because they might be the victim of some other teen's violent actions.
- Because "Circle Justice" is an alternative to jail or other harsher forms of punishment, and it brings healing to victims and abusers; also readers might not be familiar with "circle justice" and they can learn this alternative way of responding.

Mickle, Shelley Fraser: *The Queen of October*
Published by Algonquin Books, reprint edition May 1992, ISBN 1565120035

Sally Maulden is 13 in the summer of 1959, and her parents are getting a divorce. Sally is shuttled between her grandparents' home in Coldwater, Arkansas, and Memphis, Tennessee, but she feels most comfortable in Arkansas. She moves through a series of relationships with adults, including an unrealistic love for an older man. Sally matures with the help of her grandparents and a range of adults in Coldwater.

Teaching Ideas and Resources

1. Consider pairing this novel with *A Member of the Wedding* by Carson McCullers, particularly if you are teaching an American literature course. *The Queen of October* may be the more accessible novel for your students, so you could read McCullers' novel in class. The main characters in each novel can be compared and contrasted; each novel holds potential journal topics as well.
2. "Divorce: A Common Thread Which Binds Us Across Geographic and Cultural Boundaries," by Catherine Hritz in "Adolescent Literature: Making Connections with Teens" (special issue, *Virginia English Bulletin*, vol. 44, no. 2 [Fall 1994]), offers insights on the central topic of this novel and can help you discuss this all-too-common topic with your students. Encourage students to write about their experience being children of parents who separate or divorce. Have them discuss

why divorce should or should not be an option for those caught in troubled relationships.

3. For more about the author and teaching ideas, see the following websites:

   www.shelleymickle.com
   www.shelleymickle.com/biography.htm
   coe.uca.edu/ArkansasAuthorsIndex/mickle.html

Why Give This Book to Teens?

- Because they may be experiencing or have experienced their parents' separation or divorce.
- Because they may have a crush on someone older and need to see how Sally handles that kind of situation and how she finds support to move beyond her infatuation.
- Because Sally learns a good deal about adults and some of their struggles, and her story can help teen readers.

Other books by Shelley Fraser Mickle to consider reading: *Replacing Dad* and *Moms on the Loose.*

Myers, Walter Dean: *Monster*
Published by HarperCollins Juvenile Books, reprint edition 8 May 2001, ISBN 0064407314
Teen Recommended

Steve Harmon is 16 and African American—he's one of the many young African American males who is at risk to be destroyed by drugs, guns, imprisonment, or some other kind of disaster. He has been at the "wrong place at the wrong time" and now is in jail facing trial for being an accomplice to a felony murder. Is he guilty? Is his life over? This powerful novel captures Steve's story in a screenplay, named *Monster* because that's what the prosecutor calls Steve.

Teaching Ideas and Resources

1. Think about teaching this novel with *Native Son* or *Black Boy* or other novels about the African American male experience. *Monster* is a captivating read that students could do outside of class, allowing you to work with the more difficult novels like *Native Son*, *Black Boy*, or *Invisi-*

ble Man in class. *Monster* would fit well in a unit on racism, coming in on the contemporary end of the unit.

2. The novel is actually in screenplay format; consider having students write a screenplay on a current topic in their school or community setting.
3. "Popular Postmodernism for Young Adult Readers: *Walk Two Moons*, *Holes*, and *Monster*" by Stephenie Yearwood in the *ALAN Review* (Summer 2002) presents an additional perspective on the novel.
4. Teaching guides and resources on Walter Dean Myers are available at the following sites:

   www.Authors4Teens.com
   www.harperchildrens.com/hch/parents/teachingguides/myers.pdf
   www.indiana.edu/~reading/ieo/bibs/myers.html
   faculty.ssu.edu/~elbond/monster.htm
   greenwood.scbbs.com/servlet/A4TStart?authorid=wmyers&source=introduction

5. This site specifically addresses African American students and their challenges in school:

   www.putnamschools.org/Karen/literacypdf/multicultural.pdf

6. This site addresses violence and other challenges facing students and schools—it includes a book list and recommended readings:

   empowered.org/Resources/books.htm

Why Give This Book to Teens?

- Because they might have been at "the wrong place at the wrong time" and have suffered from that or need to learn from Steve's story about the dangers of being with certain groups or individuals.
- Because peer pressure is a strong force and can make people do things they would never do under other circumstances.
- Because they might be trying to make some tough decisions about belonging to or getting out of a gang.
- Because they might be African American or others who need to understand more about what so often happens to African American males.
- Because they should know about the realities of imprisonment, especially if they are tempted to think they might be doing harmless pranks and get caught up in more serious actions.

Paterson, Katherine: *Jacob Have I Loved*
Published by HarperTrophy, reissue edition 31 March 1990, ISBN 0064403688
Teen Recommended

Twin daughters of a Chesapeake waterman, Caroline and Louise grow up on a remote island during the Depression Era. Caroline is blessed with beauty, talent, and even the love of Louise's friend Coll. Feeling somehow cursed like the biblical Esau, Louise discovers that love and purpose lie beyond her island shores and her sister's shadow.

Teaching Ideas and Resources

1. Read with your students the story of the blessing of Isaac and the disinheriting of Esau in Genesis. Together, make a chart of blessings and difficulties that the twins Louise and Caroline seem to have. Using a different color pen, consider what blessings Louise/Esau may ultimately experience. Discuss whether Louise and Esau can ever be considered blessed.
2. Jacob, the favored twin, actually journeyed far and waited a long time for his "blessing." In what ways may Louise be the Jacob of this story, not the Esau? Does Louise finally come to her promised land? Use these questions for a journal entry and subsequent class discussion.
3. Lois Stover and Connie Zitlow, in "Using Young Adult Literature as a Companion to World Literature: A Model Thematic Unit on the 'Clash of Cultures' Centered on *Things Fall Apart*" (chapter 5 in Kaywell, *Adolescent Literature as a Complement to the Classics*, vol. 2, 1995), use *Jacob Have I Loved* to look at the clash of generations in *Things Fall Apart*. Use their ideas to discuss with your students the clashes of culture they experience in their lives.
4. "Exploring the American Dream: *The Great Gatsby* and Six Young Adult Novels," by Diana Mitchell, (chapter 9 in Kaywell, *Adolescent Literature as a Complement to the Classics*, vol. 1, 1993) uses this novel as one of the six YA novels in the unit. How is the American Dream a factor in this novel?
5. Lynne Alvine and Devon Duffy, in "Friendship and Tensions in *A Separate Peace* and *Staying Fat for Sarah Byrnes*" (chapter 8 in Kaywell, *Adolescent Literature as a Complement to the Classics*, vol. 2, 1995), use *Jacob Have I Loved* as one of the five YA novels to supplement the unit. Reading their essay will give you ideas for teaching a range of novels.

6. "The 'I' of the Beholder: Whose 'Truth'?" by Joanne Brown, in "Adolescent Literature: Making Connections with Teens" (special issue, *Virginia English Bulletin* (vol. 44, no. 2 [Fall 1994]), uses this novel as one of the YA novels in the unit.
7. For more on Katherine Paterson and this book, check the following websites:

   www.terabithia.com
   www.neiu.edu/~gspackar/INDEX.html
   www.indiana.edu/~reading/ieo/bibs/paterson.html
   scholar.lib.vt.edu/ejournals/ALAN/spring94/Liddie.html

8. See the following web page and the section on identity definition in relation to spirituality:

   scholar.lib.vt.edu/ejournals/ALAN/spring96/mendt.html

9. See the following web page for an *ALAN Review* essay on this novel:

   scholar.lib.vt.edu/ejournals/ALAN/spring94/Liddie.html

Why Give This Book to Teens?

- Because they might feel like the blessed or the "disinherited" in the family and can learn from Louise's story how they might respond.
- Because relating to siblings, especially if they are from a stepparent, may be difficult, and siblings from stepparents are common in the family experience of many teens.
- Because it isn't always easy to see the reasons behind what happens in our lives, so reading a novel like this one can help teens sort out the reasons for what happens in their lives.

Other books by Katherine Paterson to consider reading: *The Great Gilly Hopkins*, *Lyddie*, and *The Tale of the Mandarin Ducks*.

Pelzer, David: A *Child Called It*
Published by Health Communications,
reissue edition 1 September 1995, ISBN 1558743669
****Teen Recommended****

This graphic and incredibly tragic book reveals the horrible abuse David Pelzer experienced from the time he was a first grader until he was rescued, through the efforts of teachers and other school personnel, and placed into foster care. Pelzer tells the events as he remembers them and unfolds issues revealing a family in great pain—with Pelzer taking the brunt of his mother's psychotic behaviors.

Teaching Ideas and Resources

1. You might best use this book in teaching about respect in a character education unit. With all the pain an abused child or young person has already experienced, teachers and classmates should not add to the suffering. Possibly a segment of the book could be read aloud and used for a discussion of how students could have responded differently to Dave. If a segment is used for discussion, begin with a written response to the reading and then move to discussion.
2. The book is terribly graphic and would need to be used with mature students, but sadly, the abuse of children continues to increase. You and your students need to know about resources and ways to survive the situation—hearing David's story is one way to come to greater understanding of those resources for surviving such terrible situations.
3. Use resources from David Pelzer located at the following websites:

   www.davepelzer.com
   shop.store.yahoo.com/monkeynote/chilcalititb.html

4. The following sites are from resource libraries for training and educational support of child welfare reform:

   www.midsouth.ualr.edu/resources/DCFS/library/index/A-B.html
   www.preventchildabuse-ri.org

Why Give This Book to Teens?

- Because someone in their school, in their classes, might be smelly or disgusting and an easy target for ridicule as Dave was, and they might need to know why ridiculing such a person is so harmful.
- Because they or their peers may be too afraid to tell anyone—social workers, teachers, other adults—of being abused and need to know that they can get help.
- Because this book was recommended by many teens as one other teens should read.

Pelzer, David: *The Lost Boy*

Published by Health Communications, revised edition 1 August 1997, ISBN 1558745157

****Teen Recommended****

In this sequel to *A Child Called It*, Pelzer narrates his continuing journey to wholeness, describing the series of foster homes he lives in. This book is probably more for teachers and social workers; however, any young person who has faced abuse can learn from David's story. Pelzer does not hide his continuing struggles and seemingly illogical choices that land him in more trouble and difficult situations. His point is that the horrible scar of abuse affects a person's self-esteem, particularly as the person goes through the teenage years and is trying to find identity and acceptance.

Teaching Ideas and Resources

1. A fiction work that would be good for you to pair with *The Lost Boy* is *Ruby Holler* by Sharon Creech. In this novel, twins Dallas and Florida are in the orphanage run by the Trepids, a ruthless couple out for their own advancement and heedless of the real needs of the children in their care. Dallas and Florida are victims of numerous foster homes until they end up with Tiller and Sairy in Ruby Holler. Reading *Ruby Holler* with *The Lost Boy* will give your students Creech's gentle humor that effectively conveys the problems of foster homes in cases where the foster parents are not concerned with the good of the children.
2. Another fiction work that you could use with *The Lost Boy* is *Ellen Foster* by Kaye Gibbons. Ellen, the narrator, weaves several stories together, revealing the death of her mother, her father's alcoholism, and his subsequent remarriage. Ellen is another child experiencing the shift from birth mother and father to stepmother to grandmother to aunts and cousins. She is never well liked or treated—except when taken in for a short period by her art teacher and the teacher's husband. Eventually Ellen identifies the woman she wants as a mother, Mrs. Foster, and Ellen moves there. Ellen's story, again, is "softened" by its presentation as fiction, but her reality is nonetheless harsh and representative of the many children seeking a parental figure who cares. Because Pelzer's books are so graphic, it might be best to read his books in class and have students read *Ellen Foster* or *Ruby Holler* outside of class.
3. "Finding Your Way Home: Orphan Stories in Young Adult Literature,"

by Dirk P. Mattson, in the *ALAN Review* (vol. 24, no. 3 [Spring 1997]) is a helpful essay for the theme of foster children and orphans.

4. These sites list many books and resources helpful for the issue of child abuse:

   www.sfasu.edu/AAS/SOCWK/REACH/booksdescription.htm
   www.cec-ohio.org/Links.htm
   partners.is.asu.edu/~techprep/levels/Level-III/EdProfess/Epirl5-03.pdf

Why Give This Book to Teens

- Because they may be in foster care situations or have friends who are.
- Because Dave doesn't find foster family life that easy, even after escaping the horrible abuse he's been facing.
- Because Dave experiences, though to an extreme given the abuse he's experienced, the huge need for acceptance from his peers, and that's a common experience for teens.
- Because they need to understand classmates who might be in foster care.

If you want to read more about David Pelzer, a third book is called *A Man Called Dave*.

Sachar, Louis: *Holes*
Published by Yearling Books, reprint edition 9 May 2000, ISBN 0440414806
Teen Recommended

Stanley Yelnats (the last of four generations of the same name) has just arrived at Camp Green Lake, Texas, which is not really a camp and which has no lake. It is actually the site of a juvenile detention center run by a corrupt warden who should be imprisoned. Stanley is innocent, but he has to go through all the experiences of the "camp" before his innocence is proved and before the long-standing curse on the Yelnats (from the time of Stanley's great-grandfather) is overcome.

Teaching Ideas and Resources

1. Many of the statements in the book are ironic, so the book works well for teaching the often difficult concept of verbal irony. Have your stu-

dents select statements from the quotations below to explain how irony operates in the novel.

> "The campers are forbidden to lie in the hammock. It belongs to the Warden. The Warden owns the shade." (*Holes*, 3)
>
> "If you take a bad boy and make him dig a hole every day in the hot sun, it will turn him into a good boy." (*Holes*, 5)
>
> "My name is Mr. Sir." (*Holes*, 13)
>
> "They all have nicknames,"explained Mr. Pendanski. "However, I prefer to use the names their parents gave them—the names that *society will recognize them* by when they return to become useful and hardworking members of society." (*Holes*, 18)
>
> That was the worst part for Stanley. His hero [Clyde Livingston] thought he was a no-good-dirty-rotten thief. (*Holes*, 23)
>
> "Now you be careful out in the real world," said Armpit. "Not everyone is as nice as us." (*Holes*, 221)
>
> Zero, who couldn't read until Stanley taught him, is able to figure out that Stanley's name is on the suitcase. (*Holes*, 216)
>
> Zero is the great-great-great grandson of Madame Zeroni and Stanley is the great-great grandson of Elya Yelnats. (*Holes*, 229)

2. After reading the novel with your students, consider showing the film version of *Holes* and have your students write an essay comparing the text to the visual presentation.
3. "Popular Postmodernism for Young Adult Readers: *Walk Two Moons*, *Holes*, and *Monster*" by Stephenie Yearwood in *the ALAN Review* (Summer 2002) presents an additional perspective on the novel. Use this essay to help students recognize characteristics of postmodern novels.
4. "What's Good about the Best?" by Ted Hipple and Amy B. Maupin in the *English Journal* (vol. 90, no. 3 [January 2001]) describes *Holes* as one of the three highest-ranking novels of the 1990s and includes a rationale for teaching the novel. You can use this essay to support selection of this novel to read with your students.
5. "*Holes*: Folklore Redux," by Elizabeth G. Mascia in the *ALAN Review* (Winter 2001) looks at the folktale aspects of this novel. Students can write their own urban legends or folktales connected to people or incidents in their community.

6. Some websites with ideas for teaching the novel include:

   www.indiana.edu/~reading/ieo/bibs/sachar.html
   itc.gsu.edu/NewberyBooks/holesweb.pdf
   falcon.jmu.edu/~ramseyil/sachar.htm
   www.lessonplanspage.com/LAHolesByLouisSachar2-TeacherPagesEachChapter36.htm
   eduscapes.com/newbery/99a.htm
   www.thinkquest.org/library/site_sum.html?tname=J0113061&url=J0113061/
   emintsteachers.more.net/FY03/frickev/holes.html
   garnet.acns.fsu.edu/~msd3378/virtuallesson.html

Why Give This Book to Teens?

- Because maybe they've been falsely accused like Stanley and have felt helpless to explain their innocence.
- Because they may have been part of a group that feared the strongest person, like the Lump; reading Stanley's story might help them know how to handle the "bully" type.
- Because they might need to figure out how to help someone who is an underdog.

Other books by Louis Sachar to consider reading: *Wayside School*, *Dogs Don't Tell Jokes*, *Sideways Stories*, and the *Marvin Redpost* series.

Sparks, Nicholas: A *Walk to Remember*
Published by Warner Books, 1 September 2000, ISBN 0446608955
Teen Recommended

In the prologue to his latest novel, Nicholas Sparks makes the rather presumptuous pledge "first you will smile, and then you will cry," but sure enough, he delivers the goods. With his calculated ability to throw your heart around like a yo-yo (try out his earlier *Message in the Bottle* or *The Notebook* if you really want to stick it to yourself), Sparks pulls us back to the perfect innocence of a first love.

In 1958, Landon Carter is a shallow but well-meaning teenager who spends most of his time hanging out with his friends and trying hard to ignore the impending responsibilities of adulthood. Then Landon gets roped into acting the lead in the Christmas play opposite the most renowned goody two-shoes in town: Jamie Sullivan. Against his best intentions and the taunts of his buddies, Landon finds himself falling for Jamie and learning some central lessons in life.

> Like John Irving's *A Prayer for Owen Meany*, Sparks maintains a delicate and rarely seen balance of humor and sentiment. While the plot may not be the most original, this boy-makes-good tearjerker will certainly reel in the fans. Look for a movie starring beautiful people or, better yet, snuggle under the covers with your tissues nearby and let your inner sap run wild. (From a review by Nancy R. E. O'Brien for Amazon.com)

Teaching Ideas and Resources

1. You may or may not be able to teach this book in connection with a unit or class, but teen readers recommended it and if you are familiar with the book, you can decide which students might enjoy reading it.
2. If you do read the book with students, consider having students discuss the "credibility" of the novel—are there really such experiences? Can life be "happily ever after"? Consider using this book to help students gauge the difference between "just for escape" fiction and literature with greater depth.
3. More information can be found at

   www.nicholassparks.com/FAQS/Walk/FAQ_Book_Walk.html

Why Give This Book to Teens?

- Because they might be in a relationship that can grow from reading about others in relationships.
- Because they may not want to risk the peer pressure that comes when they relate to and befriend someone less popular.
- Because they may be in "the dating game."

Steinbeck, John: *Of Mice and Men*
Published by Penguin USA, reissue edition September 1993, ISBN 0140177396
****Teen Recommended****

Lennie and George are the main characters in this Steinbeck novel set in the time of the Great Depression. They are drifters, migrant workers who are constantly looking for jobs, though they have a dream of finding a place of their own. Lennie is the character that elicits the greatest pathos from readers—he's physically strong and mentally like a child. George acts as a father figure to Lennie, and in this role is called to make a difficult decision to save Lennie from death by a mob.

Teaching Ideas and Resources

1. The book's title is connected to the poem by Robert Burns, *To a Mouse*; explore Burns's poem with the students and have them discuss why (or why not) the title is fitting for the novel. (The *American Heritage Dictionary*'s definition of bindle stiff is "Slang = a migrant worker or hobo who carries his own bedroll [bindle is an alteration of bundle].") The poem is as follows:

   To a Mouse
   Wee, sleeket, cowrin, tim'rous
   beastie, . . .

   But, Mousie, thou art no thy lane
   In proving foresight may be vain:
   The best laid schemes o' mice an' men
   Gang aft agley,
   An' lea'e us nought but grief an' pain
   For promis'd joy.

   Still thou art blest, compar'd wi' me!
   The present only toucheth thee:
   But, och! I backward cast my e'e
   On prospects drear!
   An' forward, tho' I canna see,
   I guess an' fear!

2. An excellent novel to pair with *Of Mice and Men* is Lois Lowry's *The Silent Boy*. This novel could be read aloud in tandem with *Of Mice and Men* and students could write about how they might respond if Jacob, from *The Silent Boy*, is treated any more fairly than Lennie. Both characters can teach students about the condition of those with mental deficiencies. Students could also examine the roles of Katy and George in befriending Jacob and Lennie.
3. The following websites are helpful for teaching *Of Mice and Men*:

   us.penguinclassics.com/static/cs/us/10/teachersguides/ofmiceandmen.html
   www.sdcoe.k12.ca.us/score/mice/micetg.html
   www.yale.edu/ynhti/curriculum/units/1985/3/85.03.04.x.html
   www.greatbooks.org/library/guides/steinbeck.shtml
   www.ac.wwu.edu/~stephan/Steinbeck/mice.html

Why Give This Book to Teens?

- Because this is a book about friendship and everyone needs some true friends.
- Because George has to make a very difficult decision to "save" the life of his friend, and real friendships often call for similar decisions.
- Because they might be someone who is an outcast or treated poorly by others.
- Because they might be lonely and looking for friends.
- Because this book also teaches about the Great Depression and it is good for teens to learn about different eras in American history.

Twomey, Cathleen: *Charlotte's Choice*
Published by Bt Bound, March 2001, ISBN 0613515374

On May 9, 1905, a train pulls into Turner's Crossing, Missouri, and changes the life of Charlotte Matthews and everyone else in her community. This train is bringing orphans from the Children's Aid society; among them is Jesse Irwin, also 14, who has been abandoned by parents in New York City and hardened by living a life of survival. Charlotte and Jesse become best friends, and ultimately Charlotte must make a choice of whether to reveal a confidence Jesse has shared. Revealing Jesse's secret is one way she can save her life, but how does Charlotte break the trust of someone who has had trust broken too often?

Teaching Idcas and Resources

1. This book deals with orphans and abandoned children; it also raises issues about a small town's prejudice toward those children. Students can research background on the current state of adoption and foster care. A related research topic might be the changing status of care for orphans throughout the history of the United States.
2. "Finding Your Way Home: Orphan Stories in Young Adult Literature," by Dirk P. Mattson, in the *ALAN Review* (vol. 24, no. 3 [Spring 1997]), is a helpful essay for the theme of foster children and orphans; the essay offers additional novels to use in a themed unit.
3. If possible, invite someone from social services, specifically an adoption agency, to come to speak to the class. Have your students prepare questions for the speaker. A helpful website is www.childstudy.org/fostercare.

4. Students could read books from the following site—all the books deal with orphans and adoption:

   www.booksbytesandbeyond.com/books/JUV013050.html

5. A site that shows students "real children" awaiting adoption:

   adopt.org/servlet/page?_pageid=289&_dad=portal30&_schema=PORTAL30

6. If your students do service learning or some projects to connect their learning to real life, here is a website that may provide opportunities:

   www.orphanhelpers.com

Why Give This Books to Teens?

- Because they might be adopted and can read the story of someone who went through the challenges of foster homes.
- Because someone in the class or among their peers may be orphaned and reading this book will help teens learn something about the life of those who have been adopted.
- Because, like Charlotte, they may face the decision of revealing a secret that could save someone's life or keeping silent.
- Because this book also deals with sexual abuse and how teens are often trapped in this horrible situation.

Wells, Rebecca: *The Divine Secrets of the Ya-Ya Sisterhood*
Published by Perennial, 7 May 1997, ISBN 0060928336
Teen Recommended

The book is a blend of voices from Sidda, the now 40-year-old daughter of Vivi, to the women who make up the "Ya Yas": Necie, Teensy, Vivi, and Caro. It provides a southern Louisiana perspective to relationships and friendship, to mothers and daughters, to Catholicism before Vatican II, and to the stress of parenting and marriages that are not always one's first choice. The book reveals how much parents' pain and suffering can affect children and how the effects on the children are often not known for many years.

Teaching Ideas and Resources

1. Teaching this book in tandem with *The Sisterhood of the Traveling Pants* would give a contemporary perspective on a group of young women

bonding as the Ya Yas did. You could direct your students to write a memoir about their own childhood friends. Or in a senior year creative writing project, students could write about the gang or group they "hung around with" in their junior high or middle school years. How do these friendships change, grow, and develop? Why are such friendships important?

2. Your male students might like to read *Catcher in the Rye* by J. D. Salinger, *The Chosen* by Chaim Potok, or *A Separate Peace* by John Knowles—then have all your students discuss the differences between female and male bonding situations.
3. *Master Teacher's Guide: A Collection of Forty Guides for Middle and High School Teachers* has a teaching guide for this novel. See HarperCollins Publishers—www.HarperAcademic.com.
4. Reading group guides and other resources for the book are at the following sites:

   www.readinggroupguides.com/guides/divine_secrets.asp
   www.dragonladies.net/dragonladies_book_list.htm
   teachers.net/gazette/AUG02/jones.html
   empowered.org/Resources/books.htm

Why Give This Book to Teens?

- Because they may have trouble relating to their mothers and need to understand some of what might have happened in their mother's life.
- Because they might want to read the story of friendship that the "Ya Yas" share.
- Because they might be considering marriage and need to know more about why relationships and commitment can be challenging.
- Because if they're males, they might want insights on how to better understand females—mothers, sisters, or girlfriends.

Another book by Rebecca Wells to consider reading: *Little Altars Everywhere*.

White, Ruth: *Weeping Willow*

Published by Aerial, reprint edition 1 April 1994, ISBN 0374482802

As the novel opens, Tiny, who would have been called Ernestina if her mother had dared to defy Tiny's grandfather, is beginning high school. She is living with her stepfather, Vern, and the three children born to him and

Tiny's mother. Tiny's biological father went to fight in World War II in 1941 and was never heard from again; five months after he left, Tiny was born. In the years she and her mother lived with her mother's parents, Tiny had an imaginary friend, Willa. After her mother's marriage to Vern, many terrible things began happening to Tiny, including sexual abuse by Vern. The novel, set in Appalachia, demonstrates Tiny's courage and her struggles to grow to womanhood.

Teaching Ideas and Resources

1. In some ways this book is for "teachers too" in the sense that you need to understand that many of the students you teach come from families that are troubled. While you cannot take on all the problems your students face, you do need general knowledge of behaviors and warning signs associated with abuse and how those teenagers who have been abused might be affected.
2. Tiny has an imaginary friend, Willa. Willa is part of the years before Tiny's mother remarries and then appears again after Tiny has been abused. For a character lesson, students could write about the importance of having someone—real or imagined—as a confidante.
3. Another literary device is the interior or dramatic monologue. Invite your students to assume the persona of any of the characters in the novel and write that character's response to growing up in the "Holler" or to another event in the novel.
4. Tiny uses letters to Mr. Gillespie—under the guise of anonymity—to express hopes and fears. Have students write to Tiny or Phyllis or to someone in the students' lives.
5. "Reading from a Female Perspective: Pairing *A Doll's House* with *Permanent Connections*," by Patricia P. Kelly (chapter 8 in Kaywell, *Adolescent Literature as a Complement to the Classics*, vol. 1, 1993) uses this novel as one of the additional works in the unit.
6. "Who Am I? Who Are You? Diversity and Identity in the Young Adult Novel" by Lois Stover in *Reading Their World: The Young Adult Novel in the Classroom*, 2nd ed. (Monseau and Salvner 2000) discusses this novel in talking about minority cultures within the United States.
7. A book that fits well with *Weeping Willow* is *Forged by Fire* by Sharon Draper. Draper's setting and characters are urban and African American, but the abuse and confusion of a second marriage and a stepfather who molests are common elements in both books. Draper's book is a

Coretta Scott King Genesis Award winner. *Tears of a Tiger*, also by Sharon Draper, is another good read for those who like Draper's books.

8. For more information on Ruth White, check the following websites:

   www.carr.lib.md.us/authco/white.htm
   www.indiana.edu/~reading/ieo/bibs/whiter.html
   www.randomhouse.com/teachers/catalog/display.pperl?isbn=0-440-22921-9
   scholar.lib.vt.edu/ejournals/ALAN/winter95/Cole.html

Why Give This Book to Teens?

- Because they may have been abused and not known who they could tell.
- Because they may have friends who need them to listen to their stories of abuse.
- Because they may have struggled to be accepted as they moved into high school.
- Because they may come from a rural area and be considered an outsider.
- Because they might have heritage in Appalachia.

Other books by Ruth White to consider reading: *The Bus to Bluefield*, *Sweet Creek Holler*, and *Memories of Summer*.

Wolff, Virginia Euwer: *Make Lemonade*

Published by Scholastic, reprint edition February 2003,
ISBN 059048141X
****Teen Recommended****

Fourteen-year-old LaVaughn accepts a part-time job caring for the two children of another teen. Jolly, mother of Jilly and Jeremy, is desperate for help feeding, clothing, and raising her two small children, and she's lucky to have found a babysitter like LaVaughn, who is able to help her juggle the demands of single parenting on a small budget. LaVaughn is the narrator of this story, and she describes in realistic details how challenging it can be to help Jolly with her parenting, since Jolly has had no stable home life of her own and has few resources to draw upon as she tries to teach her children life's basics.

Together, the two teens forge an interesting connection, in which they take the worst—life's lemons—and try to make the best—lemonade—out of it. LaVaughn is able to pursue her schoolwork despite the demands of caring for Jolly's kids, and with the help of a supportive mother and understanding teachers, it looks like she might make some progress toward her goal of attending college. And Jolly might actually learn something from LaVaughn about the value of education and make some positive changes in her own life. A realistic, gritty, and often touching story about parenting, friendship, and overcoming obstacles.

Teaching Ideas and Resources

1. Encourage your students to use many of the wisdom sayings LaVaughn's mom "preaches" at LaVaughn, and the wise actions that LaVaughn takes, to make a collection of ways to "make lemonade" of the "lemons" in their own life situations. Have students share their sayings/actions and compile a list of the best ones to display in the classroom. Here are some examples:

   "Mostly you don't quit what you start." (*Make Lemonade*,11)

   "You can't trust the city to keep the bad element out; Public Housing doesn't protect private citizens." (*Make Lemonade*,14)

   LaVaughn is choosing to focus on getting to college so she'll "never live where they have Watchdogs and self-defense." (*Make Lemonade*,19)

   "If you want something to grow and be so beautiful you could have a nice day just from looking at it, you have to wait." (*Make Lemonade*, 25)

   "Steam Class"—a take-off on esteem where "they tell you how you can't be blamed for your burdens; your burdens are things not your fault, you didn't do them, but you carry them around." (*Make Lemonade*, 51)

2. "The Problem of Poverty in Three Young Adult Novels: *A Hero Ain't Nothin' But a Sandwich*, *Buried Onions* and *Make Lemonade*" by Myrna Dee Marler (*ALAN Review*, Fall 2002) provides insights into and helps for teaching *Make Lemonade* and other novels.
3. "The Urban Experience in Recent Young Adult Novels" by Sandra Hughes-Hassell and Sandy L. Guild in the *ALAN Review* (Summer 2002) presents insights about *Make Lemonade* and how it fits with urban novels.
4. "Growing Strong Family Ties" by Pamela S. Carroll (chapter 4 in Gregg and Carroll, *Books and Beyond*, 1998) uses this novel for activities in the unit.
5. The following websites offer information about Virginia Euwer Wolff and help for teaching *Make Lemonade*:

www.Authors4Teens.com
literacy.kent.edu/Oasis/Pubs/0300-17.html
stanleymusic.org/features/wolff_interview/index.php
teachers.altschools.org/tnellen/ftp/pdf/thematicteaching.pdf
www.readingmatters.co.uk/books/make-lemonade.htm

Why Give This Book to Teens?

- Because they can learn from the example of LaVaughn who is going on to college no matter what, even if no one else in their building or their family ever went.
- Because they can learn from LaVaughn who helped Jolly become motivated to return to school and get her GED.
- Because they can bring a presence of acceptance where there is none, as LaVaughn does for Jeremy and Jill, Jolly's two young children.
- Because even though life may have been cruel to them, they can survive and succeed.

Other books by Virginia Euwer Wolff to consider reading: *The Mozart Season*, *Probably Still Nick Swanson*, *Bat 6*, and *True Believer* (a sequel to *Make Lemonade*).

CHAPTER FIVE

Books about Facing Death and Loss

Albom, Mitch: *The Five People You Meet in Heaven*
Published by Hyperion Press, 23 September 2003, ISBN 0786868716

Eddie is 83; today is his birthday and he is at work at the carnival where he has been a maintenance man, servicing the rides. This is also the day that Eddie will die—he dies while trying to save a child from being crushed when a ride has gone awry. What we as readers get is Mitch Albom's notion of heaven as he traces Eddie's meetings with five people who teach him the meaning of his life. Eddie learns from the "Blue Man," the first person he meets in heaven, "the human spirit knows, deep down, that all lives intersect. [That] death doesn't just take someone, it misses someone else, and in the small distance between being taken and being missed, lives are changed" (*Five People*, 49).

Teaching Ideas and Resources

1. Albom has many "quotable quotes" in the book. Select any of the following for journal prompts or other writing activities to use with your students:

> "That there are no random acts. That we are all connected. That you can no more separate one life from another than you can separate a breeze from the wind." (*Five People*, 48)
>
> "Time," the Captain said, "is not what you think." . . . "Dying? Not the end of everything. We think it is. But what happens on earth is only the beginning." (*Five People*, 90)
>
> "You didn't get it. Sacrifice is a part of life. It's *supposed* to be. It's not something to regret. It's something to *aspire* to. Little sacrifices. Big sacrifices. A

> mother works so her son can go to school. A daughter moves home to take care of her sick father . . ." (The Captain speaking to Eddie, *Five People*, 93)
>
> "That's the thing. Sometimes when you sacrifice something precious, you're not really losing it. You're just passing it on to someone else." (*Five People*, 94)
>
> "Things that happen before you are born still affect you," she [Ruby] said. "And people who come before your time affect you as well. We move through places every day that would never have been if not for those who came before us." (*Five People*, 123)
>
> "Learn this from me. Holding anger is a poison. It eats you from inside. We think that hating is a weapon that attacks the person who harmed us. But hatred is a curved blade. And the harm we do, we do to ourselves." (*Five People*, 143)
>
> "Lost love is still love, Eddie. It takes a different form, that's all. You can't see their smile or bring them food or tousle their hair or move them around a dance floor. But when those senses weaken, another heightens. Memory. Memory becomes your partner. You nurture it. You hold it. You dance with it. Life has to end. Love doesn't." (*Five People*, 173)

2. Ask your students: Who are the five people you think you'd meet in heaven? Why would it be these five people? What do they have to teach you? Use these prompts for an essay, but also have your students give an oral presentation (a good and easy way to incorporate some speaking activities in your class) about their five people.
3. Consider pairing Albom's book with Dante's *Inferno* or with any work that deals with the end of life. It can also be used for students to create what they conceive the afterworld to be.

Why Give This Book to Teens?

- Because they might be struggling with why someone they loved has died.
- Because they can learn some wise lessons about life and loss.
- Because they might have people in their life they don't understand, as Eddie does.
- Because they might be able to help a peer or a friend who is facing grief and who feels isolated.

Albom, Mitch: *Tuesdays with Morrie*
Published by Broadway, 8 October 2002, ISBN 076790592X
Teen Recommended

Mitch Albom tells the story of the remarkable life of Morrie Schwartz, a prominent professor of sociology, one of Albom's favorite professors. In 1994, Schwartz was diagnosed with ALS, or Lou Gehrig's disease, a brutal disease that attacks the neurological system. Instead of dying "quietly," Morrie decides his ending days, his dying, will be his final class—this great teacher teaches about life's greatest mystery, death. Mitch Albom is in the prime of his life and far too busy to see and experience life. The book narrates how Albom reconnects with Morrie and takes the time to learn how to die with grace.

Teaching Ideas and Resources

1. One of the best ways to work with this book is simply to read it aloud to your students, a bit every day. The work is powerful enough that it can teach some important lessons that otherwise might not be part of the curriculum. If your school requires character education units, consider using this book so your students can learn from master teacher Morrie about "a guide to living well so that we might die well."
2. This book is filled with quotable quotes. Direct your students to choose any of the following and write why they like the quote or what they learn from it:

   > "There are some mornings when I cry and cry and mourn for myself. Some mornings, I'm so angry and bitter. But it doesn't last too long. Then I get up and say, 'I want to live . . .'" (*Tuesdays with Morrie*, 21)

   > "I'm on the last great journey here—and people want me to tell them what to pack." (*Tuesdays with Morrie*, 33)

   Key points to reflect on (Morrie asks Mitch the following questions):

   > "Have you found someone to share your heart with? Are you giving to your community? Are you at peace with yourself? Are you trying to be as human as you can be?" (*Tuesdays with Morrie*, 24)

   > "The culture we have does not make people feel good about themselves. And you have to be strong enough to say if the culture doesn't work, don't buy it." (*Tuesdays with Morrie*, 42)

> "So many people walk around with a meaningless life. They seem half-asleep, even when they're busy doing things they think are important. This is because they're chasing the wrong things. The way you get meaning into your life is to devote yourself to loving others, devote yourself to your community around you, and devote yourself to creating something that gives you purpose and meaning." (*Tuesdays with Morrie*, 43)

3. Morrie has a "living funeral" so that he can be present with all his friends and family. Though it may be hard because people think they can't cry or show emotion, discuss with your students the value of a "living funeral." If some student in your teaching context has a terminal disease or if someone has recently died from suicide, illness, or accident, consider holding the "living funeral" in your classroom.
4. Helpful websites for teaching the book include:

   www.randomhouse.com/resources/bookgroup/tuesdaysmorrie_bgc.html
   maincc.hufs.ac.kr/~theargus/370/theory_01.htm
   www.1800volunteer.org/learn/family/attitude.jsp
   www.fsc.edu/ffy/morrie.html

Why Give This Book to Teens?

- Because they may be caught up in stressful things and losing sight of what's really important.
- Because they might have someone close to them who is dying and who wants them to be able to "be with" him or her.
- Because there is a great deal of wisdom in this book.
- Because Mitch Albom learned a lot and they can, too.

Blume, Judy: *Tiger Eyes*
Published by Laurel Leaf, reissue edition 15 July 1982, ISBN 0440984696
Teen Recommended

Davey has been enjoying a walk with her boyfriend, Hugh, and now they are in the backyard of Davey's home. Her dad is working on his paintings in the store, located in the lower level of the family home. Davey and Hugh hear what sounds like firecrackers; unfortunately it is not firecrackers, but a gun, and soon Davey's father is lying in a pool of blood. Davey, her younger brother Jason, and her mother face the daunting task of dealing with the murder of their father and husband.

Davey will further struggle when Bitsy, her father's sister, and Walter, her husband, try to make Davey, Jason, and their mother completely change their lives and resettle in New Mexico. This novel shows how 15-year-old Davey learns to grieve and grow.

Teaching Ideas and Resources

1. This book is another one that you can share with individual students who have lost parents. It could also be a good book for you to read aloud in a character education unit on being supportive of peers who have experienced violence, death, or loss. The book fits for many of those "teachable moments" arising when students in your classes or school face a tragedy.
2. "Exploring the American Dream: *The Great Gatsby* and Six Young Adult Novels" by Diana Mitchell (chapter 9 in Kaywell, *Adolescent Literature as a Complement to the Classics*, vol. 1, 1993) uses this novel as one of the six YA novels in the unit.
3. Many of Judy Blume's books are among those that are censored. The following website provides teaching ideas about censorship:

   www.randomhouse.com/highschool/resources/guides3/

4. Some websites with recommended reading for grieving children:

   www.cgcmaine.org/docs/subdocs/bibliography.htm
   homepages.stmartin.edu/students/cbrown/articles.htm (This site has accompanying activities for the young person or child who has lost someone through a difficult circumstance.)

Why Give This Book to Teens?

- Because they might have lost a parent and have had to work through grief.
- Because they might be living with extended family and having a difficult time relating.
- Because they might have a mother or father who has lost her/his spouse and maybe they feel like they have to help her/him survive the loss.
- Because they might feel as Davey does about trying to talk about the fact her father has been murdered.

Other books by Judy Blume to consider reading: *Places I Never Meant to Be*, *Letters to Judy*, and *Forever*.

Creech, Sharon: *Walk Two Moons*
Published by HarperTrophy, reprint edition 30 September 1996, ISBN 0064405176

Sal (Salamanca Tree Hiddle) is 13 and has lived most of her life in Bybanks, Kentucky. The book tells two stories simultaneously. The first story is that of Sal and her father, of her mother who died, of the baby who was born prematurely and died, and of Sal's grandparents, the Hiddles—paternal grandparents (Gramps and Gram) who are taking her on a trip to Idaho, actually tracing the path of Sal's mom's last journey. Sal's family is Native American; both Sal and her mom wanted to be called Indian or American Indian. The second story is of Phoebe Winterbottom, a young girl Sal's age. Phoebe and Sal become pals when Sal and her dad move to Euclid, Ohio. They have been there a year when Margaret Cadaver (a very significant woman in the story) finds a job there for Mr. Hiddle.

Phoebe's mom is frightened when a young man appears in the area of the Winterbottom home; eventually readers learn that Phoebe's mom had a son out of wedlock. Her husband, Prudence (one of Phoebe's sisters), and Phoebe are all shocked—and Phoebe has been further upset because her mom disappeared for several weeks before all this came out. The family has also had several mysterious messages left on their porch, saying things like "do not judge a person until you've walked two moons in his moccasins."

Teaching Ideas and Resources

1. With this book and other books on death, you could teach the five stages of grief identified by Dr. Elisabeth Kübler-Ross: denial and isolation, anger, bargaining, depression, and acceptance. Have your students trace the stages in Sal's life and write about how these five stages can connect to other losses.
2. Borrowing a theme from *The Memory String* by Eve Bunting, your students can create an "In Honor Necklace." Students string beads or tokens, each symbolizing a special wish, thought, or trait that they are grateful for, onto a filament, yarn, or thread. The beads can also symbolize a positive change they want to make because of the life of the person they are honoring. (Credit for this idea is given to Denise and

Carin Beasley, who describe the idea in "Giving Words to Grief: Using *Two Moons in August, Saying It Outloud,* and *Tiger Eyes* to Explore the Death of a Parent," chapter 3 in Allen, *Using Literature to Help Troubled Teenagers Cope with End-of-Life Issues*, 2002).

3. While it may sound a little "morbid," another suggestion from the same book is to create a funeral. Often adolescents are left out of the process of doing anything to plan the funeral or the memorial. They can select favorite songs, poetry, sayings, or stories, or other artifacts to be included in the funeral.
4. A third idea from Beasley and Beasley is the Memory Book. This is a book that symbolizes the relationship between the deceased parent and the person creating the book. Bringing together mementos, photos, lessons taught, or wisdom shared helps the young person know that memories can help the deceased parent "live on."
5. "The Motherless Daughter: An Evolving Archetype of Adolescent Literature" by James Lovelace and Laura Howell Smith (*ALAN Review*, Winter 2002) looks at *Walk Two Moons* as one book on the theme of motherless daughters.
6. "Popular Postmodernism for Young Adult Readers: *Walk Two Moons, Holes*, and *Monster*" by Stephenie Yearwood (*ALAN Review*, Summer 2002) presents an additional perspective on the novel.
7. Some websites for teaching ideas include:

   www.indiana.edu/~reading/ieo/bibs/creech.html
   www.sharoncreech.com/meet/interview.asp
   www.multcolib.org/schoolcorps/creech.html

Why Give This Book to Teens?

- Because they might have experienced the death of a parent.
- Because they may have friends who have lost a parent and need to know how to listen to them.
- Because maybe their parents have "secrets" about their past and the teens become disillusioned when they learn about these secrets.
- Because they need to understand the wise saying, "Do not judge a person until you have walked a mile in his moccasins."

Other books by Sharon Creech to consider reading: *Absolutely Normal Chaos, Bloomability, Chasing Redbird,* and *Ruby Holler.*

Creech, Sharon: *The Wanderer*
Published by HarperTrophy, reprint edition 26 March 2002, ISBN 0064410323
Teen Recommended

Sophie, the narrator, says her father calls her "Three-sided Sophie: one side is dreamy and romantic; one is logical and down-to-earth; and the third side is hardheaded and impulsive" (*The Wanderer*, 3). Is it a dream that she and three of her uncles and two of her cousins sail across the ocean? Is Bompie, her grandfather, really alive? Are Sophie's parents her real parents or an aunt and uncle who have taken her in? *The Wanderer* takes Sophie on a journey to learn who she is and what she's lost.

Teaching Ideas and Resources

1. This novel was an ALA (American Library Association) Best Book for Young Adults in 2001 and would make for a quick read aloud in your classroom. It has the potential for generating discussion on death; on adventures—real or imaginary; on relationships with parents, grandparents, and other relatives; and on being orphaned.
2. "Finding Your Way Home: Orphan Stories in Young Adult Literature," by Dirk P. Mattson (*ALAN Review* 24, no. 3 [Spring 1997]) is a helpful essay for the theme of foster children and orphans; Sophie is essentially an orphan.
3. For author information and teacher resources, check the following websites:

   falcon.jmu.edu/~ramseyil/creech.htm
   eduscapes.com/sessions/land/land3.htm
   www.indiana.edu/~reading/ieo/bibs/creech.html

Why Give This Book to Teens?

- Because they might want to trace their family history and learn some of the tales that make up their heritage.
- Because they may have lost someone they love and need to feel their story is heard.
- Because they might love the sea or the ocean, and the journey Sophie and her uncles and cousins make might be one they'd enjoy.

Other books by Sharon Creech to consider reading: *Fishing in the Air* and *Pleasing the Ghost*.

Crutcher, Chris: *The Crazy Horse Electric Game*
Published by HarperTempest, 1 April 2003, ISBN 0060094907

Willie Weaver (he's Willie Jr., whose dad has been a well-known athlete for the Washington State Huskies and played in the Rose Bowl when the Huskies beat the Michigan Wolverines) is 16 at the time of the remembered event. Several of his friends are on the baseball team with him, a team that's part of the Eastern Montana American Legion. The game against Crazy Horse Electric is a major rivalry; Willie is the pitcher, and he wins the game with an amazing catch behind his back and a throw out to first.

Willie and his dad take daring rides on the Honda motorcycle. Willie's mom does not approve because she has already lost one child—Missie was born when Willie was 12, and when she was three months old, she died of SIDS. Willie blames himself since he didn't know what to do and his mother was across the street talking to a friend.

Then an additional sorrow comes: Willie is in a water skiing accident. While his dad is trying to get the lifejacket off Willie, the dad almost strangles Willie. Jenny, Willie's girlfriend, actually saves Willie. But with the brain damage that results, Willie has speech problems and is physically no longer who he once was. His dad "clams up"; life at home is incredibly tense. No one "really talks." At school, Willie struggles with the tension of not wanting to be pitied and trying to fit in.

Teaching Ideas and Resources

1. Direct your students to write letters from the perspectives of Willie, his dad, and his mom—choose topics that explain the breakdown of communication in the family.
2. Willie eventually meets a number of people who can offer him guidance and help him turn his life around. Let your students assume the role of one of these wisdom figures and write a letter to Willie with their advice.
3. Bonnie O. Ericson, in "Heroes and Journeys in *The Odyssey* and Several Works in Young Adult Literature" (chapter 1 in Kaywell, *Adolescent Literature as a Complement to the Classics*, vol. 2, 1995), describes how to teach *The Crazy Horse Electric Game* in conjunction with *The Odyssesy*.
4. For author information and background, check the following websites:

   www.Authors4Teens.com
   greenwood.scbbs.com/servlet/A4TStart?authorid=ccrutcher&source

5. "A Sense of Balance: Realism in the Characters of Chris Crutcher," by Susan Stevens (in "Adolescent Literature: Making Connections with Teens," special issue, *Virginia English Bulletin* 44, no. 2 [Fall 1994]) gives insights on this novel.
6. An essay by Shirl Chumley on *The Crazy Horse Electric Game* is available in *Rationales for Teaching Young Adult Literature* (Reid and Neufeld 1999).

Why Give This Book to Teens?

- Because they might be dealing with loss and be unable to handle the pain.
- Because they might feel guilty for something totally beyond their control.
- Because they might need to learn from the mistakes that Willie makes.
- Because they might need to know that there are people like Lisa and Sammy who believe in saving those who are hurting.

Frank, Anne: *The Diary of a Young Girl*
Published by Bantam, 1 June 1993, ISBN 0553296981
Teen Recommended

Anne and her family, who are German Jews living in Amsterdam, go into hiding in a part of a warehouse where Mr. Frank had an office; the hiding place becomes known as the "Secret Annex." Mr. and Mrs. Van Daan, their son Peter, and a dentist all share the small four-room space with the Franks. Living in constant fear of discovery by the Nazis, the families remain stressed and tense. Anne's diary is her journal of courage and growth.

Teaching Ideas and Resources

1. "Anne and Me: A Frank Talk with Cherie Bennett and Jeff Gottesfeld" by Melissa Comer (*ALAN Review*, Summer 2002) presents this couple's response about writing *Anne Frank and Me*, a good piece of literature to use in tandem with *The Diary of a Young Girl*. Share with your students what Bennett and Gottesfeld have to say.
2. Use the book *Anne Frank: Beyond the Diary; A Photographic Remembrance* by Ruud van der Rol and Rian Verhoeven (Viking Press, 1993) for further background, and have your students write about any particular photograph that strikes them.

3. "Notes from Girl X: Anne Frank at the Millennium" by Holly Levitsky (*ALAN Review*, Winter 2002) is a good place to begin to get recent insights on the novel and to give you ideas about connecting Anne Frank's story with those of contemporary refugees.
4. "Parallel Lives: Anne Frank and Today's Immigrant Students" by Mitzi Witkin, an essay in *United in Diversity: Using Multicultural Young Adult Literature in the Classroom* edited by Jean E. Brown and Elaine C. Stephens (NCTE, 1998) is another source of teaching ideas.
5. "Anne Frank's *The Diary of a Young Girl*: World War II and Young Adult Literature" by Joan Kaywell (chapter 2 in Kaywell, *Adolescent Literature as a Complement to the Classics*, vol. 1, 1993) offers extensive teaching ideas for this novel.
6. The following sites are good resources:

   www.webenglishteacher.com/frank.html
   www.annefrank.eril.net/teaching/re1.htm
   womenshistory.about.com/cs/frankacurr
   t3.preservice.org/T0301006/lifelp.html
   home.earthlink.net/~jesmith/BiogAutobiog.html
   www.teach-nology.com/teachers/subject_matter/social_studies/holocaust
   www.standards.dfes.gov.uk/schemes2/ks1-2citizenship/cit07/?view=activities
   www.edutech.org/student/courses/care/index.cfm?Group_ID=0&SessionID=43 5
   www.bookrags.com/notes/daf/PART1.htm

7. Specifically for teaching human rights, the following sites are helpful:

   scholar.lib.vt.edu/ejournals/ALAN/spring00/ariew.html
   www.cfep.uci.edu/ProDevel/uci-sati/faculty/rodebaugh_unit.html

8. "Letters as a Tool in Teaching about the Meaning of the Holocaust"

   www.yad-vashem.org.il/download/education/conf/Berlin.pdf

Why Give This Book to Teens?

- Because despite the horrible suffering Anne and her family face, she is still able to find good in life.
- Because they need to know that other teenagers have lived through

such devastation and see that what is happening in their lives can be survived.

- Because they can learn about parents willing to do anything to save their children's lives.
- Because they can learn how to live peaceably even in cramped and dehumanizing conditions, as Anne and her family did.

Guest, Judith: *Ordinary People*
Published by Penguin USA, reprint edition January 1993, ISBN 0140065172
Teen Recommended

This story demonstrates the strain on a family from death and loss, particularly when the grief and accompanying feelings are unresolved. Conrad Jarrett's perfectly ordinary world comes undone when his older brother Buck drowns in a boating accident that he (Conrad) survives. Beth, the perfect suburban mother, escapes her grief in denial. Her husband, Calvin, hides in work. The story of how these ordinary people cope with their loss begins when Conrad returns from hospitalization for a breakdown and attempted suicide.

Teaching Ideas and Resources

1. This book is written from two viewpoints: Conrad's in first person and his father Calvin's in third person. Italics indicate an interior monologue of more uncontrolled thoughts or of dreaming/flashbacks. Have your students chart Conrad's and his father's discoveries of their own hurts and strengths/healing. Then have them make a parallel chart of descriptions about their family relationships before and after Buck's death. A hint for your students: things are not what they seem on the surface.
2. Love and loss are strong themes in Guest's book. Have your students choose incidents in the book that most strongly illustrate that both losing and loving can lead to personal strength and healing.
3. Ask your students to assume the role of friend of Conrad; how would they help him talk about his experience? What advice would they give him?
4. "Catcher as Core and Catalyst" by Ted Hipple (chapter 4 in Kaywell, *Adolescent Literature as a Complement to the Classics*, vol. 1, 1993) discusses language and Guest's novel.

5. "Using Young Adult Literature to Modernize the Teaching of *Romeo and Juliet*," by Arthea J. S. Reed (chapter 6 in Kaywell, *Adolescent Literature as a Complement to the Classics*, vol. 1, 1993) uses this book as a text on suicide.
6. Ideas for teaching the novel can be found at the following websites:

   scholar.lib.vt.edu/ejournals/ALAN/fall96/f96-11-Research.html
   www.uen.org/Lessonplan/preview.cgi?LPid=1528

Master Teacher's Guide

- Have students read Margery Guest's interview with her sister Judith in *Writer's Digest* (vol. 77, no. 8 [August 1997]: 30–34).
- Discuss this quote with your students: "Our whole lives are an education toward realizing that we don't conquer. If you get through life with grace and a certain amount of happiness and good humor, you're doin' well. I'm sure this is a boring cliché, but it comes into my mind all the time: You're given this hand to play, and it makes no difference if it's a winning hand or a losing hand or a mediocre hand. It's your hand and you play it the best way you know how" (Judith Guest).

Why Give This Book to Teens?

- Because they might be in a family experiencing some of these same kinds of trauma.
- Because they may have a friend who has undergone therapy to help him/her cope, and reading this book might help them relate to that friend as he/she tries to come back to "regular life."
- Because they might feel guilt about someone or something they could have dealt with in a different way.
- Because life can throw tough things at us and we wonder if we can cope.
- Because parents are human, too, and often that scares teens.
- Because we all have strengths we never imagined.
- Because even when it's filled with pain, life is worth living.

L'Engle, Madeleine: *A Ring of Endless Light*
Published by Laurel Leaf, reissue edition 15 July 1981, ISBN 0440972329
Teen Recommended

In *A Ring of Endless Light*, L'Engle's protagonist, Vicky Austin, is facing death and loss on several fronts, from companioning her grandfather who is dying of leukemia to supporting three young men who have all experienced death. The novel opens with a funeral; the Austins have joined others to grieve the death of Commander Rodney, a family friend on the small island. Rodney, the same age as Vicky's parents, died of a heart attack after rescuing a young man who'd gone out sailing, disregarding all weather warnings.

Ironically the young man who Commander Rodney rescued, Zachary Gray, was attempting to commit suicide. Zachary is wealthy and spoiled, confused and in late adolescence, acting out his response to his mother's recent death and loss by engaging in risky behavior. Vicky is Zachary's grip on sanity; she also becomes a main support for Leo, Commander Rodney's oldest son, and for Adam, who is doing summer marine research on the island. Vicky becomes the one Adam will trust to reveal his own inner tragedies. When a young girl dies in Vicky's arms in the hospital emergency room as Vicky is awaiting word about her grandfather who has had to be admitted for a transfusion, she succumbs to the burdens of all these losses.

Teaching Ideas and Resources

1. Have your students make a gift to give Vicky. The idea of giving something to a person experiencing loss comes from Kyle Gonzales, Cynthia Clark, and Denise Beasley in chapter 4 of *Using Literature to Help Troubled Teenagers Cope with End-of-Life Issues* (Allen 2002); this chapter deals with loss of a sibling. Students can discuss what they gave and why.
2. Anne Cobb and Maribeth Ekey (in chapter 5, on loss of grandparents, in Allen, *Using Literature to Help Troubled Teenagers Cope with End-of-Life Issues*, 2002) share a series of Quick Writes—quotes from the novel that lead to writing. Many of these prompts build on my favorite quotes from the novel as well—I've made some changes to Cobb and Ekey's ideas. Use these quotes for quick writes as an alternative to giving reading quizzes.

> "Thou art all replete with very thou" (*Ring of Endless Light*, 24). What does this quote mean? Have you known a time when you were "all replete"? Describe it.
>
> "When one tries to avoid death, it's impossible to affirm life" (*Ring of Endless Light*, 50). Describe ways you affirm life.
>
> "All life lives at the expense of other life" (*Ring of Endless Light*, 98). What are examples of this quotation?

"It's hard to let go anything we love. We live in a world, which teaches us to clutch. But when we clutch we're left with a fistful of ashes" (*Ring of Endless Light*, 111). Describe a time when you "clutched" and came up with ashes. Grandfather says, "I thought I could die with you around me, and I didn't realize how much it would hurt you and that I cannot stand that hurt." His son, Vicky's dad, responds, "Perhaps you ought not deprive us of that hurt" (*Ring of Endless Light*, 123). What does Vicky's dad mean? Can pain be good for us? Explain.

"Every death is a singularity" (*Ring of Endless Light*, 155). This is built on Grandfather's belief that a butterfly's death can cause an earthquake in another galaxy. Do you believe this? Why?

Adam tells Vicky about Jeb's two losses and comments "But he still isn't over it" (*Ring of Endless Light*, 164). Is death something we can "get over"? Explain.

3. "Exploring the American Dream: *The Great Gatsby* and Six Young Adult Novels," by Diana Mitchell (chapter 9 in Kaywell, *Adolescent Literature as a Complement to the Classics*, vol. 1, 1993) uses this novel as one of the six YA novels in the unit.

Why Give This Book to Teens?

- Because, like Vicky, they might need to be a support to a friend or peer who has experienced a sudden death in the family.
- Because often teenagers have their first experiences with death when their grandparents die, so like Vicky, they can learn about how to "say goodbye" to grandparents.
- Because they may have a friend who is contemplating suicide and can learn through Vicky how they might be able to help.

Lowry, Lois: A *Summer to Die*
Published by Laurel Leaf, reissue edition 1 December 1983, ISBN 0440219175

This story is told from the viewpoint of Meg, the younger sister and less beautiful (especially from Meg's perspective) daughter of the Chalmers. Molly, the older sister, is the popular one, the prettier one; she has just become a cheerleader. Mr. Chalmers has been given a year from the university to finish a book—he's an English professor. The family rents a small house in the country so Mr. Chalmers can have the quiet to write. They move right before Thanksgiving.

The owner of the house is Will Banks, 70, a kind and creative man who befriends the Chalmers, especially Meg. Will quotes poetry—in particular, one great poem, Gerard Manley Hopkins' "Spring and Fall." He tells Meg, "It's Margaret you mourn for," and at the time Meg doesn't understand what he means. Meg can do photography, and she eventually gets a darkroom—her father builds it when he is "stuck" on his writing—and is able to teach (as well as learn with) Will Banks.

In the midst of all this, Molly gets ill. It starts with nosebleeds; but one night as Meg awakens knowing "something is wrong," Molly is in a pool of blood. What Molly develops is a kind of leukemia, but for a long time, Meg doesn't realize how ill Molly is. Her parents don't tell her since there is some hope that medication will work. The book conveys how a family deals with death and offers some great images of friendships.

Teaching Ideas and Resources

1. This book is a central one in chapter 4 of *Using Literature to Help Troubled Teenagers Cope with End-of-Life Issues* (Allen 2002). A good teaching idea from the writers of that chapter suggests having students design a gift for Meg.
2. Teach the Gerard Manley Hopkins' poem "Spring and Fall"; lead a discussion about who we really "mourn for" when we experience death.
3. Some teaching resources are located at:

    endeavor.med.nyu.edu/lit-med/lit-med-db/webdocs/webdescrips/lowry1015-des-.ht ml
    scils.rutgers.edu/~kvander/lowry.html
    www.crinkles.com/authorAuthor.html
    www.indiana.edu/~reading/ieo/bibs/lowry.html

Why Give This Book to Teens?

- Because they might have to deal with the death of a sibling.
- Because someone they know might be dealing with the death of a sibling.
- Because the book offers great images of friendships among people of different ages.
- Because they might need to know how to deal with grief and loss.

Myers, Walter Dean: *Fallen Angels*
Published by Scholastic, reprint edition February 2003,
ISBN: 0590409433
Teen Recommended

The book is dedicated to Walter Dean Myers' brother, Thomas, "whose dream of adding beauty to this world through his humanity and his art" ended in Vietnam on May 7, 1968. The book opens with a group of soldiers en route to Vietnam, on a flight from Massachusetts to Anchorage, Alaska. The narrator, Richie Perry, is not even supposed to go—he has a bad knee, but his paperwork has been messed up; he says the war will be over soon anyway. Perry has graduated from high school and plans to go college and be a writer like James Baldwin; he goes into the army hoping to earn and send money home to his mother and younger brother Kenny.

Peewee, Jenkins, and Perry are sent out to Chu Lai, their first trip into combat—they are in Alpha Company. Johnson, a large African-American, is also in their group. Jenkins is afraid he is going to die in Nam. Peewee and Perry are in a foxhole; they had to kill a Vietcong to be there. When leaving the hole and trying to get to a pickup area, Perry realizes Peewee is injured. Monaco is also in danger; all three get on a chopper, but Perry is again injured. Perry does recover, Peewee also recovers—for a time, and Monaco has to go back to the "Boonies."

Monaco, Peewee, and Perry have all "tasted what it feels like to be dead." They are "not all right." "We would have to learn what it was like to be alive again" (*Fallen Angels*, 304). Peewee and Perry fly "back to the world" together.

Teaching Ideas and Resources

1. The following are a few of the powerful lines from the novel. Use these and others that you select as writing prompts to lead to discussion:

    On a first little trial, Jenkins steps on a land mine by accident; he's killed. Perry never is able to forget Jenkins. A description of how Perry feels about Jenkins says, "I wanted to say the only dead person I had ever seen before had been my grandmother" (*Fallen Angels*, 43).

    Seeing the body bags gets to Perry: "It was only inside that I was numb" (*Fallen Angels*, 43).

    Lieutenant Carroll's prayer: "Lord, let us feel pity for _____, and sorrow for ourselves, and all the angel warriors that fall. Let us fear death, but let it not live within us. Protect us, O Lord, and be merciful unto us. Amen" (*Fallen Angels*, 44).

Carroll says his father used to call all soldiers angel warriors because usually they get boys to fight wars. Most are not old enough to vote; Carroll is 23.

"The air in Nam was always hard to breathe; it was heavy, thicker than the air back home. Now it was harder" (*Fallen Angels*, 67).

2. "Connecting with Students through Multicultural Young Adult Novels" by Diana Mitchell, an essay in *United in Diversity: Using Multicultural Young Adult Literature in the Classroom* edited by Jean E. Brown and Elaine C. Stephens (NCTE 1998), discusses ways for teaching the novel.
3. Bonnie O. Ericson, "Heroes and Journeys in *The Odyssey* and Several Works in Young Adult Literature" (chapter 1 in Kaywell, *Adolescent Literature as a Complement to the Classics*, vol. 2, 1995) describes how to teach *Fallen Angels* in conjunction with *The Odyssey*.
4. Pam Cole, in "Bridging *The Red Badge of Courage* with Six Related Young Adult Novels" (chapter 2 in Kaywell, *Adolescent Literature as a Complement to the Classics*, vol. 2, 1995), uses *Fallen Angels* as one of the YA novels to pair.
5. In "John Wayne, Where Are You? Everyday Heroes and Courage" by Pamela S. Carroll (chapter 2 in Gregg and Carroll, *Books and Beyond*, 1998), this novel is one of the YA novels that supplement the unit.
6. Check the following websites for information on Walter Dean Myers and teaching guides for the novel:

   www.Authors4Teens.com
   www.neiu.edu/~gspackar/INDEX.html
   www.mcdougallittell.com/disciplines/_lang_arts/litcons/fallen/guide.cfm
   www.indiana.edu/~reading/ieo/bibs/myers.htm

7. An essay on *Fallen Angels* by Jolene Borgese and Susan Ebert is available in *Rationales for Teaching Young Adult Literature* (Reid and Neufeld 1999).

Why Give This Book to Teens?

- Because they may wonder what it would be like to have to kill others in war, especially civilians.
- Because they may have a father or another relative who has been in

Vietnam, Korea, the Gulf War, or Iraq, and need to understand how that person's life may be affected.
- Because so many men and women, not much older than these teens and sometimes known by the teens, are dying in Iraq and other countries.
- Because males are often put into a stereotype of not being able to cry or to be afraid, and this book shows how important those emotions are for every person.

Park, Barbara: *Mick Harte Was Here*
Published by Random House Books for Young Readers, 27 August 1996, ISBN 0679882030
Teen Recommended

Phoebe, the almost-14-year-old sister of Mick, tells the story. Mick is just 10 months younger than Phoebe and is a classic clown and annoying younger brother. The day he is fatally injured in a bike accident changes the lives of Phoebe and her parents. One of the amazing things Phoebe learns is that Mick in death is not "lost," but is actually present everywhere. She is also able to talk to her peers in an assembly at school about the importance of wearing a helmet while riding a bike—had Mick worn a helmet, his life would have been saved.

Teaching Ideas and Resources

1. Because this book deals with the sudden death of a sibling, it works well for any students in your class who have experienced similar losses. Phoebe's best friend in the book has to remind Phoebe that others are feeling Mick's death too. This makes the book good as well for classmates of those who have lost a sibling. The following website lists books for dealing with grief and loss:
   www.bereavement.net/Bibliography.pdf
2. Phoebe learns about death in experiencing her brother's death. Create an "I've been there" bulletin board which allows those who have had similar experiences to share their insights on death, grief, and the guilt they often feel about not being able to prevent the death.
3. In the book, Phoebe talks about helmets and bike safety. The following sites reinforce this message:

   www.dhs.cahwnet.gov/EPIC/bike/documents/MickHarteTeachersGuide.pdf
   www.ohsu.edu/hosp-thinkfirst/tf_parent-teacher.shtml

Why Give This Book to Teens?

- Because they may have experienced a death of a sibling or family member.
- Because they might feel some of the same emotions that Phoebe experiences.
- Because they might have peers, classmates, or friends who have lost a family member and need to know how to understand their experience.

White, Ruth: *Belle Prater's Boy*
Published by Yearling Books, reprint edition 12 January 1998, ISBN 0440413729

Woodrow is the 12-year-old son of Everett and Belle; as the novel begins his mother has disappeared—no one knows where she is. It's very mysterious since the family lives in a very isolated hollow, Crooked Ridge, near Coal Station, Virginia. His cousin Gypsy is also 12; she's the narrator of the book.

Gypsy's mom is named Love. Love was the family beauty; her sister Belle (Woodrow's mom) always longed to be the beautiful one. Belle had been in love with a man named Amos, and all seemed right; then Amos saw Love and they were an instant "match." Belle was humiliated and hurt; she eventually went out and met/eloped with the first miner she saw, Everett. Gypsy only later realizes that her father, Amos, was actually in love with Woodrow's mom first, and then feels sorry for him. Amos, who loved Gypsy dearly, died suddenly after being seriously disfigured in a fire (he was a volunteer fireman)—he shot himself and Gypsy saw the shooting through the bedroom window. She has blocked that memory, though she keeps having nightmares of some hurt animal. Her mom, Love, has remarried to Porter Dotson, though Gypsy refuses to accept Porter; she sees him as "taking her dad's place."

Teaching Ideas and Resources

1. The book deals with "what essential is invisible to the eye": from the ugliness of Belle (or her lesser beauty) which plagued her; to Woodrow's severe cross-eyed situation; to Gypsy's dislike of her long hair—which though beautiful, she sees as a bother and something that hides her richer qualities; to Amos' inability to live after he's been disfigured; to Blind Benny, who was born with some disfigurement and no eyes. This central theme can be connected to many other selections of literature where the theme is appearance versus reality, or to focus students on the essentials of inner beauty rather than physical beauty. You can

also use this book as part of a unit on respect or on other positive qualities that may be part of character education units.

2. The following is the poem, written by Jalal al-Din Rumi in the thirteenth century, that Woodrow's mom was often reading right before she disappeared; use it with your students to discuss his mother's actions:

   The breeze at dawn has secrets to tell you
   Don't go back to sleep.
   You must ask for what you really want.
   Don't go back to sleep.
   People are going back and forth across the doorsill where two worlds touch.
   The door is round and open.
   Don't go back to sleep.

3. Teaching guides and author background are available at the following websites:

   theliterarylink.com/belle_lessons.html
   www.successlink.org/great2/g1768.html
   www.indiana.edu/~reading/ieo/bibs/whiter.html
   www.csulb.edu/org/childrens-lit/proj/nbgs/nbgs-lists/nbgs1997.html
   www2.sjsu.edu/testupdates/faculty/patten/belle_lessons.html

Why Give This Book to Teens?

- Because they may be someone who is judged on appearance only and who has been hurt by what others haven't "seen."
- Because they might be someone who doesn't always look beyond the surface of things, and who can learn more about why seeing beyond surface beauty is important.
- Because they may have lost a parent and might be trying to deal with that loss.

Zindel, Paul: *The Pigman*
Published by Bantam, reissue edition 1 February 1983, ISBN 0553263218
Zindel, Paul: *The Pigman's Legacy*
Published by Bantam, reissue edition 1 May 1984, ISBN 0553265997
****Teen Recommended****

John and Lorraine are typical teenagers who are very creative. These books are narrated by John and Lorraine, alternating each chapter as they tell of meeting Mr. Angelo Pignati, whom they later dub "The Pigman," and in the second book, Colonel Glenville. A combination of curiosity and adolescent daring cause John and Lorraine to become involved with both these elderly gentlemen. John and Lorraine also come to understand a good deal about loneliness, loss, and death as they try to make the last days of the Pigman and the Colonel the happiest they can be. The teens also experience fear and guilt about the role they play in the Pigman's death. Paul Zindel's ability to create realistic adolescent characters makes these books classics no adolescent should miss.

Teaching Ideas and Resources

1. Both books are written in first person, with chapters alternating between John and Lorraine. These books both work well for teaching point-of-view. Your students could be paired and do a team-writing of an experience similar to John's and Lorraine's, particularly focused on elderly relatives in their lives.
2. "Time and Tradition Transforming the Secondary English Class with Young Adult Novels," by Gary Salvner (in Monseau and Salvner 2000) discusses both these novels, giving insights on how you can teach them.
3. "The 'I' of the Beholder: Whose 'Truth'?" by Joanne Brown (in "Adolescent Literature: Making Connections with Teens," special issue, *Virginia English Bulletin* 44, no. 2 [Fall 1994]) uses *The Pigman* as one of the novels central to the unit.
4. "Gaining Understanding about Human Relationships through Young Adult Fiction" by Elizabeth Poe (in "Adolescent Literature: Making Connections with Teens," special issue, *Virginia English Bulletin* 44, no. 2 [Fall 1994]) uses this novel as one of the works in the unit.
5. For author information and background, check the following websites:

   www.Authors4Teens.com
   greenwood.scbbs.com/servlet/A4TStart?authorid=pzindel&source=
   scholar.lib.vt.edu/ejournals/ALAN/spring95/Russick.html
   www3.pei.sympatico.ca/gordie.cox/pigman.htm
   www.sdcoe.k12.ca.us/score/pigman/pigmantg.html

6. The *ALAN Review* has several articles on Paul Zindel:

   "The Effect of Gamma Rays on the Man and the Writer Zindel: *The*

Pigman Plus Twenty Years and Counting" (*ALAN Review* 16, no. 3 [Spring 1989]: 21–25, 43).

"Welcome Back, Zindel" by John A. Davis (*ALAN Review* 9, no. 1 [Fall 1981]: 2–4, 10).

"Something Wonderful, Something Beautiful: Adolescent Relationships Through the Eyes of Paul Zindel" by Kim Hansen (*ALAN Review* 18, no. 2 [Winter 1991]: 41–43).

7. www.webenglishteacher.com/zindel.html is a good site for teaching ideas.

Why Give This Book to Teens?

- Because maybe like John and Lorraine, they are curious about older people and want to have a relationship with them.
- Because maybe they need to learn that not all teenage pranks are harmless.
- Because John and Lorraine learn much about themselves, especially about how to be sensitive to the elderly.
- Because John and Lorraine are honest and realistic in their narration.

CHAPTER SIX

~

Books about Identity, Discrimination, and Struggles with Decisions

Bauer, Marion Dane (editor): *Am I Blue?*
Published by HarperTrophy, reprint edition 30 May 1995, ISBN 0064405877
Teen Recommended

This collection of short stories focuses on adolescents and sexual identity. One of the most powerful stories is that of Bruce Coville, for whom the collection is named. Coville's narrator is a young man who has just been attacked and harassed. Melvin, a fairy godfather, appears to the young man and grants him three wishes. One of the wishes involves an experiment—anyone who is gay or lesbian turns blue, to varying degrees. The narrator is surprised to realize who and how many people have kept their sexual orientation hidden.

Other stories in the book are written by many well-known YA literature writers including Francesca Lia Block, Lois Lowry, Jacqueline Woodson, M. E. Kerr, William Sleator, and Jane Yolen.

Teaching Ideas and Resources

1. In her introduction to the collection, Marion Dane Bauer shares a powerful statement of a friend of hers: "I have never met a bigot who was a reader as a child." This statement offers a key purpose for you to teach or direct your students to these short stories. Most often, teens know little about sexual identity and those who are gay or lesbian live in fear of others finding out. If for no other reason, teaching this collec-

tion of short stories may help those adolescents who attempt suicide because of their sexual identity. Consider selecting stories to read for character education units.

2. Your students may have read books by authors included in this short story collection. If so, allow students to read the story by the author they are most interested in and compare the short story to the novel.
3. "Honoring Their Stories, Too: Literature for Gay and Lesbian Teens" by Michael Cart (*ALAN Review* 25, no. 1 [Fall 1997]) is a good essay relating to this book. Use this essay for ideas about how to relate the short stories in this book to your classroom situation.
4. Nancy Prosenjak has an essay on *Am I Blue?* in *Rationales for Teaching Young Adult Literature* (Reid and Neufeld 1999). In addition to analysis of the collection, Prosenjak includes related works—collections of short stories, novels, and nonfiction.
5. Some teaching ideas are available at the following site, which presents a summary of each story in the collection:

   www.hu.mtu.edu/~evjohnso/amIblue.pdf

Why Give This Book to Teens?

- Because they might be wondering about sexual identity and need to learn more about it. Teens seldom feel comfortable talking to adults about sexual identity or other issues related to sexuality.
- Because they might be gay or lesbian and wondering how to share that reality with parents, family, or friends.
- Because too many teenagers face harassment and ridicule and they may be one of those hurting others or being hurt themselves.
- Because reading and knowledge can reduce fear and bigotry, and sexual identity is the target for many hate crimes.

Bennett, Cherie: *Life in the Fat Lane*
Published by Delacorte Books for Young Readers, 9 February 1998, ASIN 0385322747
Teen Recommended

Lara is 16 and everything in her life seems to be perfect; she's the perfect weight and size, she's dating a perfect guy, and she has the opportunity, though only a junior, to become homecoming queen. Lara is also in a very dysfunctional family, though she isn't truly aware of the dysfunction until she develops a rare syndrome, Axell-Crowne, which causes her to gain an inordinate amount of weight. Now her mother, obsessed with physical beauty, and her father, who thinks all Lara needs is willpower, practically disown her. Lara also experiences the taunts and ridicule that others who are overweight face and she no longer wants to be Lara.

Teaching Ideas and Resources

1. This book provides a great segue into the whole topic of body image that our culture thrusts at us in so many ways. Your students can analyze ads and media that promote the "thin is beautiful" image. They can make a bulletin board showing the negative ads and design counter ads that are positive. They can also research the problems of bulimia and anorexia that cause serious damage to themselves or to many of their peers—males as well as females. Consider having students do an I-Search paper on these topics.
2. Body image and weight issues related to popularity can be a good topic for a "Take a Stand" activity and follow-up discussion. Create a series of statements with which students can take a stand somewhere along the continuum of strongly disagree to strongly agree. Then have students listen to each statement and move to a location in the room indicating their position on the continuum. It might also work well to have students submit statements related to the topic and use those anonymously to create the list for the activity.
3. "Gender Issues and the Young Adult Novel in the New Millennium" by Pam B. Cole and Patricia P. Kelly (in Monseau and Salvner 2000) looks specifically at Bennett's book and the issue of body image.
4. "Eating Disorders: A Recollection and a Review of Some Relevant Young Adult Fiction," by Elizabeth M. Myers, and "The Portrayal of Obese Adolescents," by Rachel Beineke (both in *ALAN Review* 25, no 3 [Spring 1998]) are two essays worth reading in connection with this novel.
5. In the "Research Connection" of the *ALAN Review*, Fall 2003, Jeffrey Kaplan presents researcher Beth Younger's findings on "Female Body Issues in Young Adult Literature"; see this journal for other books related to female body issues.
6. The following websites have helpful teaching information and resources:

   www.teencybercenter.org/lists/food.htm
   www.caringonline.com/eatdis/books/stories.htm

www.womens-studies.ohio-state.edu/peerpower/EatingDisorders.htm
www.signonsandiego.com/news/metro/clifford/20021207-9999_1c7clifford.html
www.ala.org/Content/NavigationMenu/Our_Association/Divisions/YALSA/For_Members_Only/YAttitudes/Archives1/Summer_2002/Resource_Roundup3/The_Shame_List/The_Shame_List.htm
www.kelleyrose.org/disorderly/books.html
www.drrecommend.com/lst/Health/Mental_Health/Disorders/Eating/20.html

Why Give This Book to Teens?

- Because they might be overweight and facing ridicule about it.
- Because they might be one who thinks that body image is everything and are struggling with bulimia or anorexia.
- Because they might be someone who harasses others about weight and body image, and they should know the harm it can cause.
- Because they might face parental pressures and expectations that are unreasonable, and reading Lara's story might help them.

Brashares, Ann: *The Sisterhood of the Traveling Pants*
Published by Delacorte Books for Young Readers, reprint edition 11 March 2003, ISBN 0385730586
****Teen Recommended****

Could a pair of jeans have magical powers? Carmen, Lena, Tibby, and Bridget think so. The four friends are wildly different in size, shape, and personality, but a pair of thrift store jeans fits, flatters, and empowers each of the teens. In fact, as they try the pants on—one after another—they feel that anything might be possible. The pants couldn't have come at a better time. This is the first summer they'll be apart. Lena will visit her grandparents in Greece. Bridget is on her way to soccer camp in Baja. Carmen has been invited to stay with her father in another city, and Tibby is dreading the thought of spending the summer at a dumb summer job without her good friends. They make a pact: the magical pants will travel among them throughout the summer. They all will be able to feel like the goddesses they are during part of the long summer ahead.

Such an imaginative set-up for a novel! Readers follow the pants into the lives of these engaging girls. We watch them face difficult situations—Carmen faces her father's remarriage, Bridget struggles with a sexual attraction to a coach in her camp, Lena gets caught in a language and cultural barrier while trying to explain that she was physically assaulted, and Tibby confronts leukemia and its cruelty in twelve-year-old Bailey's life. Each of the girls learns to deal with the consequences of their actions, discover new stores of inner strength, and learn about the power of true friendship. Without moralizing, author Ann Brashares weaves in delicious ideas about celebrating our differences and loving ourselves as we are.

Teaching Ideas and Resources

1. Each chapter of the book opens with a quote, frequently the words of a famous person. Ask your students to select their favorite ones and explain how the quotes fit the characters and their actions. Some of the quotes to choose from:

   "Not all who wander are lost."—J. R. R. Tolkien

   "Luck never gives: it only lends."—ancient Chinese proverb

   "Can you make yourself love? Can you make yourself be loved?"—Lena Kaligaris (one of the four friends)

   "There is no such thing as fun in the whole family."—Jerry Seinfeld

   "Love is like war: easy to begin. Hard to end."—proverb

   "I have seen the future and it's like the present, only longer."—Dan Quisenberry

   "The problem is not the problem. The problem is your attitude about the problem. Got that?"—Coach Brevin

   "You will make all kinds of mistakes: but as long as you are generous and true and also fierce you cannot hurt the world or even seriously distress her."—Winston Churchill

2. The pants are the object that unites these four friends; have your students write about an object or symbol that could keep them connected to friends. For an oral presentation opportunity, allow the students to share their choice and explain how the object could work.
3. Using Montaigne's essay "On Friendship" or something from Emerson,

have your students make a comparison of the advice presented in these "canonical" writings with that presented by Brashares.

Why Give This Book to Teens?

- Because they might need the support of friends and can learn from the way these four young women were friends despite all kinds of differences.
- Because they might be faced with the remarriage of a parent and with the anger or feelings of abandonment that come with it and, by reading this novel, can learn to cope with their situations.
- Because they might need to know how to relate to someone younger than they are who is terminally ill.
- Because this book teaches about some of life's biggest issues: friendship, death, desires, and loss.

Cormier, Robert: *The Chocolate War*
Published by Laurel Leaf, reissue edition 1 August 1986, ISBN 0440944597

This book is set at Trinity High School, a school run by an order of Roman Catholic brothers. Brother Leon is acting headmaster and a despicable man; the "Vigils," a student group not totally unlike a college fraternity, really "runs" the place. Archie Costello is the "assigner"; he devises schemes for underclassmen to fulfill. There is a black box; if Archie draws a black marble from the box he has to do the assignment—neither ever happens.

Archie is asked by Brother Leon to help enlist the support of the Vigils behind the annual chocolate sale. Jerry Renault, a freshman who has just lost his mother to cancer in the spring and who lives with a father who can't bear the loss of his wife, first is ordered not to sell; then Jerry refuses on his own. The motto he has on a poster in his locker is "Do I dare disturb the universe?" (a T. S. Eliot line from "The Wasteland"). Jerry is eventually beaten terribly in a fight (arranged by the Vigils) against Emile Janza, a cruel, amoral young man. Roland Goubert—called the Goober, is Jerry's only friend, yet he's unable to save Jerry and feels as though he betrayed Jerry.

Teaching Ideas and Resources

1. This is another book that lends itself to the "Take a Stand" Activity. Once more, you might involve students in creating the questions/state-

ments about peer pressure and other topics they see as related to the novel. Their statements could be submitted anonymously in a box and then used for class discussion.

2. "Do I dare disturb the universe?"—Use this central quote from the book for a writing prompt and then have a discussion of the responses. Some related questions you can ask your students: Can you really get away from a gang or group to which you belong? Is it worth the suffering or ridicule you might face? Is it really possible to go against the majority?
3. Chapter 11, "Alienation from Society in *The Scarlet Letter* and *The Chocolate War*" by Elizabeth Ann Poe; chapter 12, "The Beast Within: Using and Abusing Power in *Lord of the Flies*, *The Chocolate War*, and Other Reading" by Barbara G. Samuels; and chapter 13, "Dealing with Abuse of Power in *1984* and *The Chocolate War*" by Kay Parks Bushman and John H. Bushman (all in Kaywell, *Adolescent Literature as a Complement to the Classics*, vol. 1, 1993) present units for teaching this novel.
4. *Stargirl* by Jerry Spinelli (**Teen Recommended**) is a good book to compare or read simultaneously with *The Chocolate War*. The narrator is again a young male, but this time it is the unconventional goodness of Susan/Stargirl that becomes the "affront" to her peers. They can't stand to see someone so different. In many ways, Stargirl acts heroically, particularly because she doesn't need recognition. Students could work the "Take a Stand" activity with this novel as well.
5. See the *ALAN Review* Fall 2003 issue for an article by Jen Menzel, "Intimidation in Cormier's *Tunes for Bears to Dance To*, *We All Fall Down*, and *The Chocolate War*." This article gives insights on themes in *The Chocolate War*.
6. Patricia L. Daniel, in "Relationships and Identity: Young Adult Literature and *The Tragedy of Julius Caesar*" (chapter 7 in Kaywell, *Adolescent Literature as a Complement to the Classics*, vol. 2, 1995), uses *The Chocolate War* as one of the YA novels to compare with the play.
7. Several teaching lessons are available at the following sites:

   www.webenglishteacher.com/cormier.html
   www.csis.pace.edu/schools/wp/dcronk/ChocWar.html
   www.mcdougallittell.com/disciplines/_lang_arts/litcons/chocolat/guide.cfmwww.carr.lib.md.us/mae/cormier/cormier.htm
   www.fsu.edu/~CandI/ENGLISH/webq/chocolate/Chocolate.html

Why Give This Book to Teens?

- Because they may have felt pressured to do something they really don't agree with.
- Because they may be struggling with how to fit in—especially if they have had some loss in their family like Jerry had in his.
- Because sometimes they deal with adults who knowingly or unknowingly add to the problems and pressures they experience.
- Because they may feel guilty about not being able to help or save another person they like.

Danticat, Edwidge: *Behind the Mountains*
Published by Orchard Books, October 2002, ISBN 0439372992

Celiane Esperance is a young Haitian woman; she lives with her mother and older brother, Moy, in the mountain area of Beau Jour, Haiti. Her father left for the United States in 1995, five years before Celiane's diary entries begin. Her father has been working to get the money for Celiane, Moy, and their mother to come to New York. Celiane's story includes the fear she faces in preelection Haiti; one day in Port-au-Prince a seven-year-old girl is killed when a bomb is thrown at the school bus on which she's riding. Celiane's question at this news is "Why must children be killed? They are not involved in politics" (*Behind the Mountains*, 53). This novel also reveals the tension 19-year-old Moy faces—he is not allowed to be an adult, but in his father's absence he takes on many adult responsibilities.

Once the family is reunited in New York, Celiane's diary describes the world of Haitian immigrants trying to assimilate. Moy wants to follow his dream of painting; his father wants him to pursue education. Papa's and Moy's values clash and Celiane sees it all; her story is one common to many immigrants in early twenty-first-century America.

Teaching Ideas and Resources

1. This book, as well as *Flight to Freedom* by Ana Veciana-Suarez, is part of a new series, First Person Fiction, a line of novels about today's immigrant experience published by Scholastic. These novels are both first-person narratives; you can use them to teach point-of-view in novels while helping your students learn about other cultures and about the realities that exist for many students who are from immigrant families. Scholastic also provides a discussion guide including a summary

of each novel; discussion points on character, setting, and theme; a comparison of the novels; related readings; and the following websites:

www.historyofcuba.com (The Timetable History of Cuba)
www.odci.gov/cia/publications/factbook/geos/cu.html (CIA—The World Fact Book)
www.encarta.msn.com/find/concise.asp?ti = 06082000 (Encarta Encyclopedia Article on Haiti)
www.infoplease.com/ipa/a0107612.html (information on Haiti)

2. Suggest that your students look for newspaper articles and other news reports on immigrants or refugees trying to come to the United States. Have them compare these news stories with the experiences Celiane has in her life.
3. Other websites include:

www.wehaitians.com/diaries%20of%20desperation.html
www.litwomen.org/Complist/complearn_a.html
teacher.scholastic.com/products/tradebooks/bookupdate/janfeb04.htm
www.libraries.phila.k12.pa.us/misc/SummerReading/SummerRead-Grade6.html

4. A printable file on the novels is available at:

www.nysreading.org/BookBanter/banspring03.pdf

5. A site on Historical Fiction for Teens:

www.webrary.org/rs/bibhistfict.html

6. Multicultural Books for Young Readers:

education.umn.edu/CI/NBFYR/MultiCultural.html

7. Reading Around the World:

www.seattleschools.org/schools/hamilton/Library/world_read.htm

Why Give This Book to Teens?

- Because many students are international, and all students need to learn more about different cultures and their peers who come from different countries.
- Because people in the United States sometimes have difficulty accept-

ing people from other nations, particularly after September 11, 2001, and a book like this can let young adults know what their peers who are immigrants are experiencing.
- Because Celiane's family struggles with many of the same tensions that their own families may face, regardless of cultural experience.
- Because many young people today are growing up in places where there is violence.

Greene, Bette: *The Drowning of Stephan Jones* Published by Laurel Leaf, reissue edition 1 January 1997, ASIN 0440226953

Carla Wayland is 16 and living with her mother in Rachetville, Arkansas; Carla's father left the family when she was a baby. Her mother, a librarian at the public library, faces a barrage of issues around censorship, but nevertheless keeps working for the rights of all. Sometimes Carla is embarrassed by her mother's tough stances. When a gay couple moves into neighboring Parson's Springs, Carla faces her greatest test. Andy Harris, a popular and handsome high school senior, appears to be a devout Christian; however, he is also homophobic and his actions toward Frank and Stephan (the gay couple) erupt with increasing hatred. Carla struggles as she believes she's in love with Andy, but in the face of Andy's violent actions, she wants to say, "I really, really hate it when you're hating. I hate it even more when you try to force me into hating, too" (*Drowning of Stephan Jones*, 81). This is a tragic and powerful novel.

Teaching Ideas and Resources

1. Once again, consider doing the "Take a Stand" activity to determine students' responses to the topic. If you do the activity as part of prereading, you could use statements or actions of the characters of the novel and see what students think before and after the novel.
2. This novel could be used in a character education unit—particularly in connection with response to bullying, harassment, or hate crimes. Students could write about hate crimes or situations they have witnessed, read about or heard about; have the students submit their writings anonymously, and you could use these for discussion.
3. After reading the novel, have students debate the fate of Andy and his peers. They might also research the Matthew Shepard case or do follow-up reading of *The Laramie Project*.

4. There are two articles from the Winter 1994 *ALAN Review* that could enhance the teaching of this novel: "America's Designated Victims: Our Creative Young" by Bette Greene (*ALAN Review* 21, no. 2 [Winter 1994]: 2–4) and "Understanding Adolescent Homophobia: An Interview with Bette Greene" by Lynne Alvine (*ALAN Review* 21, no. 2 [Winter 1994]: 5–9). These two articles can be found at the following websites:

   scholar.lib.vt.edu/ejournals/ALAN/winter94/Greene.html
   scholar.lib.vt.edu/ejournals/ALAN/winter94/Alvine.html

5. "Drowning in Dichotomy: Interpreting *The Drowning of Stephan Jones*" by Patrick K. Finnessy (*ALAN Review* 25, no. 3 [Spring 1998]) is a resource for teaching this novel.
6. "Honoring Their Stories, Too: Literature for Gay and Lesbian Teens," by Michael Cart (*ALAN Review* 25, no. 1 [Fall 1997]) is a good essay relating to this book.
7. Some other websites with resources for teaching the novel:

   www.ncac.org/issues/bettegreene.html
   www.ncac.org/projects/l_gbooks.html
   scholar.lib.vt.edu/ejournals/ALAN/spring98/finnessy.html
   www.glsen.org/binary-data/GLSEN_ARTICLES/pdf_file/751.pdf
   scholar.lib.vt.edu/ejournals/ALAN/winter96/webunder.html
   www.tamucc.edu/~swolff/ENGL3360/youngadultEJ.pdf
   www.ccsu.edu/library/nadeau/Bibliographies/BannedBooks.htm
   www.glsen.org/binary-data/GLSEN_ARTICLES/pdf_file/67.pdf

Why Give This Book to Teens?

- Because no one deserves to be hated and harassed; we all need to learn this.
- Because they might be in a position like Carla—where they love someone without being able to see his or her worst qualities.
- Because like Carla, they want to see the "deeper, more real qualities, those qualities which the eyes alone could never penetrate" (*Drowning of Stephan Jones*, 203).
- Because we all need to understand more about sexual identity and acceptance of diversity.
- Because they might have been harassed for being different.
- Because using religion for hate is not acceptable.

Hesse, Karen: *Witness*
Published by Scholastic, reprint edition February 2003, ISBN 0439272009

This powerful book is based on actual events related to the Ku Klux Klan in Vermont in the 1920s. We hear the events conveyed through the voices of ten characters, each presenting varying perspectives. Most poignant are the voices of six-year-old Esther Hirsch, whose mother has died, and of Leanora Sutter, age 12, whose mother is also dead. Esther and her father are Jewish and become objects of Klan attacks for "corrupting a Christian woman," Sara Chickering, into taking Jews into her home. Leanora and her father are Black and experience harassment as well from Klan members. Eighteen-year-old Merlin Van Tornhout is caught between the acceptance he feels from the Klan and the desire to be something more. The "religious figure" clergyman, Johnny Reeves, is one of the book's most appalling figures, locked in bigotry and believing in his own righteousness.

Teaching Ideas and Resources

1. This book would be a very effective opening for any unit on discrimination or on the Holocaust. You could use the book in a read-aloud, readers' theater format. Then you could follow with a write-around activity where students respond to the book and its "voices." After writing their own thoughts, they pass their paper to a student on their right; this student comments on the first response, signs his or her name, and passes the paper on. (The same exercise can be done in a computer classroom by having students move from one computer to the next.) You end up with a written dialogue on which to build discussion.
2. The dramatic monologue style of the book is reminiscent of Edgar Lee Master's "Spoon River Anthology." If you are teaching American Literature, use *Witness* in tandem with "Spoon River Anthology."
3. "Consider the Source: Feminism and Point of View in Karen Hesse's *Stowaway* and *Witness*" by Wendy J. Glenn (*ALAN Review*, Winter 2003) offers a perspective for teaching the novel.
4. Web resources for teaching the novel include:

   www.indiana.edu/~reading/ieo/bibs/hesse.html
   www.csulb.edu/org/childrens-lit/proj/nbgs/nbgs-lists/nbgs2002.html
   205.213.162.11/stairs_site/workshop_pages/TeacherLine/childrens_authors/activity1_shared_resources.html#kh
   www.emporia.edu/libsv/nom0304bcurr.htm

Why Give This Book to Teens?

- Because they might have people who judge them by skin color, religion, or other external factors.
- Because teenagers were those most hurt in this real-life incident.
- Because hate crimes continue today and teens can help their peers stop such violent behavior.
- Because it is easy to get caught up in an activity or group when it is supported by a religious group we belong to.

Other books by Karen Hesse to consider reading: *Phoenix Rising*, *Just Juice*, and *The Music of Dolphins*.

Kerr, M. E.: *Night Kites*
Published by Demco Media, September 1987, ISBN 0606035230

The narrator is Erick Rudd, now 17. His family story includes a brother, Pete, ten years older than Erick, who develops AIDS. Erick himself is an average 17-year-old with friends like Jack Case (also 17) who are exploring the world of sexuality and, for a good part of the novel, bemoaning their lack of sexual activity. At the heart of this book are a young man's struggle and his parents' struggle to accept an older brother and son who is "different" and whose difference has brought him into contact with a deadly disease.

Teaching Ideas and Resources

1. Your students may find this book best to respond to anonymously, particularly because the central characters are males and teen males are often more reluctant to share feelings on sexuality, let alone sexual identity. Consider having them write using pseudonyms or assumed names and have them write to Jack, Erick, Pete, or his parents.
2. Teaching resources for the novel include the following:

   Mellon, Constance. "Critical Essay on *Night Kites* by M. E. Kerr." In *Masterplots II: Juvenile and Young Adult Literature Series Supplement*. Pasadena, CA: Salem Press, 1997.

   journals.cec.sped.org/EC/Archive_Articles/VOL.33NO.6JULYAUGUST2001_TEC_P rater.pdf (About Using Juvenile Literature to Teach about HIV/AIDS)

   www.ric.edu/astal/authors/mekerr.html

3. Many of the resources—especially websites—included in the teaching

ideas for *The Drowning of Stephan Jones* are also applicable for teaching this novel, so consider using those.

4. "Honoring Their Stories, Too: Literature for Gay and Lesbian Teens," by Michael Cart (*ALAN Review* 25, no. 1 [Fall 1997]) is a good essay relating to this book.

Why Give This Book to Teens?

- Because they might know of someone who has AIDS.
- Because they might also be in the "dating game" and be wondering how to relate.
- Because this story is told by a 17-year-old male and not many books are presented in the voice of young men.
- Because no one deserves to die alone.
- Because parents are struggling too, and teens don't often realize that their parents have difficulties with sexual identity also.

Latifa: *My Forbidden Face: Growing Up Under the Taliban—A Young Woman's Story*
Published by Miramax, 9 July 2003, ISBN 1401359256

Latifa is a teenager in Kabul, Afghanistan, on September 27, 1996, when the Taliban take control of Kabul. From this day, her family, her city, and her country are never the same. Yes, she lived a childhood that was seldom free of bombing and attacks, but she had never faced the oppression that came with the Taliban controlling Kabul. Her mother, who is a doctor, can no longer practice medicine especially not medicine for women; after the Taliban, women cannot get any medical treatment. Latifa had just passed the first part of the university exams and was hoping for a career in journalism. After the takeover, she cannot attend school and all hopes of a "normal" career are gone. She and many others, especially women, become prisoners in their own homes.

Teaching Ideas and Resources

1. In the introduction to the book, Latifa writes that she hopes this book will be important to other women, "those whose words are locked away, those who have hidden what they have witnessed in their hearts and in their memories." She dedicates the book to all the Afghan girls and women who have kept their dignity to their last breath, to all who

have been deprived of rights in their own countries, and to those who "live in darkness even after the dawn of the twenty-first century." You should use this book to teach—especially to teach the many young people of the United States who have never known such violations of freedom and basic human rights.

2. Latifa's story is a memoir. The book can demonstrate an example of this genre. You could also use it in a nonfiction unit on biography. The following site provides a further list of biographies to pair with *My Forbidden Face*:

   www.fahan.tas.edu.au/libraries/senior/biography.htm

3. Students could do a web quest on Afghanistan, on the Taliban, on the various religious groups in Afghanistan, and on other topics related to the book and do oral presentations on their findings. Afghanistan is frequently in world news or written about in newspapers. Your students could compare Latifa's view of Afghanistan to the 2006 realities.
4. For some web resources on the book, check the following sites:

   www.csmonitor.com/2002/0530/p17s01-bogn.htm
   www.usatoday.com/life/books/2002/2002-03-21-burqa.htm
   www.developmentgateway.org/node/134111/
   rawa.fancymarketing.net/zoya-nd.htm
   hotburrito.100megsfree5.com/books/taliban.html
   www.angelfire.com/ca/miroo/womenbiblio.html
   www.womenforafghanwomen.org/press/womensreview.html

Why Give This Book to Teens?

- Because many in America are afraid of the Taliban and most often we fear what we don't know.
- Because the post-9/11 United States has made us more aware of countries like Afghanistan, but we seldom know stories of the "everyday" citizens there.
- Because we need to understand the oppression and violence that marks our world so we can learn how to end it.
- Because if they feel restricted, they can learn about how much freedom countries like the United States provide for them.
- Because all over the world there are teens like Latifa who live amid war and oppression, and we need to understand more about their world.

Martel, Yann: *Life of Pi*
Published by Harvest Books, 1 May 2003, ISBN 0156027321

Piscine Molitor Patel, nicknamed Pi, is the son of a zookeeper in India. Pi spends his precocious teen years studying zoology, and, over his family's protests, three unique religions. He practices all three! When the economy fails, his family emigrates to Canada on a freighter, taking with them many of the animals, which they've sold to North American collectors. When the ship sinks and all others are lost, a zebra, an orangutan, a hyena, a Bengal Tiger, and Pi share a lifeboat. To survive, Pi must tame the tiger, named Robert Parker. In a series of environmental and psychological adventures, the author creates a coming-of-age survival story.

Teaching Ideas and Resources

1. Some questions to begin your discussion of the novel include the following: How does Pi use the lessons of childhood? What childhood characteristics and beliefs must Pi discard? In what ways do Pi's 227 days in a lifeboat at sea, his escape from the carnivorous seaweed island, and the lessons he learns from his relationship with Robert Parker the tiger—whether real or a creation of his imagination—create the beliefs by which he will live as an adult? Your students could also write about how they might survive if they were in Pi's situation and about the choices they would make.
2. Martel uses intensely descriptive passages to show Pi discovering his "place" in the "universes" of the lifeboat, the sea, and his own sense of self. Direct your students to make lists of what some of these discoveries are.

Master Teacher's Guide

- "They didn't know that I was a practicing Hindu, Christian, and Muslim. Teenagers always hide a few things from their parents, isn't that so? All sixteen-year-olds have secrets, don't they?" How do your students react to this quotation and Pi's practicing of three religions?
- See Jonathan Keifer's "Fascinating 'Life of Pi' gives readers a reason to believe." (*San Francisco Chronicle*, June 23, 2002.) Use this essay for background on the novel.
- Add Pi's scientific thinking to his mix of three religions, and Pi's experiences become an interesting laboratory. How might Pi be an allegory,

an illustration, or even a model for today's teens who must grow up on a very small and complicated planet?

- "Pi comes to realize that survival involves knowing when to assert himself and when to hold back, when to take the upper hand and when to yield to a power greater than himself." What has he learned about the use and the futility of power?
- A review by Gary Krist, "Taming the Tiger: for the hero of this novel, survival depends on knowing when to yield" (*New York Times Book Review*, July 7, 2002, p. 5), is another resource to help you teach the novel.

Why Give This Book to Teens?

- Because the instincts to survive are stronger than they know.
- Because even tough times hold magical and beautiful experiences.
- Because "the tigers" in their lives may help them discover their strengths.
- Because they may be in a search for what to believe and can learn from Pi's searching.

Mickle, Shelley Fraser: *The Turning Hour*
Published by Thomas Rivera Center, 15 January 2004, ISBN 1579660088

It's early December, she's 16 years old, and Bergin has decided to commit suicide. She swallows a bottle of aspirin, but she is found by her 14-year-old stepbrother before she dies and now her question is "how do I get back?" Bergin's story is revealed as she goes through counseling, and as her mother, Leslie, recalls her own mother's alcoholism and her father's strength. Leslie and Doug's divorce and subsequent remarriages all play a role. The novel traces carefully the significance of each person in Bergin's life, but especially the significance of her father and mother, who separated when Bergin was six years old. Like a detective novel, it aims at discovering why Bergin attempted to take her life.

Teaching Ideas and Resources

1. Set up a question and answer box. Have your students write out the questions they want answered by characters in the book, especially by Bergin. Select students who are willing to assume the roles of characters and hold a question/answer session.

2. It is likely that one of your students, or someone your students know, has committed or attempted suicide. As a pre-reading activity, ask your students to write why they think suicide is or is not justified. After reading the novel, have them again write their response and compare the two responses.
3. For background on this book and the author, check the following websites:

   www.shelleymickle.com/biography.htm
   aol.teenreads.com/reviews/0913515221.asp
   www.bookreporter.com/reviews/0913515221.asp
   www.readinggroupsguides.com
   www.sitescraper.co.uk/books/Suicidal%20behavior.html
   www.childadvocacycentergainesville.org/board.htm

Why Give This Book to Teens?

- Because they might be tempted to commit suicide.
- Because they might be suicide survivors, trying to rebuild their lives.
- Because they might be overwhelmed with problems and need to know there are other ways to handle seemingly insurmountable difficulties.
- Because they might have friends, peers, or family members who have committed suicide.
- Because they might be children of parents who have separated or divorced and never have been able to piece all the feelings together.

Napoli, Donna Jo: *Song of the Magdalene*
Published by Point Signature, August 1998, ISBN 0606137890

The narrator of the book is Miriam, who from the age of ten experiences "fits." Miriam's mother has died and her family has a servant, Hannah, who has a crippled son, Abraham. Set in the time of Jesus (known as Joshua in the Jewish tradition and in this book), the town of Magdala is filled with devout Jews who see anyone crippled as a sinner. In addition, anyone who experiences the "fits" Miriam has is considered possessed by a demon. She hides her "fits"—though she never knows exactly when she will experience one—by going alone into the valley. She doesn't go unnoticed; Abraham knows she goes and begs to be taken along. He reveals to her that he is intelligent, even going so far as to teach Miriam to read.

Now Miriam is doing several things that are unacceptable in the patriarchal Jewish world—she is going around the town and into the valley as good women should not, and she is traveling with an outcast—Abraham. In the presence of most of the Jewish community, he does not speak and appears to be mute or an idiot.

The book presents a real picture of the struggles of someone who is different; it gives the story of Mary of Magdala, who the Gospels say "was possessed by seven demons." Miriam/Mary is freed by the "great healer"—Joshua/Jesus—and follows in his company.

Teaching Ideas and Resources

1. Abraham is a mature young man who, because of his physical illness and the suffering he's experienced from being treated as an outcast and an idiot, has wise advice to give Miriam. Discuss with your students his words about his illness and Miriam's fits: "You didn't sin, Miriam. You broke no law of Moses and Israel. You're not sick because you sinned, Miriam. I'm not sick because I sinned. If there's anything I've figured out in my life, it's that invalids aren't any more sinners than anyone else" (*Song of the Magdalene*, 55).
2. Miriam is in the temple one day and hears the Levites chanting. One of the reasons they praise God is that they have not been made women. Discuss the role of women and the reality that in many cultures today women still do not have the rights that are afforded males.
3. "Fairy Tales, Myths, and Religious Stories," by Donna Jo Napoli (*ALAN Review* 25, no. 1 [Fall 1997]), provides insights to this novel.
4. Some teaching ideas can be found in the following website:

   powayusd.sdcoe.k12.ca.us/pusdphs/library/issues_of_faith.htm

Why Give This Book to Teens?

- Because they might want to know more about the lives of women who lived at the time of Jesus.
- Because they might have some kind of physical or emotional handicap that isolates them from others.
- Because they too might want to have a "reason" for some of life's difficulties—like why some people develop cancer or terminal illness.
- Because they might want to learn about a courageous woman.

Other books by Donna Jo Napoli to consider reading: *Spinners*, *Zel*, *Sirena*, *Stones in Water*, and *Daughter of Venice*.

Philbrick, Rodman: *Freak the Mighty*
Published by Scholastic, reprint edition June 2001,
ISBN 0439286069
Teen Recommended

Max, a boy who is large for his age and frequently ridiculed for his physical size and lack of intellectual ability, narrates this book. In addition, Max bears a striking resemblance to his father, a man imprisoned for killing Max's mother. Kevin Avery, alias "Freak," who has a giant mind and a deformed, dwarfish body, befriends Max. The combination is "Freak the Mighty." The sequel, *Max the Mighty*, and an 1998 video, *The Mighty*, further supplement this text displaying a range of differences.

Teaching Ideas and Resources

1. After you have read the novel, it might be a good idea to have a medical person who has knowledge about the kind of disorder that Kevin had come present to the class. As an alternative, finding information about this illness could be a good web quest activity for your students to learn about illnesses that can cause disfigurement.
2. All too often, your students have been ridiculed, or even worse, have ridiculed others who look different or have some disability. This novel is a quick read and can be used with your students to address respect or other aspects of character education.
3. In "John Wayne, Where Are You? Everyday Heroes and Courage" by Pamela S. Carroll (chapter 2 in Gregg and Carroll, *Books and Beyond*, 1998), this novel is one of the YA novels used to supplement the unit.
4. "Listening to Kids in America" by Rodman Philbrick (*ALAN Review* 28, no. 2 [Winter 2001]) gives insights by the author on this novel.
5. "Are These Parents for Real? Students' Views of Parents in Realistic and Historical Fiction" by Janis M. Harmon and Monica C. Gonzalez (*ALAN Review*, Winter 2003) looks at the parent image in *Freak the Mighty*.
6. For author information, background, and teaching ideas, check the following websites:

   www.Authors4Teens.com
   greenwood.scbbs.com/servlet/A4TStart?authorid=rphilbrick&source=
   www.rodmanphilbrick.com/teaching.html

www.moraga.k12.ca.us/JM/Teacher/Forster/Projects/Mighty/indexFreak.html
www.resourceroom.net/Comprehension/literature/ftm_toc.asp
teacher.scholastic.com/writewit/bookrev/tguide.htm
www.cinematheque.bc.ca/pdfs/mighty.pdf

Why Give This Book to Teens?

- Because they might be struggling with body image, feeling embarrassed by who they are.
- Because they might be harassed because of something their parents or family members have done.
- Because everyone should have a friendship like Max and Kevin have.
- Because they might be someone who ridicules others because of appearance and need to realize that appearances aren't everything.

Other books by Rodman Philbrick to consider reading: *Max the Mighty* and *The Last Book in the Universe*.

Reynolds, Marilyn: *Love Rules*
Published by Morning Glory Press, 1 July 2001, ISBN 1885356765

Lynn Wright is 17, beginning her senior year at Hamilton High. Her best friend, in fact, "soul mate friend," Kit Dandridge has something so important to share with Lynn that Kit won't talk about it over the phone—they have to meet at "their tree." Lynn learns that Kit is lesbian and struggles to keep their friendship. Lynn also begins dating an African American and finds herself "on the outside looking in" because she is interracial dating. Conan, her new boyfriend, struggles also to tell his family he is dating a "white girl." Kit, Lynn, and Conan learn a good deal about the hate that their peers can show and about how they can best support diversity in each other.

Teaching Ideas and Resources

1. This book, with the realistic situations at Hamilton High, provides a cast of characters with whom students can relate. Have your students select a character to whom they feel they can best relate. Write a series of diary entries in the voice of that character.
2. Marilyn Reynolds' website has helpful teaching guides for *Love Rules* and other books in her Hamilton High series. Check the following site for these guides:

   www.morningglorypress.com/pages/fictrite.html

3. "Honoring Their Stories, Too: Literature for Gay and Lesbian Teens," by Michael Cart (*ALAN Review* 25, no. 1 [Fall 1997]) is a good essay relating to this book and why you should teach it.
4. In Jeffrey Kaplan's "Research Connection" in the Fall 2003 *ALAN Review*, Barbara Smith shares her research on "Sexual Orientation and Young Adult Literature"—this essay includes other books that address the same topic as *Love Rules*.
5. Resources addressing the topic of gay and lesbian young adults are found at:

   www.glsen.org/templates/resources/record.html?section = 16&
   record = 1523
   teens.denverlibrary.org/find_pages/genre_pages/glbtq.html
   www.framinghamlibrary.org/teen/bglt.htm
   www.usd320.k12.ks.us/whs/lmc/alternative.html
   www.alexsanchez.com/gay_teen_books.htm

Why Give This Book to Teens?

- Because they might have friends whose sexual identity is different from theirs, but who need them to continue being a friend.
- Because they might need to learn more about sexual identity, particularly that it is not just a choice; homosexuality is a biological and psychological reality.
- Because bullying and harassment are unacceptable for any person.
- Because they might be teens who need courage to accept their sexual identity.

Rinaldi, Ann: *Wolf by the Ears*
Published by Scholastic, reissue edition January 1993, ISBN 0590434128

The novel is narrated from the perspective of Harriet Hemings, probable daughter of Thomas Jefferson and Sally Hemings, an African American woman. Harriet, Beverly (a male), Madison, and Eston are the Hemings children still living at Monticello; their brother Thomas has already left—"passing as white" into a different world. Thomas left when Harriet was 10; he apparently bore such resemblance to Jefferson that when anyone came to the plantation, he was sent elsewhere. Harriet's mother has been the keeper of Jefferson's wardrobe and the only one allowed, most times, into the inner sanctum of the Master's rooms. Harriet always feels she must call Jefferson "the Master"—yet that sets a slave relationship, despite that fact that all of the Blacks at Monticello (definitely the Hemings) are given papers saying they are free; these papers are accessible when the Hemings reach age 21.

Harriet speaks of the pain she sees in Jefferson; "I'm watching him. Me. Harriet. I watch the great Thomas Jefferson at the time when he doesn't know it. And I see things others don't see. I can do that with people. Especially with white folk. They don't know how to keep what's in their hearts from showing in their eyes like we do" (*Wolf by the Ears*, 12). Harriet records how others want her to leave when she is 21; she doesn't want to leave; she believes Jefferson doesn't want her to leave either. Thomas Mann Randolph, son-in-law of Jefferson, wants Harriet to "go for freedom."

Eventually Harriet does decide to leave the plantation. As Harriet is preparing to leave, and she has now shared this with Jefferson, who seems saddened, yet tolerant, Harriet finds out that Beverly is leaving—he won't tell Jefferson before he goes. Also only after their farewell meeting does Harriet learn from her mother that Beverly was also "passing." The end chapter—a final scene with Jefferson—is very powerful.

Teaching Ideas and Resources

1. American history gives us one perspective on Thomas Jefferson; how do this book and other recent knowledge about Jefferson most likely fathering children with slaves affect your perspective on this man? Have your students answer this question and relate it to the larger issue of what is expected of someone in a position like the president of the United States.
2. The book's title is based on the following quote by Jefferson:

   > "Gradually, with due sacrifices, a general emancipation and expatriation could be effected. But, as it is, we have the wolf by the ears, and we can neither hold him, nor safely let him go. Justice is in one scale, and self-preservation the other."

   Discuss the quote with your students and how it fits with the issue of slavery or other political issues.
3. The key to this work is the alienation of non-recognition. This novel is a great one to "pair with a classic," specifically *Absalom, Absalom*. You could have your students read Rinaldi's book on their own while you are reading *Absalom, Absalom* in class, since it is a much more difficult novel.

4. Teri Lesesne, in "Exploring the Horror Within: Themes of the Duality of Humanity in Mary Shelley's *Frankenstein* and Ten Related Young Adult Novels" (chapter 10 in Kaywell, *Adolescent Literature as a Complement to the Classics*, vol. 2, 1995) uses *Wolf by the Ears* as one of the YA novels in this unit.
5. "Making Valid Connections: Historical Fiction Set in Virginia" by Cheryl Christian (in "Adolescent Literature: Making Connections with Teens," special issue, *Virginia English Bulletin* 44, no. 2 [Fall 1994]) focuses primarily on *Wolf by the Ears*.
6. Some web resources for teaching this book can be found at:

   www.scils.rutgers.edu/~kvander/rinaldi65.html
   education.boisestate.edu/bdavies/wolf_by_the_ears.htm
   www.scils.rutgers.edu/~kvander/rinaldi.html
   www.springfieldlibrary.org/reading/womenYA.html
   www.hpl.lib.tx.us/gala/bhm03/readings_ya.html
   falcon.jmu.edu/~ramseyil/rinaldi.htm

Why Give This Book to Teens?

- Because identity and recognition of who you are is one of the most important things in life.
- Because often we have glorified images of historical figures, such as presidents, and we need to know these people are also human and imperfect.
- Because they may be people of color who have experienced racism.
- Because they may need to know more about the lives of African Americans and about the ways African Americans and others have been persecuted.

Other books by Ann Rinaldi to consider reading: *A Break with Charity*, *The Last Silk Dress*, and *Broken Days*.

Ryan, Pam Muñoz: *Esperanza Rising*
Published by Scholastic, reprint edition 1 June 2002, ISBN 043912042X

Esperanza is anticipating her thirteenth birthday; she's used to living a life as the landowner's daughter, not as a day laborer or migrant worker. Her father has always been sympathetic to the workers, but not everyone knows that nor respects that. Just before her birthday, her father is killed by bandits and Esperanza's life is changed forever. Eventually she and her family escape to California, and Esperanza truly needs to live on hope, as her name implies.

Teaching Ideas and Resources

1. The book contains a number of proverbs or wise sayings. Ask your students to select one of these to explain and apply to a situation in their life:

   "You can only feel the earth's heartbeat when you are still and quiet." (*Esperanza Rising*, 2)

   "Wait a little while and the fruit will fall into your hand." (*Esperanza Rising*, 2)

   "There is no rose without a thorn." (*Esperanza Rising*, 14)

   "He who falls today may rise tomorrow." (*Esperanza Rising*, introduction)

   "The rich person is richer when he becomes poor, than the poor person when he becomes rich." (*Esperanza Rising*, introduction)

   "In Mexico we stand on different sides of the river." (Miguel, a worker's son, to Esperanza, *Esperanza Rising*, 37)

   "The rich take care of the rich and the poor take care of those who have less than they have." (*Esperanza Rising*, 79)

2. "The Migrant Experience in the Works of Mexican American Writers" (*ALAN Review*, Fall 2002) has insights on this and other novels related to migrant workers.
3. Resources on the author and the novel can be found at the following:

   www.pammunozryan.com/books.html
   www.bluffton.edu/lionlamb/biblio/conflict
   www.simsbury.lib.ct.us/ya2001.htm

Why Give This Book to Teens?

- Because they might know what it means to have money and enough to live on, but not how to survive if they lost all they had.
- Because like Esperanza, they might be used to having people wait on them, but they might need to learn to take care of themselves.

- Because Esperanza's story is reflective of many of the immigrant people coming to the United States—they need to understand the situation of those people, especially of those young people who may be their classmates.

Salinger, J. D.: *The Catcher in the Rye*
Published by Little Brown & Company, reissue edition 1 May 1991, ISBN 0316769487
Teen Recommended

Holden Caulfield is about to be expelled from Pencey Prep. He cannot relate to or confide in anyone except his little sister Phoebe, so he skips out four days early for Christmas break and heads for New York City. Labeling nearly everything he encounters as phony—his favorite word, Holden rarely lets others see his real self. Disgusted with the uselessness of the adult world, he goes back to his parents' apartment to talk to his sister Phoebe about his dream to become a "catcher in the rye." He visits his history teacher, Mr. Antolini, who makes sexual overtures; Holden panics and runs back to Phoebe.

Teaching Ideas and Resources

1. Holden Caulfield is the master of cynical "cool" that disguises deep caring about lots of things. Ask your students to make a list of things they view cynically and note those about which they also care or worry.
2. View the film *Finding Forrester*. Have your class list the parallels and differences between William Forrester and Salinger. Then have them make comparisons between Holden Caulfield, the New York teen of the 1940s, and Jamal Warner as the model of today's New Yorker.
3. "Catcher as Core and Catalyst" by Ted Hipple (chapter 4 in Kaywell, *Adolescent Literature as a Complement to the Classics*, vol. 1, 1993) presents numerous teaching ideas.
4. The following site lists novels that can be compared with *The Catcher in the Rye*:

   www.yabookscentral.com/cfusion/index.cfm?fuseAction=guides.guide&guide_id;eq31&book_id=127

5. The following websites are helpful for teaching Salinger and *The Catcher in the Rye*:

www.webenglishteacher.com/salinger.html
www.cwrl.utexas.edu/%7Eailise/teaching/lesson/catcher/index.html
www.teachnet-lab.org/MBHS/scragg/catcher/Catchernovel.html
www.umsl.edu/~gryan/amer.studies/amst.catcherwegquest.html
www.educeth.ch/english/readinglist/salingerjd/seclit.html

Master Teacher's Guide

- For the alienated and cynical Holden, there is no spiritual salvation. Instead, Holden dreams of *himself* as the savior figure, "the catcher in the rye." Ask students: Do any of your vocational dreams contain similar "save the world" elements? How do they differ from or compare to Holden's?
- "Holden Caulfield's Legacy" by David Castronovo (*New England Review*, Spring 2001) provides background on the novel.
- Coles, Robert. *Secular Days, Sacred Moments* (*America* 181, no. 3 [July 31, 1999]: 8) gives insights on the novel.
- *Contemporary Authors Online* provides author background. See www.gale.com.
- "Holden Caulfield, Alex Portnoy, and *Good Will Hunting*: Coming of age in American films and novels" by Lawrence E. Ziewacz (*Journal of Popular Culture* 35, no.1 [June 2001]: 211–218) gives insights for pairing *Catcher* with more contemporary works.

Why Give This Book to Teens?

- Because they might feel that no one understands them or their world.
- Because they might be struggling with what the future holds for them—and whether it has any meaning at all.
- Because Holden has been the classic teenager for half a century.
- Because they're smarter, kinder, and more honest than Holden.
- Because Holden is still funny, modern, and cool.

Staples, Suzanne Fisher: *Shabanu*
Published by Laurel Leaf, 12 August 2003, ISBN 0440238560
Teen Recommended

Shabanu, a young Pakistani girl, and her family are desert people who follow a water supply throughout the year. Her family has no sons and Shabanu is allowed some freedoms many Muslim girls are not. According to Muslim tradition, Shabanu and her older sister Phulan are betrothed to their male first cousins. Shabanu accepts the betrothal even though it will end her freedom. When a tragic encounter with a wealthy landowner ruins the marriage plans of Phulan, Shabanu is called upon to sacrifice the life she has dreamed of with her future husband. She must choose between upholding family honor or following her own inner voice.

Teaching Ideas and Resources

1. "I AM: Coming to Know Thyself through Literature" (chapter 1 in Gregg and Carroll, *Books and Beyond*, 1998) presents an extensive unit for teaching *Shabanu*. It gives pre-reading, during-reading, and after-reading activities as well as pairing the novel with *Antigone*.
2. Bonnie O. Ericson, in "Heroes and Journeys in *The Odyssey* and Several Works in Young Adult Literature" (chapter 1 in Kaywell, *Adolescent Literature as a Complement to the Classics*, vol. 2, 1995) describes how to teach *Shabanu* and several other YA novels along with *The Odyssey*.
3. Lois Stover and Connie Zitlow, in "Using Young Adult Literature as a Companion to World Literature: A Model Thematic Unit on the 'Clash of Cultures' Centered on *Things Fall Apart*" (chapter 5 in Kaywell, *Adolescent Literature as a Complement to the Classics*, vol. 2, 1995), use *Shabanu* to discuss clashes of generations in *Things Fall Apart*.
4. Teaching activities for the novel can also be found at:

   atozteacherstuff.com/stuff/literature4.shtml
   www.indiana.edu/~reading/ieo/bibs/staples.html
   www.glencoe.com/sec/literature/litlibrary/pdf/shabanu.pdf

5. "What about Our Girls? Considering Gender Roles with *Shabanu*" by Colleen A. Ruggieri (*English Journal*, January 2001) provides some excellent approaches to the novel.

Why Give This Book to Teens?

- Because it is particularly important in "post 9/11" United States culture to understand more about Muslims.
- Because Shabanu has to make difficult decisions regarding her family and her future happiness.
- Because this novel shows the challenges in growing from adolescence to adulthood.

Taylor, Mildred: *Roll of Thunder, Hear My Cry*
Published by Scholastic, 1991, ISBN 0590982079
Teen Recommended

The book, as do all of Taylor's writings, presents the experience of Black Americans in Mississippi in the 1930s and the period preceding the Civil Rights Movement. Cassie, Taylor's protagonist, is female, Black, and part of a land-owning family in an area of White sharecroppers, who are themselves besieged by the Depression but further blinded by racist reactions. Taylor's novel is easily paired with *To Kill a Mockingbird.*

Teaching Ideas and Resources

1. Many English programs require *To Kill a Mockingbird* as one of the novels in American Literature or in ninth-grade novel units. Harper Lee's book presents situations of racism from the perspective of narrators who are White; Mildred Taylor's protagonists are Black. Read the two novels simultaneously—perhaps have half of your students read *To Kill a Mockingbird* and the other half read *Roll of Thunder, Hear My Cry*—and do a comparison of the texts. For a graphic organizer, a Venn diagram would work well in seeing the parallels between the novels.
2. *Roll of Thunder, Hear My Cry* is the first book in a trilogy. The other two novels are *Let the Circle Be Unbroken* and *The Road to Memphis.* Suggest that your students read the trilogy, which is an easy and gripping read, particularly as part of a unit of study on slave narratives or the Black experience in America.
3. Here are more suggestions for pairing these novels with "classical" American literature units: Consider pairing *Let the Circle Be Unbroken* or *Roll of Thunder, Hear My Cry* by Mildred Taylor, *To Kill a Mockingbird* by Harper Lee, or *Native Son* or *Black Boy* by Richard Wright with nonfiction about racism and civil rights or with *The Autobiography of Miss Jane Pittman.* Also consider pairing Mildred Taylor's novels with *The Grapes of Wrath* by John Steinbeck or other literature of the Great Depression. Two other books that could be paired with those listed above are *Nightjohn* and *Sarny* by Gary Paulsen.
4. "'Do they TRUST Me?': White Teachers, African American Students, and an African American Young Adult Novel," by Pamela S. Carroll (in "Adolescent Literature: Making Connections with Teens," special issue, *Virginia English Bulletin* 44, no. 2 [Fall 1994]) focuses specifically on this novel.

5. In "John Wayne, Where Are You? Everyday Heroes and Courage" by Pamela S. Carroll (chapter 2 in Gregg and Carroll, *Books and Beyond*, 1998), this novel is used as one of the YA novels to supplement the unit.
6. "Anne Frank's *The Diary of a Young Girl*: World War II and Young Adult Literature" by Joan Kaywell (chapter 2 in Kaywell, *Adolescent Literature as a Complement to the Classics*, vol. 1, 1993) uses this novel to show the impact of World War II on families.
7. "*Their Eyes Were Watching God* and *Roll of Thunder, Hear My Cry*: Voices of African American Southern Women," by Pamela S. Carroll (chapter 10 in Kaywell, *Adolescent Literature as a Complement to the Classics*, vol. 1, 1993) presents a unit for using this novel.
8. An essay on Mildred Taylor in *Contemporary Southern Writers*, 1999, provides background on Taylor's many excellent books.
9. The following websites provide more information on Mildred Taylor and her books:

   falcon.jmu.edu/~ramseyil/taylor.htm
   www.indiana.edu/~reading/ieo/bibs/taylor.html
   www.penguinputnam.com/static/packages/us/yreaders/educate/guides/taylor/content.htm
   websites.ntl.com/~nchs/NCHS_PROSE.html
   www.planetbookclub.com/teachers/civil.html
   www.penguinputnam.com/static/packages/us/yreaders-new/tl-guide-landmildredtaylor.html

Why Give This Book to Teens?

- Because they may be people of color who have experienced racism.
- Because they may need to know more about the lives of African Americans and the ways these people have been persecuted.
- Because Cassie can be a good role model for other African Americans.

Other books by Mildred Taylor to consider reading: *Let the Circle Be Unbroken*, *The Road to Memphis*, and *The Gold Cadillac*.

CHAPTER SEVEN

Books about Courage and Survival

Bagdasarian, Adam: *Forgotten Fire*
Published by Laurel Leaf, reprint edition 9 April 2002, ISBN 0440229170

In 1915, Vahan Kenderian is 12 and the youngest son in a wealthy Armenian family. Historic Armenia was at the crossroads between Europe and Asia. Repeatedly the Armenians were controlled by invaders—Greek, Persian, Roman, and Mongolian. By 1900, one-ninth of the Ottoman Empire's population was Armenian; in the eyes of the Turks who ruled the Empire, the Armenians were a threat to the government's security. Vahan narrates the terrible suffering that came upon his family, his village, and his culture. His story is based on the true story of an Armenian child in 1915.

Teaching Ideas and Resources

1. The epigraph to the book reads, "Who does now remember the Armenians?" This is a quote from Adolf Hitler in 1939, before he launched into so many parts of Europe and annihilated peoples. He made the statement in support of his argument that the world would soon forget the extermination of a people. Use the quote to find out if any of your students have heard of Armenians and the genocide of these people in 1915.
2. Discuss with students their knowledge (or lack of knowledge) about any current situation similar to the destruction of the Armenians; have students locate news articles on similar situations and share their findings with the class.
3. The Dell Laurel-Leaf Books paperback edition has an interview with

the author at the end of the book, providing insights into the novel and why he wrote the book. If you can get a copy of this edition, use these resources to teach the book.

4. Use the following websites for further background on the book:

   www.education-world.com/a_curr/curr401.shtml
   www.ala.org/Content/ContentGroups/ALSC1/ALSConnect1/March_2003.htm
   www.cms.edu.do/Teachers%20Folders/willian%20farren/Pages/pdfs/comp/readlists/t c_2001.pdf

Why Give This Book to Teens?

- Because Vahan Kenderian represents another group of people who have been tortured and annihilated.
- Because Vahan's story of courage is a powerful one.
- Because we all need to learn how to live in peace and acceptance with others of different races, religions, and cultures.
- Because someone like Hitler arose years after the Armenians were destroyed and he counted on humans being forgetful and unaware.

Crew, Linda: *Children of the River*
Published by Laurel Leaf, reissue edition 1 August 1991, ISBN 0440210224

Cambodian refugees are the central characters; the narrator at the beginning of the novel is Sundara, age13. She is living with her aunt Soka (her mother's sister) and Soka's husband, Naro. Soka has just given birth. Ravy is 6; his little brother Pon is about 3. Chamroeun is the boyfriend Sundara left back in the city (Phnom Penh) when she came to be with her aunt's family. The family is warned that the Khmer Rouge (Communists) are coming. Soka does not want to leave, having just given birth and having been unable to complete the rituals accompanying birth.

The grandmother also sees no reason to leave, but Naro, upon returning for work, forces everyone to go. They get on board ship; then everyone gets sick. Soka can't provide milk for the baby. Sundara is caring for it, but eventually the baby dies and Sundara is forced to throw the baby into the water.

Later, the family is settled in Oregon. When Sundara is in school, she writes a poem about her experiences but is embarrassed as her teacher reads it aloud. Sundara's writing is so much more serious and full of big issues than that of her classmates—most of whom are White.

Jonathan McKinnon, son of a doctor who helped Sundara's family when they first arrived, is a star football player. He becomes intrigued with Sundara and her life. Much of the book is about her trying to explain the difference in customs between her world and his.

Teaching Ideas and Resources

1. Very often the "average" American teenager—many of the students in our classes—do not know what it means to have to leave behind family, friends, the homeland . . . everything. Have students make a list of the things and people they'd find most difficult to leave and explain why they have listed what they have.
2. Have students write about the best aspects of our culture that they want to share with immigrants—they might focus on why they are happy to be living in the United States. Have them also write about what is weak or faulty in American culture. After they've written about the pros and cons, have a class discussion on the topic.
3. Students could do a web quest related to Ellis Island and the conditions of immigration during some of the major immigration periods in the late nineteenth and early twentieth centuries. They might like to focus specifically on the cultures from which they and their families have come.
4. "America: Mother of Exiles" by Gail Gregg, Melinda Miller, and Nan Vollgracht (in Gregg and Carroll, *Books and Beyond*, 1998) uses this novel as one of the YA novels depicting immigrant life in America.
5. Bonnie O. Ericson, in "Heroes and Journeys in *The Odyssey* and Several Works in Young Adult Literature" (chapter 1 in Kaywell, *Adolescent Literature as a Complement to the Classics*, vol. 2, 1995), describes how to teach *Children of the River* in conjunction with *The Odyssey*.
6. "*The Awakening* and Young Adult Literature: Seeking Self-Identity in Many Ways and in Many Cultures" by Pamela Sissi Carroll (chapter 4 in Kaywell, *Adolescent Literature as a Complement to the Classics*, vol. 2, 1995) uses *Children of the River* as one novel to complement *The Awakening*.
7. Lois Stover and Connie Zitlow, in "Using Young Adult Literature as a Companion to World Literature: A Model Thematic Unit on the 'Clash of Cultures' Centered on *Things Fall Apart*" (chapter 5 in

Kaywell, *Adolescent Literature as a Complement to the Classics*, vol. 2, 1995), use *Children of the River* as one of the novels in this unit.

8. Resources for teaching the novel can be found at:

   www.webenglishteacher.com/lcrew.html
   www.randomhouse.com/teachers/authors/crew.html
   www.classroom.com/edsoasis/TGuild/Lessons/Cambodia.html

Why Give This Book to Teens?

- Because many students in their schools may come from different cultures and they can learn about these immigrant students' lives.
- Because sometimes Americans have limited perspectives about immigrants and think they are coming to the United States to take our jobs.
- Because many immigrants who are teens have to struggle to hold on to their family's values and culture while trying to fit into U.S. teenagers' culture.

Elliot, Laura: *Under a War-Torn Sky*
Published by Hyperion Books for Children, 2001, ISBN 0786817534

Henry Forrester is only 19 years old, but he wants to become a pilot in World War II. He is on his fifteenth bombing mission, but every airman in his company of the Eighth Air Force bombing crew had come to realize that 15 missions were the "average life span" for pilots. Few made it to 25 missions and were able to go home alive.

Henry's plane is shot down, and he knows most of his crew has died. He survives the parachute landing, but he is injured and alone in enemy territory. Henry's story is a powerful survival story—he overcomes not only the physical injury, but also the psychological pain he has from his relationship with his father that has haunted him from childhood.

Teaching Ideas and Resources

1. Early in the novel, Henry is reflecting on a poem, "High Flight," written by a 19-year-old American pilot flying with the Royal Air Force, just before his death. Give students a copy of the poem and have them compare the ethereal images in the poem to the reality that Henry and other pilots experienced. "High Flight" could also be compared to poetry by Sigfried Sassoon, Wilfred Owen, and other poets of war.
2. The novel presents a number of topics related to World War II—the

French Resistance Movement; the Royal Air Force; the B-24, B-17, and other aircraft; the life of pilots and bombing crews; the Luftwaffe and German air force—students could do a web quest on any of these topics.

3. This novel would make an excellent, easier-to-read companion novel to *All Quiet on the Western Front.*
4. Another book by Laura Elliot for younger readers is described at the following site:

   www.harpercollins.com/hc/aboutus/subrights/Fiction%20Notebook%20-%20Spring%20Summer%202003.pdf

5. Other websites related to World War I and World War II include:

   www.websterschools.org/classrooms/willinklib/world_war_i_and_world_war_ii_fic.htm
   www.scrantonlibrary.com/teen/guybooks.htm

Why Give This Book to Teens?

- Because they might have family members or friends who have been in war, and by reading this book, they can learn more about what these people have experienced.
- Because they might be worried about having to fight in war.
- Because they might need to learn that those we fight in war are also humans.

Gordon, Sheila: *Waiting for the Rain*
Published by Laurel Leaf, reprint edition 6 October 1996, ISBN 0440226988

The main characters are Frikki, an Afrikaner/Dutch boy who comes frequently to his uncle's (Oom Koo) farm, and Tengo, a Black South African boy. Though the boys become friends, their worlds are indeed separate. Tengo's mom works in the house of the Koo family; his father works as a hired hand. Tengo and other natives are referred to by the term "kaffir." Tengo is a voracious learner; he eventually gets to go to Johannesburg and study; it is the time soon after the massacres in Soweto and other places. Joseph, Tengo's cousin, is an active member of resistance groups such as the ANC (African National Congress). The novel traces the two boys' stories up through young adulthood; ultimately they end up with Tengo unknowingly beating Frikki (now a soldier in the Afrikaner military—doing his two years of mandatory service) over the head to prevent Frikki from killing him (Tengo). Neither knows the other right away—when they do recognize each other, Tengo is holding Frikki's gun and has the power most Blacks in South Africa never know.

Teaching Ideas and Resources

1. This is a great novel to pair with *Cry the Beloved Country*. This book can also be used for teaching about apartheid. *Waiting for the Rain* is also another one of the novels that builds on the friendship of two young males, so it could make a good pairing with *The Chosen* by Chaim Potok.
2. Have students do a web quest on apartheid, South Africa, and the reasons for the violence in that country; they could also look for newspaper articles or news reports on other nations struggling with racial discord.
3. Lois Stover and Connie Zitlow, in "Using Young Adult Literature as a Companion to World Literature: A Model Thematic Unit on the 'Clash of Cultures' Centered on *Things Fall Apart*" (chapter 5 in Kaywell, *Adolescent Literature as a Complement to the Classics*, vol. 2, 1995), use *Waiting for the Rain* as a YA novel addressing clashes of culture.
4. Teacher resources on African countries are located at:

   www.ohiou.edu/internationalstudies/ovic/Africa1.htm

Why Give This Book to Teens?

- Because the friendship these two boys experience proves that we *learn* hate and discrimination.
- Because we need to know that humans are not always kind to others.
- Because we need to learn ways to end hatred and prejudice.

Hesse, Karen: *Out of the Dust*
Published by Scholastic, 1997, ISBN 0590371258

Billie Jo is 13 as the book opens; in a loosely poetic and extremely powerful text, she tells of her life in Oklahoma during 1934–1935 in the days of the dust bowl. Her family—mother, father, and the child her mother is carrying in her womb—are all managing in the dust and depression, until the day of a tragic accident, when Billie Jo's hands are severely burned; her mother is also burned and the unborn child dies. Billie Jo then no longer wants to do much of what she had done in the past, including playing the piano.

Teaching Ideas and Resources

1. Students can learn a good deal from older family members or relatives about specific periods in U.S. history. This book provides the springboard for them to learn about and explore the era of the Great Depression. A community interview activity would work well.
2. This book would be a good companion to *The Grapes of Wrath*, *Of Mice and Men*, or other literature connected to the Depression Era. Hesse's book, as the easier read, would be good for reading outside of class.
3. "What's Good about the Best?" by Ted Hipple and Amy B. Maupin (*English Journal*, January 2001) discusses why *Out of the Dust* is such a highly rated young adult novel and provides a rationale for teaching this book.
4. There are excellent teaching resources for this book at the following websites:

   www.knowledge.state.va.us/cgi-bin/lesview.cgi?idl=297
   www.indiana.edu/~reading/ieo/bibs/hesse.html
   205.213.162.11/stairs_site/workshop_pages/TeacherLine/
   childrens_authors/ activity1_shared_resources.html#kh
   www.fsu.edu/%7ECandI/ENGLISH/power/dust.htm

5. "The Motherless Daughter: An Evolving Archetype of Adolescent Literature" by James Lovelace and Laura Howell Smith (*ALAN Review*, Winter 2002) looks at *Out of the Dust* and the motherless daughter.
6. An essay by Jackie Swensson on *Out of the Dust* is available in *Rationales for Teaching Young Adult Literature*, edited by Louann Reid and Jamie Hayes Neufeld (Portsmouth, NH: Heinemann, 1999).

Why Give This Book to Teens?

- Because they need to know about some of the difficult times in American history, and this book presents a good understanding of the years of drought during the Great Depression.
- Because, like Billie Jo, they might have to live through hard days.
- Because Billie Jo has to overcome great grief and sadness and her story is inspiring.

Hesse, Karen: *Letters from Rifka*
Published by Puffin Books, 1993, ISBN 0140363912

Rifka is 12 as this work opens; the time is 1919–1920. The book is a series of letters written by Rifka to her cousin Tovah. Rifka and her family are trying to flee Russia; three of Rifka's older brothers have already escaped conscription into the Russian army and gone to America. Now, Rifka, her parents, and her other brothers, Nathan and Saul, are fleeing.

At the Polish border, they are stripped and searched; only then can they board the train for Warsaw. Rifka contracts typhus; then the rest of the family, except for Saul, gets it as well. After they are all better and are en route, Rifka sees a Polish peasant girl with a baby. Rifka tells the young woman she (Rifka) will help style her hair. While doing so, Rifka catches ringworm from the peasant girl. Thus when the rest of the family is "cleared" for passage to America, Rifka must stay behind and be treated for the ringworm. People from the Hebrew Immigrant Aid Society (HIAS) help Rifka get settled in Antwerp. A Catholic sister helps with the treatments for Rifka; in the process, she loses all her hair. To make matters worse, the rest of her family is now in America and Rifka is constantly homesick.

Rifka is writing in a book of Pushkin's poetry; eventually she also writes some poetry, which she doesn't feel is very good. On the ship over, she grows to love Pieter—tragically, he is drowned in a terrible storm at sea. Rifka experiences loss after loss as she befriends those in need. She is detained on Ellis Island since she has no hair, and the officials fear she'll become a "social responsibility"—unable to get a husband.

Rifka is a powerful young heroine based on a real person, Karen Hesse's great-aunt Lucy.

Teaching Ideas and Resources

1. This book uses the genre of letters. Have your students look for letters from family members or use websites to locate letters from earlier historical periods, then compare these letters with Rifka's. They can write letters to Rifka or to those whose letters they locate.
2. Throughout the book, Hesse includes excerpts from Pushkin's poetry. These excerpts provide a good way to study this poet and the tradition of Russian poetry of which Pushkin was a part.
3. This novel came after the publication of "Anne Frank's *The Diary of a Young Girl*: World War II and Young Adult Literature" by Joan Kaywell (chapter 2 in Kaywell, *Adolescent Literature as a Complement to the Classics*, vol. 1, 1993), but it would work well in the unit.

Why Give This Book to Teens?

- Because they will read a story of tremendous courage.
- Because Rifka faces separation from her family and other connections and has to rely on her own strength.
- Because we need to learn from the past about the terrible ways people have treated others and how to change our world for the better.
- Because Rifka's family wanted to immigrate to the United States, as so many people today do—this book gives insights into the struggles immigrants face.

Houston, Jeanne Wakatsuki, and James D. Houston: *Farewell to Manzanar* Published by Bantam Books, reissue edition 1 March 1983, ISBN 0553272586

Jeanne is telling the story of her family and other Japanese people who experienced the internment camp at Manzanar. The book reveals much of the subtle racism against the Japanese, particularly once the camps were closed. Jeanne, who is about seven in 1942 when Pearl Harbor is bombed, tries to come to understand the major impact of the experience on her family, her culture, and her world, especially the deep fears of the "other." It is well presented from the female voice of a young girl who has to keep struggling with the mix of cultures; though her heritage is Japanese, she is American-born and caught up in what it takes to be American.

Teaching Ideas and Resources

1. If possible, have a survivor of the Japanese internment come and talk to your class or have students try writing to those who have been survivors.
2. *Legends from the Camp*, a book of poetry by Lawson Fusao Inada, presents in poetry form many of the experiences of the Japanese Americans. Locate this book and share some readings with the class. You might also have students respond to a prompt about what they would have taken with them if they were forced from their homes into the camps as the Japanese Americans were. Students should be prepared to explain why they would take what they've listed.
3. This novel is good to pair with *Summer of My German Soldier*. Websites that are particularly helpful with the historical context of these two novels are:

www.cfep.uci.edu/ProDevel/uci-sati/faculty/rodebaugh_unit.html
www.intranet.csupomona.edu/%7Etassi/manzanar.htm
www.smith.edu/fcceas/curriculum/mayewil.htm

4. Pair this novel with *Snow Falling on Cedars*—you might also consider using the film version of *Snow Falling on Cedars* and then having your students write about their impressions after seeing this visual portrayal.
5. "Anne Frank's *The Diary of a Young Girl*: World War II and Young Adult Literature" by Joan Kaywell (chapter 2 in Kaywell, *Adolescent Literature as a Complement to the Classics*, vol. 1, 1993) uses this novel in the portion that deals with the Japanese.
6. "Reconciling Memories of Internment Camp Experiences During WWII in Children's and Young Adult Literature" by Jacqueline N. Glasgow (*ALAN Review*, Fall 2002) has good ideas for this novel and others on the same topic.
7. Lois Stover and Connie Zitlow, in "Using Young Adult Literature as a Companion to World Literature: A Model Thematic Unit on the 'Clash of Cultures' Centered on *Things Fall Apart*" (chapter 5 in Kaywell, *Adolescent Literature as a Complement to the Classics*, vol. 2, 1995), use *Farewell to Manzanar* to compare to the clash of generations in *Things Fall Apart*.
8. "Japanese and Japanese American Youth in Literature," by Connie S. Zitlow and Lois Stover (*ALAN Review* 25, no. 3 [Spring 1998]) offers good insights to help teach this novel.

Why Give This Book to Teens?

- Because they need to know that Americans have not always been tolerant of other Americans.
- Because they need to know about this sad "chapter" of American history.
- Because since September 11, 2001, Americans have become more suspicious of immigrant peoples and this book can help them understand the suffering that Japanese Americans experienced simply because of fears of other Americans.

Lowry, Lois: *Number the Stars*
Published by Laurel Leaf, 9 February 1998, ISBN 0440227534

Annemarie Johansen is 10 years old and the story is told from her viewpoint. She and her family live in Copenhagen; Kristi is her younger sister. Lise, their 18-year-old sister, was killed in an accident two weeks before her wedding, and Peter Nielsen, her fiancé, is active in the resistance movement. During the three-year occupation, electricity and food have been rationed; no one has enough to eat and there is a nightly curfew after 8:00 P.M. No leather is available so shoes are made of fish skin (fish scales). Eventually the Nazis close all businesses that are owned or run by Jews. Using a reference made early on about the King of Denmark, "All of Denmark is his bodyguard," Annemarie says all of Denmark must be bodyguards for the Jews.

Annemarie's friend Ellen Rosen is from a Jewish family. One day the Rosen family comes and leaves Ellen with the Johansens; the Rosens are led into hiding by Peter. The Nazis come to the Johansen home; they question why Annemarie is blond and this "other daughter"—that's what they've been told about Ellen Rosen—is dark. Fortunately the Johansens have pictures of Lise when she was little—Lise was dark, so they claim Ellen is Lise, and the Nazis go away. Ellen and her parents are eventually helped to escape to a boat that Henrik is running which will take them to safety in Sweden.

Teaching Ideas and Resources

1. The title of the book comes from a line from Psalm 147: "he who numbers the stars one by one." This reference can lead to a discussion of how the title of the book fits the story. It can also lead to a connection of biblical parallels.
2. "Anne Frank's *The Diary of a Young Girl*: World War II and Young Adult Literature" by Joan Kaywell (chapter 2 in Kaywell, *Adolescent Literature as a Complement to the Classics*, vol. 1, 1993) uses this novel to discuss those who risked their lives to save the Jews.
3. Lois Stover and Connie Zitlow, in "Using Young Adult Literature as a Companion to World Literature: A Model Thematic Unit on the 'Clash of Cultures' Centered on *Things Fall Apart*" (chapter 5 in Kaywell, *Adolescent Literature as a Complement to the Classics*, vol. 2, 1995), use *Number the Stars* as a complement to *Things Fall Apart.*
4. A website that pairs this novel with *Farewell to Manzanar* is:

   www.cfep.uci.edu/ProDevel/uci-sati/faculty/rodebaugh_unit.html

5. The following website provides helpful resources on Lois Lowry:

   www.indiana.edu/~reading/ieo/bibs/lowry.html

Why Give This Book to Teens?

- Because they might learn about how they can be helpful to those who experience hatred or prejudice.

- Because they can learn stories of great courage.
- Because they may sometime have to decide whether they will help another in need even if it means risk to them.

Nolan, Han: *If I Should Die Before I Wake*
Published by Harcourt Paperbacks, 1 May 2003, ISBN 0152046798

Hilary is a member of a neo-Nazi group; she is also dealing with abandonment issues since the death of her father when Hilary was only five. Hilary's mother, unable to handle grief, had left Hilary alone for three days. Now in adolescence, Hilary finds a sense of belonging with the Aryan Warriors. After one of the group's latest attacks on a young Jewish boy named Simon, Hilary is in a motorcycle accident while riding with Brad, a leader in the Aryan Warriors. Hilary is critically injured and in a Jewish Hospital. Through time travel, Hilary "becomes" Chana, a Polish Jew who sees her family and the families of hundreds of other Jews destroyed by the Nazis. Chana ultimately ends up in Auschwitz.

Teaching Ideas and Resources

1. The first Harcourt paperback edition of the book, 1996, contains an interview with Han Nolan. This interview can be a good starting point for class discussion, since Ms. Nolan discusses why she used the time travel concept.
2. *If I Should Die Before I Wake* presents a new "take" on the Shoah (Holocaust), opening with a hate-filled monologue from Hilary and her neo-Nazi indoctrination. You could use the opening with students to address the topic of hate crimes/hate groups.
3. This novel could be paired with *The Diary of a Young Girl*, *The Devil's Arithmetic*, or *Night*, again coming from the late twentieth-century perspective of revisionism and the revival of Nazism.
4. "Bubbe," Chana's grandmother, is a woman of tremendous courage and wisdom. Use any of the passages from the book that include her advice and have students write about a wisdom figure in their lives. One possible passage is the following:

> "Hardship and suffering should not lessen our love for God. Everything we do, even here, [in Auschwitz] should remain as it has always been, a means of communion with God. Remember, there is nothing, nothing here on this earth that is apart from *Shekhinah*, God's presence." (*If I Should Die Before I Wake*, 196–97)

5. These author sites give additional background on Han Nolan:

   www.Authors4Teens.com
   greenwood.scbbs.com/servlet/A4TStart?authorid=hnolan&source=introduction

6. An essay by Jeffrey Kaplan on *If I Should Die Before I Wake* is available in *Rationales for Teaching Young Adult Literature* (Reid and Neufeld 1999).

Why Give This Book to Teens?

- Because they may need to learn about the harms and problems of groups like the Aryan Warriors.
- Because they may have known discrimination or abuse for their ethnic, religious, or sexual identity.
- Because they may need to have someone like Chana's "Bubbe," her grandmother, who can encourage them to go through any of life's difficulties.
- Because they will read about tremendous courage and terrible suffering.

Paterson, Katherine: *Lyddie*
Published by Demco Media, April 1999, ISBN 0606160671
Teen Recommended

Lyddie is not yet 15, but she and her younger brother Charlie become the sole supports for their family, trying to hold onto the farm their father had established. He's gone West to seek for riches; after he left, their mother never was "quite right." She leaves to live with Lyddie's aunt and uncle, taking the two youngest children, Rachel and Agnes. Eventually Lyddie and Charlie are "apprenticed out" to earn money for the farm. Lyddie's experiences are not as pleasant or productive as Charlie's, and she eventually leaves Vermont for Massachusetts and the life of a "factory girl" in Lowell.

Yes, she makes money, but it is hard earned. The novel reveals the cruel world of child labor at the turn of the twentieth century and shows the courage of a young woman who will not be defeated.

Teaching Ideas and Resources

1. This book would work well to companion an American history unit on the early years of the twentieth century—especially the issues of child labor and factory life.

2. For more sense of the labor reality for young women described in *Lyddie*, read the novel along with Lois Lowry's *The Silent Boy*.
3. "Organize! A Look at Labor History in Young Adult Books," by Deborah Wilson Overstreet (*ALAN Review*, Fall 2001) includes a discussion of *Lyddie*.
4. "*Lyddie* and *Oliver*: Instructional Framework for Linking Historical Fiction to the Classics," by Janis Harmon (*ALAN Review* 25, no. 2 [Winter 1998]) offers an examination of the novel.
5. "Finding Your Way Home: Orphan Stories in Young Adult Literature," by Dirk P. Mattson, (*ALAN Review* 24, no. 3 [Spring 1997]) is a helpful essay for the theme of foster children and orphans.
6. "Family Relationships As Found in Arthur Miller's *Death of a Salesman* and Cynthia Voight's *The Runner*," by Ruth Cline (chapter 5 in Kaywell, *Adolescent Literature as a Complement to the Classics*, vol. 1, 1993) uses this novel as one of the YA books on family relationships.
7. Teaching ideas and background can be found at the following sites:

   www.carolhurst.com/titles/lyddie.html
   www.lessonplanspage.com/SSLACreateJournalAndPetitionAboutWorkingConditions67.htm
   teacher.scholastic.com/authorsandbooks/events/paterson/more_info.htm
   www.webenglishteacher.com/paterson.html
   volweb.utk.edu/Schools/bedford/harrisms/novel.htm
   www.bcps.org/offices/lis/curric/middle/eng/8.html#lyddie
   www.indiana.edu/~reading/ieo/bibs/paterson.html

Why Give This Book to Teens?

- Because they may have to hold an outside job while going to school, and Lyddie's story might inspire them.
- Because sometimes they might find themselves in the role of the adult or parent, despite the fact they're still teenagers.
- Because they might have to deal with working conditions that are unjust or need to learn about others who have to face these.

Paulsen, Gary: *Hatchet*
Published by Scholastic, 1999, ISBN 059098182X
Teen Recommended

Brian Robeson is a teen—he is caught in the stress of his parents' divorce. He has seen his mother with a lover; he wants to keep this "secret" from his dad. He is off to visit his dad, going via private plane to the Canadian oilfields where his dad is working. Brian's mom has given him a hatchet—Brian is somewhat embarrassed, but having the hatchet eventually is Brian's lifesaving item. En route to Canada, seated in the cockpit with the pilot who doesn't seem all that communicative, Brian is given a "mini"-flying lesson. The pilot begins to give signals of pain—eventually he has a heart attack. Brian first tries to make contact with the ground via radio, but he loses touch. He then attempts to fly the plane, but he crashes into a lake. Brian makes it to an island—there he begins a series of learning experiences for this city boy now alone without anything except his hatchet. He survives on the island for 54 days before he is rescued.

Teaching Ideas and Resources

1. This is a good novel to pair with some of the "man versus nature" works such as Jack London's "To Build a Fire."
2. "Bringing Us the Way to Know: The Novels of Gary Paulsen" by Susan Nelson Wood (*English Journal*, January 2001) focuses specifically on *Hatchet*, but is good for teaching any of Paulsen's novels.
3. "An Overlooked Characteristic of a Good Literary Choice: Discussability" by Robert C. Small Jr. (in "Adolescent Literature: Making Connections with Teens," special issue, *Virginia English Bulletin* 44, no. 2 [Fall 1994]) examines this book as one of the novels it suggests.
4. For more information on Gary Paulsen and his books, check the following websites:

   falcon.jmu.edu/~ramseyil/paulsen.htm
   www.indiana.edu/~reading/ieo/bibs/paulsen.html
   www2.nypl.org/home/branch/kids/read2003/chats/paulsen.cfm

5. A teaching guide to *Hatchet* is located at:

   www.simonsays.com/subs/183/teacher_guide.cfm?areaid=183&asset_id=119051

Why Give This Book to Teens?

- Because this is a story of bravery and survival.
- Because Brian has had a "city life" and learns what it means to be in nature.
- Because he is experiencing the psychological pain of his parents' divorce and many teens are experiencing that as well.

Paulsen, Gary: *Nightjohn*
Published by Laurel Leaf, reissue edition 1 January 1995, ISBN 0440219361

The book is narrated by Sarny, who is, as the book opens, a slave girl of age nine. The novel deals with the horrendous treatment of slaves owned by Waller. (According to Sarny, he deserves no first name.) John is purchased and comes to the plantation very beaten and scarred. Sarny reveals much about the plight of slaves who try to run away, the women who are used as "breeders," the cruelty of dogs trained to track runaways slaves, the terrible whippings, and the other inhuman conditions (inadequate food, shelter, etc.) they must endure.

Sarny wants to learn "letters" and she realizes that John will teach her in return for tobacco. John had escaped to the North, but he returned to slavery to help others learn to read. At one point when she has learned the letters to make a word, Sarny is caught by Waller. He tries to get her to tell who taught her; Mammy takes the blame and is whipped as she is forced to have a harness around her neck and pull the master in a wagon. John admits he is the one who taught Sarny. As punishment, John has two toes cut off—the "rule" was that an appendage was cut off for each time a person was caught.

Teaching Ideas and Resources

1. This is a good novel to use with a unit on African American literature and racism. It would work particularly well companioning *Nightjohn* with Frederick Douglass' *Narrative of a Slave* or other slave narratives.
2. "Considering the Power of the Past: Pairing *Nightjohn* and *Narrative of the Life of Frederick Douglass*" by Kelly Chandler, an essay in *United in Diversity: Using Multicultural Young Adult Literature in the Classroom* edited by Jean E. Brown and Elaine C. Stephens (NCTE, 1998), offers good teaching ideas.
3. "Gaining Understanding about Human Relationships through Young Adult Fiction" by Elizabeth Poe (in "Adolescent Literature: Making Connections with Teens," special issue, *Virginia English Bulletin* 44, no. 2 [Fall 1994]) uses this novel as one of the focus novels for the unit.
4. A unit plan for incorporating *Nightjohn* with other texts in American literature is available at www2.sjsu.edudepts/english/Warner.htm/nj.htm.
5. *Sarny* is a sequel to *Nighthjohn*; your students might want to read this novel for further study about slavery. Also, the film version of *Nightjohn* is a powerful visual portrayal of the book.

6. Several good websites are the following:

   www.slaveryinamerica.org/amliterature/amlit_lp_nightjohn_overviewunit.htm
   www.learner.org/channel/workshops/makingmeaning/makingmeaning/planning/reading.html
   active.sln.org.uk/emau/resource.htm
   www.davis.k12.ut.us/curric/languagearts/grade8.html
   www.k12webworks.com/shhs/pages/115.html

7. For more information on author Gary Paulsen, check these websites:

   www.trelease-on-reading.com/paulsen.html
   www.indiana.edu/~reading/ieo/bibs/paulsen.html

Why Give This Book to Teens?

- Because it is important to know about the horrors of slavery.
- Because Sarny and John are willing to make huge sacrifices to learn to read.
- Because sometimes we take it for granted that we can read and can get an education.
- Because freedom is never given easily.

Spinelli, Jerry: *Milkweed*
Published by Knopf Books for Young Readers, 9 September 2003, ISBN 0375813748

He is called many things since no one really knows his name. He is a Gypsy living in Warsaw, Poland, during the early Hitler years, still young enough to think that he will be safe because he isn't a Jew. He's first called simply "Stopthief" since that is what he has heard many times during his smuggling incidents. Later, Uri, one of the boys who befriends "Stopthief" and takes him into the lifestyle of other young boys who are living by smuggling, creates a story of Misha Pilsudski, and that becomes "Stopthief's" new identity. The novel is a courageous story of Misha's attempts to feed and save orphans, especially Janina, amid the ghetto life of Warsaw.

Teaching Ideas and Resources

1. This novel could be paired with any that you use to teach about the Holocaust; it might work especially well with Elie Wiesel's *Night*. The

added insight of this novel is that Gypsies were among those persecuted during the Nazi genocide and often students know little about other groups who suffered.

2. The following websites connect you with the range of topics addressed by this novel and with author information:

   www.Authors4Teens.com
   topics.practical.org/browse/Jerry_Spinelli
   www.indiana.edu/~reading/ieo/bibs/spinel.html
   www.randomhouse.com/features/jerryspinelli
   www.teachervision.fen.com/lesson-plans/lesson-26381.html

Why Give This Book to Teens?

- Because they might not know that groups other than the Jews were also hated and persecuted by the Nazis in World War II.
- Because they can learn about others, even as young as 13, who have had to overcome life-and-death challenges.
- Because they might be someone who is orphaned or feels alienated from parental figures and need to know Misha's story.

Other books by Jerry Spinelli to consider reading: *Stargirl*, *Loser*, and *Wringer*.

Veciana-Suarez, Ana: *Flight to Freedom*
Published by Scholastic, 1 February 2004, ISBN 0439382009

Yara, a young Cuban woman, relates her family's story of leaving Cuba in 1967. They are leaving a Cuba where they experience a government under which "we must get approval to breathe" (*Flight to Freedom*, 6). Yara's family (except for her brother Pepito, who is conscripted into the army) leaves for Miami and joins relatives there. This novel reveals the tensions the family experiences. Papi believes they must join forces and fight for Cuba's liberation; Mami wants to adapt to American life, but only to a point. Ileana is an older daughter who becomes involved with Tommy, an Anglo activist protesting the Vietnam War. In addition, the family has relatives who have been in Miami longer and have some acculturation. Through Yara's journal, we see the world of refugees, culture clashes, and the struggle to know "where is home."

Teaching Ideas and Resources

1. Yara's diary entries reveal much about the family's tensions. Consider using this novel for teaching first-person narrative and pairing it with

The Diary of a Young Girl, which presents a family that stays and hides rather than emigrates. Discuss with your students which option they think their parents would take.

2. If you have students from other cultures in the class, have these students share stories of the cultural differences they have experienced. Which experiences of Yara or her family do these immigrant students connect with? Have the Anglo students in the class write about a country they would like to live in; if they have traveled outside the United States, have them write about some of the cultural differences they have experienced.
3. Keep a bulletin board with newspaper clippings about immigrants to raise awareness about the difficulties immigrant people face.
4. The following websites offer resources for teaching this book:

   www.webrary.org/rs/bibhistfict.html
   www.somosprimos.com/spjun02.htm
   www.greenhill.org/AISL2004/presentations/Notable2003.pdf (notable trade books for Social Studies—2003)
   db.latinosandmedia.org/bibliography/title.html

Why Give This Book to Teens?

- Because since September 11, 2001, Americans have been more suspicious of people from other countries, and this book offers the perspective of those coming to the United States.
- Because Yara and her family lived through events like the assassinations of Martin Luther King Jr. and Robert Kennedy, and she shares her sorrow even though she is new to the country.
- Because Yara has to adapt in school, and many Anglo students don't realize the difficulties they create for those who are new.

Voight, Cynthia: *Homecoming*
Published by Fawcett Juniper/Ballantine, 1983
Teen Recommended

Dicey is 13, her brother James is 10, Maybeth is 9, and Sam is 6. As the novel opens, the children's mother is telling them to stay in the car and to obey Dicey; the mother heads into the shopping mall in Peewauket, Rhode Island, and never comes back. The children stay in the car overnight; then eventually head (walking!) to Bridgeport, Rhode Island. Dicey shows incredible ingenuity for a 13-year-old: she keeps the children together; she helps them find food; she maps their route; she keeps them hidden from the police, afraid the police will separate the children and put them in foster homes. The conditions are extraordinarily demanding—walking in rain, not always getting something to eat; not always able to find shelter at night. Dicey is going on an address she has for Aunt Cilla in Bridgeport—Cilla is the children's mother's aunt.

The father of the family deserted when the two oldest could barely remember him; the mom became desperate after losing her job and having to face questions about Maybeth—teachers think Maybeth is retarded since she is very quiet and noncommunicative in school. James is intelligent and does well in school. Sam is a little fighter—he struggles particularly in trying to understand that their mom has gone.

Dicey lives an incredibly responsible life in caring for all her siblings and trying to keep the family together. Her story is a compelling one.

Teaching Ideas and Resources

1. The issue of homeless children is a growing concern. This novel offers good insight into the challenges and the courage needed for children. The novel could be an introduction to a research unit on the topic of homelessness.
2. Bonnie O. Ericson, in "Heroes and Journeys in *The Odyssey* and Several Works in Young Adult Literature" (chapter 1 in Kaywell, *Adolescent Literature as a Complement to the Classics*, vol. 2, 1995), describes how to teach *Homecoming* in conjunction with *The Odyssey*.
3. "Finding Your Way Home: Orphan Stories in Young Adult Literature," by Dirk P. Mattson (*ALAN Review* 24, no. 3 [Spring 1997]) is a helpful essay for the theme of foster children and orphans.
4. "Into the Woods Again: Three Recent Young Adult Novels of Parental Abandonment" by Gail Munde (*ALAN Review* 24, no. 3 [Spring 1997]) examines this novel as one of the three.
5. Helpful websites for teaching *Homecoming* include the following:

   www.webenglishteacher.com/voight.html
   www.randomhouse.com/highschool/guides/homecoming.html
   www.mcdougallittell.com/disciplines/_lang_arts/litcons/homecomi/guide.cfm
   scholar.lib.vt.edu/ejournals/ALAN/fall96/f96-11-Research.html
   www.indiana.edu/~reading/ieo/bibs/voight.html

Why Give This Book to Teens?

- Because they might have friends or peers who have been abandoned by parents.
- Because they can learn about the resourcefulness and courage of a teen who does all she can to keep her family together.
- Because the issue of homelessness is more a reality today than ever.

Other books by Cynthia Voight to consider reading: *Dicey's Song* and *Jackaroo.*

Wojciechowska, Maia: *Shadow of a Bull*
Published by Aladdin Paperbacks, 1992, ISBN 0689715676

Manolo Olivar is nine; he looks a good deal like his father, Juan Olivar, a famed bullfighter. At Juan's birth, the prophecy was that he would be one of the best bullfighters ever. Manolo is fearful; he sees himself as a coward. He is rapidly "taken under the wings" of six men in the village of Arcangel, who want him to begin learning all about bullfighting. He even begins to practice secretly. At the same time, Juan, the older brother of Manolo's best friend, is very eager to become a bullfighter. Juan, unlike Manolo, has the "aficinado"—the love of fighting, but his father had been injured and "rejected" by Manolo's father, so Juan does not believe he has any chance to become known. On the day Manolo first "tests" his bullfighting skills, he realizes he cannot kill the bull and that he is not "made" for fighting. He wants to be a doctor; he learned that in helping the aging village doctor help an injured "clown" bullfighter. Manolo waits two years before actually being "tested," wondering if his father was ever fearful.

Teaching Ideas and Resources

1. Because of the setting in Spain and in the bullfighting arena, this book would be a good companion to Hemingway's *The Sun Also Rises*; it could be the outside-of-class text.
2. You might consider reading the book aloud while the class is studying a novel like *The Sun Also Rises*; use the book for a discussion about what makes for true courage or for the topic of following in parents' footsteps. Your students can debate the statement: "A person should follow his or her parents' expectations."
3. Some web resources for teaching the book include:

   www.bcps.org/offices/lis/curric/middle/eng/6.html

www.schoolhousebooksweb.com/Newbery.html
clerccenter.gallaudet.edu/products/perspectives/sep-oct97/teachers.html
www.ed.uiuc.edu/YLP/Units/Mini_Units/94-95/Loos.Hispanic-cultures
www.michigan.gov/documents/Social_Studies_Trade_Books_42259_7.pdf

Why Give This Book to Teens?

- Because they might be sons or daughters who everyone thinks will do what their father or mother did/does.
- Because, like Manolo, they may need to test their courage.
- Because they might need to get a better sense of who they really are instead of what others think they are.
- Because they may wonder if their parents or other role models were/are ever fearful.

Yolen, Jane: *Briar Rose*
Published by Tor Books, reprint edition 15 November 1993, ISBN 0812558626

Rebecca, Shanna, and Sylvia are now all young adults, but each remembers their grandmother telling and retelling the "Sleeping Beauty" fairy tale. Their grandmother's stories always held some harsh and strange images that were not part of the original tale. Following their grandmother's death, Rebecca is left with her "Gemma's" parting words: "I am Briar Rose." Rebecca's search to find the real identity of her grandmother leads to another chapter in the horrendous story of the Holocaust.

Teaching Ideas and Resources

1. Have your students research their favorite fairy tale and write a new version that addresses some contemporary issue of hate, violence, or injustice.
2. Have students research a family member—preferably a grandparent or older relative—and write a short biography of that person's life. These presentations could include Power Point slides, and if the person written about is available, he or she could be invited to a "This Is Your Life" presentation.
3. If possible, invite a Holocaust survivor to the class for a presentation.

4. Students can write fairy tales with contemporary emphases. Check the following website for help with fairy tales:

   www.theliterarylink.com/fairypage.html

5. Websites that are helpful for teaching a number of Jane Yolen's books and providing author information are the following:

   www.Authors4Teens.com
   www.webenglishteacher.com/yolen.html
   www.loretonh.nsw.edu.au/english/year12_yolen/yolen_page.htm
   www.janeyolen.com/tchrsideas.html
   www.scils.rutgers.edu/~kvander/swteach.html
   www.theliterarylinks.com/questins_otherbooks.html#Briar%20 Rose
   www.stmary.pvt.k12.de.us/Lib_Holocaust_Resources.html

Why Give This Book to Teens?

- Because they may have a grandparent or older relative they want to know better.
- Because this is another story that reveals how humans can treat other humans inhumanely, and we need to learn to make peace, not hatred.
- Because reading helps us understand worlds we can never experience.

CHAPTER EIGHT

Books on Allegory, Fantasy, Myth, and Parable

Babbitt, Natalie: *The Eyes of the Amaryllis*
Published by Farrar, Straus and Giroux, 1977

This book is only a fantasy for those who do not know of the power of the sea, of the ocean. The true story behind this book deals with loss of the brig *Amaryllis* in 1850, when a hurricane "swallowed" the ship, the captain, and the crew. Babbitt begins this novel some 30 years after this event, recounting how Geneva Reade, the ship captain's widow, who had witnessed the ship's disappearance, is still waiting and hoping for some message from the bottom of the sea. Her granddaughter Geneva, known as Jenny, comes to stay with her grandmother, and together they faithfully search the sea. Jenny's father (George), then a young boy, had also witnessed the ship's disappearance. He feared the sea ever after; his daughter, by contrast, is drawn to it.

Teaching Ideas and Resources

1. The book's epigraph, "Many waters cannot quench love, / neither can the floods drown it" (Song of Solomon 8:7), presents a biblical connection that you can explore with your students. How is this biblical passage related to the book?
2. John Masefield's poem, "I Must Go Down to the Sea Again" or other poetry like "The Seafarer" or other literary works with themes connected to the allure of the waters would make good companion pieces. *The Eyes of the Amaryllis* is short enough to be read aloud during a study of *The Odyssey* to offer a prose companion. The book could also be

used in a unit on ballads and balladry, accompanied by Gordon Lightfoot's musical rendition of "The Wreck of the Edmund Fitzgerald." A current film that would work well in such a unit is *The Perfect Storm*.
3. The prologue of the book, "Seward's Warning," provides an example of dramatic monologue. Consider reading this prologue as an introduction to a writing prompt on the conflict of man versus nature.
4. The following website provides author background on Natalie Babbitt:

   www.indiana.edu/~reading/ieo/bibs/babbitt.html

Why Give This Book to Teens?

- Because maybe they've been fascinated by the ocean, the sea, or some other element of nature and want to explore it, despite nature's unpredictability.
- Because they might have witnessed death or destruction caused by nature and can relate to the fears George has for his daughter.
- Because this book might help them bond with an older relative who has lost someone he or she loves.

Babbitt, Natalie: *Tuck Everlasting*
Published by Faber and Faber Ltd, 24 October 1988,
ASIN 0571120954
Teen Recommended

Now a recently released movie, this sparse tale offers a combination of fantasy and realism, complete with a kidnapping, a murderer escaping from jail, and some difficult decision making. However, Babbitt's book also asks profound questions about the meaning of life and death. When 10-year-old Winnie Foster meets the Tuck family, she is invited to cross boundaries she never imagined. She is eventually offered the ultimate gift—eternal life from the Fountain of Youth—and begins to wonder what living forever might really cost. Winnie acts as a sort of reverse "savior" for the Tucks and their burden of protecting humankind from the knowledge that such an eternal existence is possible.

Teaching Ideas and Resources

1. Ask students to make two sketches of a spring. *On the first sketch*, label the spring, "My Thoughts about Living Forever." Ask students to write sentences, phrases, or questions that reading *Tuck Everlasting* provokes in their minds. Make these ideas "flow" out of the spring. The ques-

tions or comments can branch into puddles or rivulets, and can be "dammed up" by other comments or questions. *On the second sketch*, label the spring, "Babbitt's Hints about Everlasting Life." Ask students to copy sentences from *Tuck Everlasting* that suggest Babbitt's own views. Make these sentences "flow" out of the spring.

2. Chapter 1 presents several musings about the woods, the neighbors, and the approach to life of those living in Treegap. Have your students write about and discuss what they experience in neighborhoods or in the communities where they live.
3. Babbitt's story is like a myth or fable. Consider having students write a myth or fable about living forever.
4. Go to scholar.lib.vt.edu/ejournals/ALAN/winter95/Milner.html and read Joseph O. Milner's comments on *Tuck Everlasting* in "Hard Religious Questions in *Knee-Knock Rise* and *Tuck Everlasting*" (*ALAN Review* 22, no. 2 [Winter 1995]). Milner writes, "*Tuck Everlasting* seems to be probing difficult questions with a skeptical attitude not unlike that found in the works of two literary scourges of religion, Kurt Vonnegut and Wallace Stevens. . . . Natalie Babbitt is working in much the same territory in that she takes the basic, haunting question—if a man die, shall he live again?—and reverses it to ask, if a man were not to die, could he truly live?"
5. If you are teaching Vonnegut, consider pairing *Tuck Everlasting* with one of his works. Or look at the poetry of Wallace Stevens, which Milner cites, and consider doing a study of the poetry paralleled to *Tuck Everlasting*.
6. "An Overlooked Characteristic of a Good Literary Choice: Discussability," by Robert C. Small Jr. (in "Adolescent Literature: Making Connections with Teens," special issue, *Virginia English Bulletin* 44, no. 2 [Fall 1994]) examines this novel.
7. For more information on Natalie Babbitt and her books, check the following websites:

   www.neiu.edu/~gspackar/INDEX.html
   www.webenglishteacher.com/babbit.html
   www.indiana.edu/~reading/ieo/bibs/babbitt.html

Why Give This Book to Teens?

- Because they might have questions about life and what comes after life.
- Because they might have to make some difficult decisions and can learn from Winnie Foster's choices.

- Because someday they might find they'd like to escape the pressures of life as it is and might need to see some of the disadvantages of living forever.

Other books by Natalie Babbitt to consider reading: *Knee-knock Rise* and *The Devil's Storybook*.

Block, Francesca Lia: *I Was a Teenage Fairy*
Published by HarperCollins Juvenile Books, reprint edition 2 May 2000, ISBN 0064408620
Teen Recommended

This book beautifully combines fantasy and realism. For that reason, it might not be for all readers. Block's books are known for becoming cult classics. The setting is Los Angeles, in modern times. However typical the storyline may seem—Barbie Marks is a beautiful, successful model, her career created by her mother—this novel is anything but typical.

Barbie has a tiny, talking fairy named Mab who is her companion throughout her dysfunctional life. Is Mab real? The reader is forced to ask and answer that question repeatedly during the novel. Mab is a "straight talker"; she speaks in a way Barbie is not capable of. There are only a few other characters even mentioned in the novel. Griffin Tyler is the other character Mab helps learn to deal with himself.

Barbie and Griffin were both molested by the same photographer at an early age. Though his photographs launched their careers, Barbie and Griffin are forced to deal with the secret and the pain. Set against the glamour of the young, successful, Los Angeles lifestyle, the tragedy of their abuse is made to seem real, though it is never dealt with in graphic detail. Both characters must come to terms with themselves. Barbie must also come to terms with her family: a mother who looked the other way while her daughter was sexually abused, and a father who abandons his family to begin another.

Teaching Ideas and Resources

1. The book is a modern fairy tale and follows the fairy tales tradition—the stories were often more dark and violent than we might remember. Students can write their own modern fairy tale addressing issues that may be "too dark" to be presented in realistic fiction.
2. A teaching guide for *Dangerous Angels*, also by Francesca Lia Block, is available in *Master Teacher's Guide* by HarperCollins Publishers—

www.HarperAcademic.com. *Dangerous Angels* is **Teen Recommended** and has similar themes to *I Was a Teenage Fairy.*

3. Teaching resources for this book are located at the following website:

   ccwf.cc.utexas.edu/~funlearn/booksr4kids/teenage.html

4. "Francesca Lia Block's Use of Enchantment: Teenagers' Need for Magic in the Real World" by Lois L. Warner (*ALAN Review*, Winter 2002) is an excellent essay for examining a number of Block's books.
5. The novel may be too controversial even when taught as fairy tale, but the oppressive mother figure trying to live her life through Barbie is often a reality for teens.

Why Give This Book to Teens?

- Because they may have experienced some form of abuse.
- Because they might have friends who have had such experiences.
- Because they might have parents who have determined their future and are not really in tune with their abilities and aptitudes.
- Because sometimes an imaginary friend can help them find themselves.

Others books by Francesca Lia Block to consider reading: *The Hanged Man*, *Violet and Claire*, and *Dangerous Angels*.

Card, Orson Scott: *Ender's Game*
Published by Tor Books, reprint edition 15 August 1992, ISBN 0312853238
Teen Recommended

Andrew is six; his older siblings are Peter and Valentine. In this highly scientific and futuristic fictional world, Andrew is a "third"; his parents risked having more children than they should. Andrew, aka Ender, has been singled out, though. He is taken by the International Fleet at age six and made a commander by age nine. Has he had a childhood? Is the "programming" that happens at the school dehumanizing? Can he or should he fight the system? Supposedly Ender is "right" for the "program," but as Dink Meeker asks, "Is the program right for Ender?"

Teaching Ideas and Resources

1. The book could be paired with *Brave New World* or some of the other science fiction/Utopia works. You might also pair it with *The Giver* by

Lois Lowry. Both books recognize children and how their lives can be controlled; Ender and Jonas are both among the gifted children taken and "used" by governments or adults who are in power.

2. This book has the potential for many good discussions and writing prompts. One topic for discussion is childhood. What should the "normal" childhood be like or include? Is the training program that Ender experiences a good thing for a child as young as six? Why or why not?
3. Ender and Jonas both represent children who maintain goodness and high ideals despite the adult world; a character comparison of these two protagonists would be a good activity.
4. *Artemis Fowl* by Eoin Colfer, also **Teen Recommended**, is another novel to work into this study. Artemis Fowl, a 12-year-old, is the protagonist, but in many ways is not the hero that Ender or Jonas is. Artemis wants the fairy gold, and he has the genius to crack the ancient fairy code of writing. He is ruthless with only occasional qualms of conscience. Encourage students to analyze his character in light of Jonas, Ender, and Gollum from the *Lord of the Rings* trilogy.
5. *The Transall Saga* by Gary Paulsen, also **Teen Recommended**, is another good book to read along with *Ender's Game*. In *The Transall Saga*, Mark Harrison is transported to another world/planet. Unlike Ender and Artemis, Mark is working to save many of the people in the land as well as to save the planet Earth, which he learns had been decimated. If the class is divided into several groups, each reading one of these novels, each group could present a panel discussion on why the protagonist of the novel they read is or isn't a hero and why they believe this.
6. "Taming the Alien Genre: Bringing Science Fiction into the Classroom" by Katherine T. Bucher and M. Lee Manning (*ALAN Review*, Winter 2001) offers insights to teaching this novel.
7. Resources for teaching *Ender's Game* and background on Orson Scott Card are available at the following sites:

   www.hatrack.com
   hometown.aol.com/hostaacprofryk/endergame.html
   www.addison.lib.il.us/6card.asp
   web.mit.edu/m-i-t/science_fiction/profiles/card.html
   www.jointhesaga.com/otherviews/card.htm
   www.woodrow.org/teachers/bi/1994/science_fiction.html

Why Give This Book to Teens?

- Because they might wonder if everything technological is necessarily the best for our world.
- Because they might some time be forced to choose between what they know is right and what the adults around them are telling them.
- Because Ender's world is a political world that needs analyzing, and often our world needs analysis that we don't give it.
- Because what begins as science fiction all too quickly becomes reality.

Coelho, Paulo: *The Alchemist*
Published by Harper San Francisco, reprint edition 10 May 1995, ISBN 0062502182
Teen Recommended

Santiago is a shepherd; he is also on a journey because he wants to know the world. He has puzzling dreams about finding a treasure at the pyramids and meets a series of people as he searches for the interpretation of the dreams. An old man, Melchizedek, the king of Salem, is one of the most helpful; Melchizedek informs Santiago that Santiago has discovered his "Personal Legend." En route to Egypt, Santiago finds himself duped a number of times, but he stays rooted in the wisdom of Melchizedek and uses the Urim and Thummin, sacred lots for determining God's will, that Melchizedek gave him.

Teaching Ideas and Resources

1. This book is filled with biblical references—have students trace the references and find their larger context in the Bible and then relate them to the novel.
2. The Alchemist, Melchizedek, and others in the book are wisdom figures. Have students locate their favorite quotation or passage and write an explanation of the wisdom contained in the passage/quote.
3. Have students write their Philosophy of Life or "Personal Legend."
4. *Master Teacher's Guide: A Collection of Forty Guides for Middle and High School Teachers* includes a guide for teaching *The Alchemist*. The guide is available from Harper Collins Publishers, www.HarperAcademic.com.
5. Paulo Coelho's official website is www.paulocoelho.com.br/engl/index.html.

Why Give This Book to Teens?

- Because they are at the beginning of their "Personal Legend."
- Because the book is a parable filled with many wise lessons about life.
- Because too often we don't know our dreams and even more often, we don't follow them.

Other books by Paulo Coelho to consider reading: *The Fifth Mountain*, *The Pilgrimage*, and *Veronica Decides to Die*.

Cooper, Susan: *The Dark Is Rising*
Published by Random House Children's Books, 31 December 1973, ASIN 0701150203
Teen Recommended

Merriman Lyon appears in a new role, this time in Buckinghamshire as teacher and Old One. He mentors Will Stanton, the seventh son of a seventh son, who wakes on his eleventh birthday to discover he, too, is one of the immortals whose mission is always to keep the dark forces in check. Will learns he must bring together the six signs that will defeat the Dark when it rises at the darkest time of the year between Christmas and Twelfth Night. Sliding through portals of time and space, Will battles the forces of darkness in his own time or in earlier centuries. He learns how the Old Ones can stand together to face the power of the rising Dark. However, Will must discover within himself the courage and wisdom required for the task.

Teaching Ideas and Resources

1. The Walker, "Hawkin," liegeman to Merriman, betrays the Light to the Dark with terrible consequences. Will is both saddened and angered by The Walker. More than anything else, the dilemma of The Walker's divided loyalties, paralleled by those of Will's selfish and giddy sister Mary, contributes to the loss of Will's innocence. Have students write a letter to Mary from Will with the emotions and allegiances of a kid brother and also those of being an Old One.
2. Merriman helps Will distinguish between the magical power of the Light, not "of magic . . . born out of foolishness and ignorance and sickness of the mind." What are some contrasts among the ways magic is used by the servants of the Dark and by the Old Ones who are sworn to unite the signs of Light?
3. Teri Lesesne, in "Beyond Camelot: Poetry, Song and Young Adult Fan-

tasy" (chapter 12 in Kaywell, *Adolescent Literature as a Complement to the Classics*, vol. 2, 1995), uses the novel as one of the additional reading elements in the unit.

Master Teacher's Guide

- Each book in Cooper's *Dark Is Rising* series is set in a specific season—Lammas, Christmas, Halloween, Midsummer—times when magic is strong, according to legend. Although *The Dark Is Rising* is more indebted to Celtic myth than to Christian story, have students list incidents and symbols of the Christmas season. How does Cooper use them to examine ideas of community, sacrifice, and redemption?
- At Oxford, Cooper heard lectures by J. R. R. Tolkein and C. S. Lewis, the great writers of Christian allegory and fantasy. Students familiar with the Lord of the Rings trilogy or the Chronicles of Narnia might look for their influences in Cooper's work.
- Check the resource: "Susan Cooper" by Margaret K. McElderry in *Horn Book* (1976), pp. 367–72, or at www.thelostland.com/mcelderry.htm.
- Cooper wrote: "A friend of mine says it's all the fault of Oxford University, where students of English had to read so much mediaeval literature that we ended up believing in dragons." Relate this comment to her works.
- www.thelostland.com/qanda.htm is a website connected to the novel.

Why Give This Book to Teens?

- Because Cooper's time and space portals are better than a movie's special effects.
- Because Will's fears can help us understand our own.
- Because we, too, may be asked to join causes that demand much of us.

Cooper, Susan: *Over Sea, Under Stone*
Published by Scholastic, 1989, ISBN 0590433202
Teen Recommended

The first book in Cooper's *Dark Is Rising* series introduces Simon, Jane, and Barney Drew, on holiday in Cornwall with their adoptive uncle Merriman Lyon (Merlin). When the three discover that an ancient map may lead to the Holy Grail, Barney, a fan of the King Arthur legends, persuades the others to join the search. They suspect that their great-uncle is not in Cornwall by accident and that he is even more mysterious than they imagined. As the children discover a timeless battle between the Light and the Dark, they meet sinister dangers when other village residents seek the Grail for their own dark purposes.

Teaching Ideas and Resources

1. For centuries the legends of the Grail have tempted scholars and inspired death-defying searches. How and when do the Drew children begin to suspect that the race to find the Grail and the manuscript decoding its runes has implications worth risking their lives to win?
2. Knowing whom to trust is a critical life skill for young people. As they read, have students list characters the children meet during their summer in Cornwall, making notes on their trustworthiness. Where are the surprises? When and why do their initial judgments change?

Master Teacher's Guide

- Cooper wrote: "Haunted places all, true springs of the matter of Britain. Bronze Age barrows littered our landscape; Celt and Anglo-Saxon merged in our faces; Arthur invaded our daydreams; the Welsh legends our darker dreams at night." How does her comment relate to the book?
- For author information, check "Meet Susan Cooper" at usitweb.shef.ac .uk/~emp94ms/ownwords.html.
- For more insights on the book, see "Susan Cooper" by Margaret K. McElderry in *Horn Book* (1976), pp 367–72, or at www.thelostland .com/mcelderry.htm.
- The standing stones and legendary sites of Cornwall take on more mystery for the Drew children as the story spins out. Read about Cooper's childhood influences and show where you see them in this book.

Why Give This Book to Teens?

- Because families working together can protect important things.
- Because not all authority figures can be trusted.
- Because some things are worth great risk.

Cormier, Robert: *Fade*

Published by Laurel Leaf, reissue edition 1 September 1991, ISBN 0440210917

What would I do if I were invisible? What power would invisibility give me and how might such power be corrupting? When Paul learns that he has inherited a family curse/gift of being able to "fade," he discovers dark secrets of family and friends. As an adult, he fears that his nephew will use the family curse/gift for ultimate evil. "Terrible power brings terrible temptations. So far the wielders of the power, the faders, have all been normal, sane and stable. But what if a fader were to grow up abused, damaged and vicious?"

Teaching Ideas and Resources

1. Go to Amazon.com and read Patty Campbell's 1998 interview with Robert Cormier at www.amazon.com/exec/obidos/tg/feature/-/5191/102-8751315-8641718. In a discussion about evil, Cormier says, "It's people who deny evil that there's no hope for. Once you know about the existence of evil, then you can start to fight it. Evil doesn't come out of a cave at night—it wears the bland face of the man who belongs to the Rotary Club, or the grocer . . ." Do parallel journal pages with these headings: Where are the revelations of evil in *Fade*? Where are the revelations of evil in my world? Across the bottom discuss: Is Cormier's conclusion supportable?
2. In the *ALAN Review* (Winter 2001), John Ritter, John H. Simmons, and ReLeah Lent and Gloria Pipkin all have articles that are tributes to Robert Cormier and provide insights into this author.
3. The *ALAN Review* vol. 12, no. 2 (Winter 1985) had several essays on Robert Cormier; all offer good resources for teaching his works.
4. See these websites for insights on the novel:

   theliterarylink.com/questions_otherbooks.html#Fade
   www.cix.co.uk/~asc/trapped/book55.htm

Why Give This Book to Teens?

- Because Paul is 13 (the age of, or close to the age of, many teens) and he possesses a power that could bring death.
- Because maybe they have some quality that allows them to do something unusual; how do they handle this quality?
- Because maybe they have a friend who has a secret he or she shares with them. What do they do about that secret, especially if it might be harmful to others?

Other books by Robert Cormier to consider reading: *I Am the Cheese*, *The Bumblebee Flies Anyway*, *Tunes for Bears to Dance To*, *The Rag and Bone Shop*, and *We All Fall Down*.

Gibran, Kahlil: *The Prophet*
Published by Walker and Co., large print edition September 1991, ASIN 0802725325
Teen Recommended

In a distant, timeless place, a mysterious prophet walks the sands. At the moment of his departure, he wishes to offer the people gifts, but he possesses nothing. The people gather round, each asks a question of the heart, and the man's wisdom is his gift. It is Gibran's gift to us, as well, for Gibran's prophet is rivaled in his wisdom only by the founders of the world's great religions. On the most basic topics—marriage, children, friendship, work, pleasure—his words have a power and lucidity that in another era would surely have provoked the description "divinely inspired." Free of dogma, free of power structures and metaphysics, consider these poetic, moving aphorisms a 20th-century supplement to all sacred traditions—as millions of other readers already have. (Review by Brian Bruya, Amazon.com)

Teaching Ideas and Resources

1. This is a book of "wisdom sayings"—it would work well while studying *Siddhartha* or Emerson's "Self Reliance" or Thoreau's *Walden*. Students could do a comparison of the "wisdom" provided by each writer and describe which they find more appealing.
2. Have students select the saying or short essay that is most fitting for their lives and then identify or explain why this saying is most appropriate for them. Have students select the wisdom most needed by people in their high school—again, ask them to provide an explanation for their choice. Have students select the advice they'd most like to give others and explain why. Have students select the advice most needed by those in political leadership in the United States and explain why.

Why Give This Book to Teens?

- Because we all need wisdom to guide our lives.
- Because the topics addressed in the book fit all ages, all times.
- Because sometimes wise words can change attitudes toward life.

Highwater, Jamake: *Anpao: An American Indian Odyssey*
Published by Scholastic, November 1991, ISBN 0590451405

Anpao means "the dawn." This book is a series of myths woven together in journey. Anpao and his twin Oapna are poor and have no parents (actually

Anpao was conceived by the Sun and a human mother), but they do love the beautiful maiden, Ko-ko-mik-e-is. She says she cannot marry because she belongs to the Sun. "Be careful, Ko-ko-mik-e-sis, and listen to me because I have great power. You must not marry. You are mine." Ko-ko-mik-e-sis tells Anpao she will marry him if he goes to the Sun and tells the Sun that Ko-ko-mik-e-sis wants to marry him, and if Anpao can get the Sun to remove the scar on his face.

The book chronicles Anpao's odyssey to the Sun; he must fight the jealousy of the Moon who constantly causes deaths, disasters, and destruction.

Teaching Ideas and Resources

1. Myths are good texts to help students learn about other cultures and periods of history. This book would be a good companion with a study of Greek and Roman mythology. If you have students write a myth, adding a culture from the United States may help students find more relevance.
2. If you are in a region of the country where you have contact with Native Americans, it would be good to have a member of a local tribe come and talk about storytelling. You might also consider taking students to some "sacred place" of Native Americans since Native American sacred stories usually cannot be told outside of these sacred sites.
3. Pair this book with the video series of Joseph Campbell, *The Power of Myth* and have your students compare the myths of Anpao to those Campbell explores.
4. Visit the following website and note the section on the "Quest for Spiritual Knowledge":

   scholar.lib.vt.edu/ejournals/ALAN/spring96/mendt.html

Why Give This Book to Teens?

- Because Anpao is on a journey into adulthood, just like they are.
- Because they can learn something about coming of age as youth in another culture experience it.
- Because Anpao overcomes many obstacles and demonstrates courage.

L'Engle, Madeleine: *A Wrinkle in Time*
Published by Yearling Books, reissue edition 11 May 1998, ISBN 0440498058

L'Engle, Madeleine: A *Wind in the Door*
Published by Yearling Books, reissue edition 15 March 1974,
ISBN 0440487617
L'Engle, Madeleine: A *Swiftly Tilting Planet*
Published by Yearling Books, reissue edition 15 December 1980,
ISBN 0440401585
L'Engle, Madeleine: *Many Waters*
Published by Yearling Books, reissue edition 1 August 1987,
ISBN 0440405483
****Teen Recommended****

Each book in this series focuses on some member of the Murry family, whose parents are talented scientists, and deals with the mysterious reality of time. *A Wrinkle in Time* draws readers through the allegory about time to the real world and challenges them to discover what each has to counteract the forces of hate and evil. The book introduces the theory of the "tesseract," a fifth dimension of time. *A Wind in the Door* examines the inner sickness that can stifle human growth, particularly the growth of the spirit. Through the fantastic environment of the mitrochondria and farandola, which are literally and scientifically too minute to be explored, L'Engle presents the all-important philosophy:

> "Remember, Mr. Jenkins, you're great on Benjamin Franklin's saying, 'We must all hang together, or assuredly we will all hang separately.' That's how it is with human beings and mitrochondria and farandolae—and our planet, too, I guess, and the solar system. We have to live together in—in harmony, or we won't live at all." (*A Wind in the Door*, 147)

The next two novels, *A Swiftly Tilting Planet* and *Many Waters*, both explore the deplorable reality of enmity between brothers or in families and communities of the world, again using the adolescent protagonists who see the reality through those who are lovers of peace and those who are not. In *A Swiftly Tilting Planet*, L'Engle introduces another concept about relationships called "kything," which allows those close to one another to bolster each other's spirits.

Many readers know Sandy and Dennys, the "normal" boys in the Murry family, from *A Wind in the Door* and *A Wrinkle in Time*. A simple hunt for a recipe on their parents' computer and a wish to go somewhere warm plunges them into a blazing-hot desert somewhere else in time. When they get acquainted with a family of tribesmen, they're feeling pretty comfortable until they realize the family belongs to THAT Noah. How will Sandy and Dennys get back to their own time before the Great Flood—the many waters—comes? They realize that Noah's beautiful daughter Yalith is not mentioned in the Genesis flood story they've read. Fearing that she may be trapped, they are determined to change history and save her. Meanwhile the fallen angels, the Nephilim, exercise powers of evil the twins had never encountered.

Teaching Ideas and Resources

1. Some animals embody goodness and majesty in L'Engle's pre-Flood fantasy. Others reflect the Nephilim. Invite students to expand L'Engle's good and evil menagerie and tell reasons for their choices.
2. Yalith's grandfather Enoch teaches her some important ways that creatures listen to and praise their Creator. How does what she learns give her strength and resources she will need?
3. Sandy and Dennys discover that, even though they've tessored into prehistory, problems of deception, violence, and jealousy feel familiar. What aspects of L'Engle's pre-Flood world seem similar to our own times?
4. The following resource has extensive ideas for working with these four novels: "Teaching the Madeleine L'Engle Tetralogy: Using Allegory and Fantasy as Antidote to Violence" (ERIC: Accession No. ED 436 785, 23 pages on microfiche).
5. "The Storyteller: Fact, Fiction, and the books of Madeleine L'Engle" by Cynthia Zarin (*New Yorker*, April 12, 2004) is a good resource for understanding L'Engle.
6. The following websites have helpful teaching ideas as well:

   www.madeleinelengle.com
   www.webenglishteacher.com/lengle.html
   www.sdcoe.k12.ca.us/score/lengle/lengletg.html
   www.lausd.k12.ca.us/lausd/offices/di/Burleson/Lessons/planet/index.htm
   www.lausd.k12.ca.us/lausd/offices/di/Burleson/Lessons/Wrinkle/index.htm
   www.proteacher.com/070104.shtml

Master Teacher's Guide

- L'Engle said: "Have courage and joy. Sometimes our moments of greatest joy come at [the] times of greatest courage. . . . Our children need

to hear over and over again that there is no such thing as redemptive violence. . . . Violence never redeems. And what we do does make a difference!" How do the actions of Sandy and Dennys illustrate L'Engle's advice to her readers?
- Check the resource "Listening to the Story: A conversation with Madeleine L'Engle," by DeeDee Risher: www.theotherside.org/archive/mar-apr98/lengle.html.

Why Give This Book to Teens?
- Because our world, for all its technological advances, is sometimes a "sick" planet.
- Because families are often torn by sibling rivalries.
- Because love of parents and siblings, and love from parents and siblings, is often the force that can save the world.
- Because, like Meg and Charles Wallace, we often are misunderstood and ridiculed by our peers.
- Because unicorns and other mythological creatures often pique curiosity.
- Because blending Bible stories and imagination allows readers to ask fresh questions.
- Because the idea of knowing what's coming and trying to escape it makes a great adventure.

Other books by Madeleine L'Engle to consider reading: *The Arm of the Starfish*, *Dragons in the Water*, *Troubling a Star*, and *The Rock That Is Higher*.

L'Engle, Madeleine: *An Acceptable Time*
Published by Laurel Leaf, reissue edition 1 November 1990, ISBN 0440208149

This novel's central character is Polly, the oldest daughter of Meg Murry and Calvin O'Keefe. Polly is with her grandparents, the famed scientists of L'Engle's tetralogy. With the Murry's friend Dr. Louise, and her brother, Bishop Columbra, she experiences a time travel all her own. In this novel, as with the earlier four, L'Engle identifies peoples of earlier times whose culture led them to greater oneness with the universe as well as peoples, not unlike some in our contemporary world, who believe force is the only way to achieve goals.

Teaching Ideas and Resources

1. Because Polly goes to a world of three thousand years earlier, this book is a good lead to exploring civilizations of the ancient world. Students could research this earlier age in history and explore what has changed in the centuries since. In groups, they could present findings about what has improved and what has changed in negative ways.
2. Groups could also examine the similarities between ancient and modern times; for example, Polly notes that the concept of human sacrifice is no more barbaric than the genocide that happened during the Nazi regime in World War II. Students could present their findings in oral presentations or in essays.

Why Give This Book to Teens?

- Because, like Zachary, they might be so focused on saving their own life that they are unaware of the danger they are causing to others, particularly someone they love.
- And like Zachary, they might feel they have done something so unforgivable that there is no hope for them.
- Because, like Polly, they might become the instrument of peace in a troubled time.
- Because sometimes we cling to outdated and problematic traditions when we are fearful of change or of challenging others' to new ways of doing things.

Lewis, C. S.: *The Chronicles of Narnia*
Published by HarperCollins, 30 October 1998, ISBN 0060281375
Teen Recommended

The Lion, the Witch and the Wardrobe is probably the one book of the series that teachers would get time to teach, but all of the books in *The Chronicles of Narnia* are worth reading. In *The Lion, the Witch and the Wardrobe*, Peter, Susan, Edmund, and Lucy come into a fantasy world controlled by the White Witch. Narnia, under this wicked witch, is a land where it is always winter, but Christmas never comes. All who have been under the power of the White Witch and those who are hiding from her are awaiting Aslan, an allegorical Christ figure.

Teaching Ideas and Resources

1. Especially if students have never been introduced to the concept of allegory, use *The Lion, the Witch and the Wardrobe* to teach what alle-

gory is. Have students identify the names, the places, the seasons, and the characters that are symbolic and explain what each of them symbolizes. You might include background on names and what these mean. For example, Lucy is connected with light. How do light and Lucy's character connect?

2. Have students write their own allegory. Begin with brainstorming, clustering, or mapping a problem/conflict/issue that needs addressing. Once students have identified a problem, then, in groups or individually, have students create an allegory to solve the problem or conflict.
3. Though *The Lion, the Witch and the Wardrobe* is on one level a children's story, it can be read on many other levels as well, one of which is biblically. If you have your students write allegories, you might consider having them design the allegory to present to younger children.
4. Check the following websites for further resources for C. S. Lewis:

   falcon.jmu.edu/~ramseyil/lewis.htm
   members.lycos.co.uk/Jonathan_Gregory76/lion.htm
   personal.bgsu.edu/~edwards/lewis.html
   cslewis.drzeus.net
   www.scriptorum.org/l.html
   www.aslan.demon.co.uk/allegory.htm

Why Give This Book to Teens?

- Because the Professor is a very positive adult figure, a wisdom figure, and sometimes it's hard for adolescents to find adults who are positive role models.
- Because as allegories, these books have many layers of meaning, so the *Chronicles* are not for children only.
- Because a fantasy world can often help us better understand the real world.

Other books by C. S. Lewis to consider reading: *Out of the Silent Planet*, *Perelandra*, *This Hideous Strength*, and *Till We Have Faces*.

Lewis, C. S.: *The Screwtape Letters*
Published by Harper San Francisco, 5 February 2001,
ISBN 0060652934
****Teen Recommended****

C. S. Lewis has developed here a powerful work of irony. He has created a series of devils, but the principal characters are Screwtape and his nephew

Wormwood. Screwtape, through a series of letters, is mentoring Wormwood on how to successfully tempt a new Christian. Do not be fooled—the book teaches more about what and who God is and what true Christianity requires than it does about devils.

Teaching Ideas and Resources

1. This book is excellent for teaching irony and satire—two difficult concepts for students. Students will need to know that the "Enemy" Screwtape speaks of is actually God. They also need to know, just as they need to know when reading Swift's "A Modest Proposal," that irony and satire call for readers to make serious "leaps." They cannot take the text at face value.
2. If you are studying any other works with representations of the Devil, for example, Dante's *Inferno*, Milton's *Paradise Lost*, or Goethe's *Faust*, this work by Lewis provides an excellent parallel text.
3. Here are some sites for teaching guides to work with *The Screwtape Letters*:

   www.readinggroupguides.com/guides/screwtape_letters-author.asp
   www.rapidnet.com/~jbeard/bdm/exposes/lewis/cs-lewis.htm

Why Give This Book to Teens?

- Because maybe they wonder if the Devil really exists.
- Because maybe they have some trouble believing in God or in some divine being.
- Because this book demonstrates that not all books on religion are unapproachable.

Lowry, Lois: *Gathering Blue*
Published by Laurel Leaf, 10 September 2002, ISBN 0440229499

Kira is young, especially young to be left alone in the world. She has fought, and her mother has fought for her, since she was born fatherless and with a twisted leg. It was the custom of the community to take such infants to the Field of Leaving, unnamed, before the spirit filled the infant, making her human. Kira, though, like two others in this novel, has gifts the community wants and needs. Kira can thread: her fingers simply "know" the stories and convey the memories in the threads. Matt, from the people of the Fen, is her only companion and support against the women of the village led by the vindictive Vandara. Kira eventually is taken by the Council of Guardians to become the one who repairs the robe for the Singer. Her privileged position does not come without cost, nor does it for the others selected to be the artists for the community.

Teaching Ideas and Resources

1. *Gathering Blue* is set in an undefined time and setting, presenting a world that is both a utopia and a dsytopia. Using a Venn diagram or similar graphic organizer, have students define what is good about Kira's world and what is troubling. Compare Kira's world to our contemporary world; again, note what is positive and what is negative about each world.
2. Several members of Kira's village hold special roles: the Council of Guardians, the Singer, the Carver, and eventually Kira, as robe-threader. Discuss with students the privileged life they lead. Does having all the comforts one wants necessarily make the person happy? Explain.
3. Kira, Thomas, and Jo, the little singer, all possess "knowledge" that no one else has; they are each artists in a village without art. What would our world be like without music? Art? Literature/story?
4. "Take pride in your pain. You are stronger than those who have none" (*Gathering Blue*, 22–23). These words are advice given by Kira's mother. Ask students to explain this statement and locate other quotes from the novel that are paradoxes or seeming contradictions.
5. Kira holds and keeps with her a small cloth weaving, a kind of talisman for her; it conveys comfort and peace but also warnings and cautions. Ask students: If you were to have such a talisman, what would it be and why?
6. "The Artistic Identity: Art as a Catalyst for 'Self-Actualization' in Lois Lowry's *Gathering Blue* and Linda Sue Park's *A Single Shard*" by Janet Alsup (*ALAN Review*, Fall 2003) is a very helpful essay for examining artistic identity, as well as providing insights into both novels.
7. Check the following websites for a sample lesson plan and teaching ideas:

   www.westga.edu/~kidreach/gatheringbluelesson.html
   www.indiana.edu/~reading/ieo/bibs/lowry.html

Why Give This Book to Teens?

- Because the life of comforts can seem enviable, especially when we face difficulties.

- Because sometimes they can feel all alone and overwhelmed by those older and in authority positions, even though their accusations may be false.
- Because they may need to rethink what freedom means, especially when others seem to have "the good life."

Lowry, Lois: *The Giver*
Published by Laurel Leaf, 10 September 2002, ISBN 0440237688
Teen Recommended

The key in this story is lack of difference. In the communal lifestyle Jonas and others experience, everything is the same. While all the regulation can present an aura of security for them, the young people in Jonas's world face the deprivation created by sameness. The ultimate horror of the sameness is "release" of anyone different. And for Jonas, destined to become the next Keeper of Memories, the reality of release is a horror he cannot allow to continue. Lowry's novel can teach readers about the richness in diversity and the problems with a world where there is supposedly no pain.

Teaching Ideas and Resources

1. This novel again presents a world that is utopic; *The Giver* makes a good companion novel to *Brave New World* or *1984*. Students could first identify the elements in Jonas's society that are the most enticing; then identify those elements that are most problematic.
2. Have your students prepare a debate: Pro—Jonas's world is the kind of world we should have; Con—Jonas's world is too problematic and it is good that Jonas would leave it.
3. "What's Good about the Best?" by Ted Hipple and Amy B. Maupin (*English Journal*, January 2001) explains why *The Giver* is such a strong novel.
4. "Character Education + Young Adult Literature = Critical Thinking Skills" by Mary Ann Tighe (*ALAN Review* 26, no. 1 [Fall 1998]) focuses on *The Giver* as one novel to use with character education.
5. "Grief, Thought, and Appreciation: Re-examining Our Values Amid Terrorism through *The Giver*" by Angela Beumer Johnson, Jeffrey W. Kleismit, Antje J. Williams (*ALAN Review*, Summer 2002) offers ideas for teaching *The Giver* in light of terrorism.
6. For more author information and teaching ideas, check the following websites:

www.carolhurst.com/authors/llowry.html
www.indiana.edu/~reading/ieo/bibs/lowry.html
www.yabookscentral.com/cfusion/
index.cfm?fuseAction=guides.guide&gude_id=14&
book_id=183
www.scils.rutgers.edu/~kvander/lowry.html
www.sonoma.edu/users/l/lord/343/Links.htm
www.sdcoe.k12.ca.us/score/giver/givertg.htm
www.learner.org/channel/libraries/makingmeaning/
makingmeaning/wholegroup/lesso nplan.html

Why Give This Book to Teens?

- Because Jonas's story is for anyone, not only for those who are 12.
- Because the idea of a world without pain and any unpredictability can be enticing.
- Because they might think about creating an ideal world and can see what works and what doesn't.

Other books by Lois Lowry to consider reading: *Anastasia Krupnik* and others in the Anastasia series, *The Silent Boy*, and *Messenger*.

Paterson, Katherine: *Bridge to Terabithia*
Published by Harper Trophy, 1987
****Teen Recommended****

Jess Oliver Aarons Jr. is the only son in a family; he's sandwiched between two older sisters, Ellie and Brenda, and two younger, May Belle (who really adores him) and Joyce Ann (who is too young and demanding). His dad isn't around much; he drives back and forth daily to Washington; his mother is too busy to seem to care. Though left with many of the household chores, Jess is creative; he loves to draw. The only one who supports his artistic talents is Miss Edmunds, a teacher at school who is unconventional compared to the rest of the teachers and to the folks in the community of Lark Creek, a kind of "backwater" area.

The Burke family, two seemingly "hippie type" adults and their daughter Leslie, move in next door. Jess likes to run; he has dreams of being the "fastest kid in the fifth grade"—he runs in the cow pasture. When Leslie moves in, she wants to run, too; she is the fastest. She also doesn't fit in since her parents are so different. The family has moved because Leslie's parents are "reassessing their value structure"; because of the uniqueness of her family and the ways students at school treat Leslie, she and Jess bond.

Leslie eventually finds a place in the woods between the two families' homes and names the place "Terabithia"; she tells Jess it will be like Narnia, and she loans Jess her books about Narnia. Their secret place becomes the site of grief and healing.

Teaching Ideas and Resources

1. Through a written description, an artistic representation, or other media, create your own "Terabithia"—your personal favorite place or private world.
2. "A Bridge Too Far—But Why?" by John Simmons (*ALAN Review* 25, no. 2 [Winter 1998]) examines this novel.
3. For more about Katherine Paterson and her books, check the following websites:

   www.neiu.edu/~gspackar/INDEX.html
   www.indiana.edu/~reading/ieo/bibs/paterson.html

4. "Characters in Realistic Fiction: Do They Change with Changing Times?" by Mary Jane Gray (in "Adolescent Literature: Making Connections with Teens," special issue, *Virginia English Bulletin* 44, no. 2 [Fall 1994]) uses this novel as one of the focus novels it examines.
5. Here are other websites related to the novel:

   www.beyondbooks.com/lit71/1.asp
   www.learner.org/channel/workshops/isonovel/Pages/Patersonpage.html
   www.learner.org/channel/workshops/isonovel/Pages/MollerPage.html

Why Give This Book to Teens?

- Because they may want to have their own private place and this story can show the importance of such a place.
- Because they might have lost a good friend and find it hard to share their grief or even to be able to grieve.
- Because they may have friends who are considered "odd" or whose lifestyle is unlike others' around them.

Other books by Katherine Paterson to consider reading: *Sign of the Chrysanthemum*, *Lyddie*, *The Great Gilly Hopkins*, and *Parzival: The Quest of the Grail Knight*.

Rowling, J. K.: *Harry Potter and the Chamber of Secrets*
Published by Scholastic, 22 October 2002, ISBN 0439420105
Teen Recommended

Can we go beyond criticizing the Harry Potter books from a Christian perspective, instead seeing them as a tool that can open new ways of thinking? Whether Rowling intended us to or not, we can use the insights we find for good purpose. In this second book of the series, Harry is confronted early on with Dobby, a house elf, bent on preventing Harry from returning to Hogwarts. This year Harry is led to explore the Chamber of Secrets and mysteries connected to it.

Teaching Ideas and Resources

1. Divide the class into four houses; each house gets a House Elf. House Elves must bring cookies and juice, run errands, straighten up the room when members of the house leave, and sit on the floor. One speaker from each "house" presents conclusions of group discussion.
2. "I've always been able to charm the people I needed. So Ginny poured out her soul to me, and her soul happened to be exactly what I wanted. . . . I grew stronger and stronger on a diet of her deepest darkest secrets. . . . Powerful enough to start feeding Miss Weasley a few of my secrets, to start pouring my soul back into her . . ." (Tom Riddle, in *Chamber of Secrets*, 310).

   Ginny Weasley gets mixed up in something really dangerous. How was Tom Riddle able to take part of her soul? Are there things that can take our "souls"? Is it just young people who experience these dangers?
3. "It is our choices, Harry, that show who we truly are, far more than our abilities." (Dumbledore, in *Chamber of Secrets*, 333.) Have your students comment on this statement of Dumbledore's. What does it mean to them? Why?
4. Ask your students: Why is Harry worried that he himself might be the Heir of Slytherin? Are Harry's fears like anything you might have felt? How does Headmaster Dumbledore explain how Harry got to be in Gryffindor? What made Tom Riddle choose the Dark Arts? What connections can you make between Tom Riddle's choices and some you yourselves might have made?
5. "Critically Thinking about Harry Potter: A Framework for Discussing Controversial Works in the English Classroom" by Joanne M. Marshall (*ALAN Review*, Winter 2003) provides a good basis for using the novels.

6. "Spiritual Quest in the Realm of Harry Potter" by Gail Radley (*ALAN Review*, Winter 2003) could be used with the any of the novels to date in the Harry Potter series.

Why Give This Book to Teens?

- Because Harry Potter faces choices between good and evil.
- Because sometimes they are afraid of who they are or of some of the qualities they possess.
- Because they, like Ginny, can get "taken in" by groups or ideas they don't really want to follow.

Rowling, J. K.: *Harry Potter and the Sorcerer's Stone*
Published by Scholastic, September 1998, ISBN 0590353403
Teen Recommended

This first book in the series introduces Harry Potter and his true background—his parents, James and Lily Potter, were wizards and were killed by Lord Voldemort. Harry lives his first year at Hogwarts, builds friendships with Ron Weasley and Hermione Granger, gets his first opportunities to play Quiddith, and has his first encounters with the Dark Lord.

Teaching Ideas and Resources

1. Rowling shows some of the influences of two other English writers of Christian allegory, J. R. R. Tolkein and C. S. Lewis. Even if she does intend to be allegorical, playing with the texts allows the author's ideas to help us explore our own beliefs. Ask your students: What ideas, connections, and affirmations do the following quotes provoke in you?

   > "These people will never understand him! He'll be famous—a legend—I wouldn't be surprised if today was known as Harry Potter day in the future—there will be books written about Harry—every child in our world will know his name."
   >
   > "Exactly," said Dumbledore . . . "It would be enough to turn any body's head. Famous before he can walk and talk. Famous for something he won't even remember. Can you see how much better off he'll be, growing up away from all that until he's ready to take it?" (*Sorcerer's Stone*, 13)
   >
   > "You'll find some wizarding families are much better than others, Potter. You don't want to go making friends with the wrong sort." (Draco Malfoy, in *Sorcerer's Stone*, 109)

"[The Mirror of Erised] shows us nothing more or less than the deepest most desperate desire of our hearts. You, who have never known your family, see them standing around you. . . . However, this mirror will give us neither knowledge or truth. . . . It does not do to dwell on dreams and forget to live." (Dumbledore, in *Sorcerer's Stone*, 214)

"To one as young as you, I'm sure it seems incredible, but to Nicholas and Perenelle [inventor of the Sorcerer's Stone], [dying] is like going to bed after a very, very long day. After all, to the well-organized mind, death is but the next great adventure." (Dumbledore, in *Sorcerer's Stone*, 297)

"Your mother died to save you. If there is one thing Voldemort cannot understand, it is love. He didn't realize that love as powerful as your mother's for you leaves its own mark. Not a scar, no visible sign . . . to have been loved so deeply, even though the person who loved us is gone, will give us some protection forever." (Dumbledore, in *Sorcerer's Stone*, 299)

"Call him Voldemort, Harry. Always use the proper name for things. Fear of a name increases fear of the thing itself." (Dumbledore, in *Sorcerer's Stone*, 298)

"There are all kinds of Courage," said Dumbledore [to Neville Longbottom] smiling. "It takes a great deal of bravery to stand up to our enemies, but just as much to stand up to our friends." (*Sorcerer's Stone*, 306)

2. "*The Sorcerer's Stone*: A Touchstone for Readers of All Ages" by Susan Nelson Wood and Kim Quackenbush (*English Journal* 90, no. 3 [January 2001]) is a good resource for teaching any of the works.
3. Here are some websites that can be useful for the Harry Potter series:

   www.learner.org/channel/workshops/isonovel/Pages/HarryPotterpage.html
   www.scholastic.com/harrypotter/reference
   www.jkrowling.com
   www.scholastic.com/harrypotter/books/guides/index.htm

Why Give This Book to Teens?

- Because they might have lost or experienced the death of someone in their family.
- Because they might know some peers who are proud and selfish like Draco Malfoy.
- Because they can learn a great deal from "wisdom figures" like Dumbledore. Who in their family or relationships is such a person?

Rowling, J. K.: *The Prisoner of Azkaban*
Published by Scholastic, 8 September 1999, ISBN 0439136350
Teen Recommended

Harry is now 13 and attending his third year of school at Hogwarts. The escape of Sirius Black from the formidable prison of Azkaban is the central focus of the book. Harry learns more about dealing with the "dark arts" that will continue to torment him, particularly about the dementors: the hooded, gray, deathly creatures who guard Azkaban and who ultimately drive a person to despair. Harry also learns the truth of who Sirius Black is and how important it is to look beyond the appearance for the truth.

Teaching Ideas and Resources

1. This book has numerous symbols that can provide creative writing ideas as well as excellent journal prompts:

    Consider the "boggarts"—the shape-shifters who can take the shape of whatever they think will frighten people most—and the response to such fears, to see the ridiculous and laugh. Students can write about what would be most fearful for them and how they could foil the fears by imagining the "boggart" in a humorous context.

    Consider the Grim—a symbol of what can cause or signal our death. Harry believes the shaggy black dog is a threat. Again students can write about what might seem negative, but in fact, can be positive.

2. Students could write/create their own "Defense against the Dark Arts"—what aspects of life seem negative or destructive to them? What can be the protection or the charm to be used in these situations or against these obstacles?
3. Harry is taught that the most potent response to the presence of dementors—those who want to lead us to despair and to see only the worst in life—is to call on a Patronus. "The Patronus is a kind of positive force, a projection of the very things that the dementor feeds upon—hope, happiness, the desire to survive—but it cannot feel despair, as real humans can, so the dementors can't hurt it" (*Prisoner of Azkaban*, 237). The other piece of the "defense" is to concentrate with all one's energy on a single, very happy memory. Using the concept of the defense against dementors, have students write about a single, very happy memory. Also, have them create a list of "patronae" —who would be their rescuers.

4. Albus Dumbledore is a wisdom figure throughout the series. Here are a few of the quotable quotes he offers in this third book in the Harry Potter series:

   > To Harry, when Harry tells Dumbledore that Harry thought he saw his father: "You think the dead we loved ever truly leave us? You think we don't recall them more clearly than ever in times of great trouble? . . . [Your father] shows himself most plainly when you have need of him" (*Prisoner of Azkaban*, 427–28).
   >
   > "Harry, in a way, you did see your father last night. . . . You found him inside yourself." (*Prisoner of Azkaban*, 428)
   >
   > "Didn't make any difference?" said Dumbledore quietly. "It made all the difference in the world, Harry. You helped uncover the truth. You saved an innocent man from a terrible fate." (*Prisoner of Azkaban*, 425)

Why Give This Book to Teens?

- Because there are many real "dementors" in life—and teens need to be able to ward off the obstacles that can drain them of hope and life.
- Because they need to remember that there are people, often family and friends, who are true "patronae" in life.
- Because they need to celebrate the very happy memories in life.
- Because they want to remember that those we love who die don't ever really leave us.

Rowling, J. K.: *Harry Potter and the Goblet of Fire*
Published by Scholastic, 8 July 2000, ISBN 0439139597
Teen Recommended

The central event of Harry's fourth year at Hogwarts is the Tri-Wizard competition. Harry finds himself more and more under suspicion; few people really believe that Harry did not put his name in the competition, knowing he is not old enough to compete. Harry (along with Hermione and Hagrid) also has to deal with Rita Skeeters and her gossipy commentaries in the *Daily Prophet*. The greatest challenge to Harry, though, is the Dark Lord's return and his relentless pursuit of Harry.

Teaching Ideas and Resources

1. This book, like the others in the series, has many elements of fiction worth exploring. The "Veela" who are present at the Quiddith World

Cup have similarities with "the Sirens" from mythology. There are also continual references to the Phoenix, the mythological bird that can rise from its ashes to new life. Harry's and Lord Voldemort's wands each have a phoenix feather in the core; Dumbledore has Fawkes, the phoenix in his office. Consider working with your students on these elements of mythology in a unit on myths.

2. Again there are numerous quotations from the book worth thinking and writing about—consider using some of the following for "Ready Writes" or class starting prompts:

> Regarding the first task of the Tri-Wizard contest: "Courage in the face of the unknown is an important quality in a wizard [could fill in other nouns than wizard]" (*Goblet of Fire*, 281).
>
> Sirius to Ron about Mr. Crouch: "If you want to know what a man's like, take a good look at how he treats his inferiors, not his equals" (*Goblet of Fire*, 525).
>
> Describing Azkaban: "Many go mad in there . . . they lose the will to live" (*Goblet of Fire*, 529).
>
> Dumbledore to Harry, who is so exhausted and does not want to tell his story of the duel with Lord Voldemort and the terrors he experienced in the cemetery: "Numbing the pain for a while will make it worse when you finally feel it" (*Goblet of Fire*, 695).
>
> Dumbledore in his end of the term speech: "We can fight it [Lord Voldemort's power] only by showing an equally strong bond of friendship and trust. Differences of habit and language are nothing at all if our aims are identical and our hearts are open" (*Goblet of Fire*, 723).

3. Harry discovers a strange device in Dumbledore's office—the pensieve. Dumbledore uses it when he has too many thoughts and memories in his mind. He removes some and places them in the pensieve; this allows him to see more clearly the patterns or links in all the ideas. How would you use a pensieve if you were able to have one?
4. Lord Voldemort wants Harry's blood more than anything since Harry's under the special protection of the supreme sacrifice his mother made for him—she died that he might live. Ironically, Barty Crouch, the younger, has a mother who sacrifices all for him, willingly assuming her son's appearance in Azkaban. Consider using these sections of the book with your students to discuss the theme of parents' sacrifices for their children.

Why Give This Book to Teens?

- Because, like Harry when he feels the pain of his scar and says what he "really wanted was someone like a parent: an adult wizard whose advice he could ask without feeling stupid, someone who cared about him" (*Goblet of Fire*, 22), they may want an adult or guidance person in their life.
- Because Harry has to deal with being teased and harassed by those who are jealous of him; they may also have this experience.
- Because Harry is called to be extremely courageous even to the point of fighting for his life—he can be an inspiration.
- Because Harry is tempted to take the glory of winning, but he doesn't let himself get trapped in gaining power; he realizes that Cedric's death is a far greater concern.

Rowling, J. K.: *Harry Potter and the Order of the Phoenix*
Published by Scholastic, 10 August 2004, ISBN 0439358078
Teen Recommended

Some have commented that *The Order of the Phoenix* is too "dark," but the book represents what a real 15-year-old who has experienced the true horrors that Harry has feels like. He is frustrated at not being kept posted on all that is happening as Dumbledore assembles the Order of the Phoenix, a band of those who are willing to fight the Dark Lord. Harry also experiences the pain of his unwilling "union" with Lord Voldemort—at times Harry actually hates Dumbledore. Also Harry "sees himself" doing the actions of the Dark Lord, as when Harry thinks he has caused Arthur Weasley's near death. Above all this book presents Harry's own sacrifice for one he loves, Sirius Black, and the Dark Lord again operating under the notion that he can best get to Harry by attacking those Harry loves.

Teaching Ideas and Resources

1. This novel is the one most connected with Harry's "coming of age." Should Harry be more in Dumbledore's confidence? Should he know more about the secret workings of the Order of the Phoenix? These questions would be good writing prompts and discussion starters for the broader issue: At what age are teens really able to make their own decisions? Why do you choose this particular age?
2. The Fidelius charm is connected with protecting one's most significant friends or family. Have students write their own fidelius charm and explain why they'd use it and for whom.

3. The phoenix is a powerful mythical symbol. How does this symbol become particularly important in the Order of the Phoenix? Why?
4. Review Dumbledore's conversation with Harry after Sirius's death. What does Dumbledore mean as he says that youth cannot know old age, but he as an older person needed to remember more about what youth experiences? How is this significant?
5. The following websites have helps for teaching *The Order of the Phoenix*:

   www.charactercounts.org/pdf/HarryPotter-guide_by-Michael-Josephson-0703.pdf
   www.waterborolibrary.org/potter.htm
   www.theorderofthephoenix.net/book-5/chapters.htm
   www.hp-lexicon.org/order-phoenix.html
   www.webenglishteacher.com/rowling.html

Why Give This Book to Teens?

- Because they may have struggled with being discounted or felt not trusted by adults when they had done actions requiring the courage and wisdom of adults.
- Because they may have had an experience like Harry's when they actually feel hate toward the very people they should love.
- Because they may have someone in their life like Dolores Umbridge.

Tolkien, J. R. R.: *The Hobbit*
Published by HarperCollins, 4 September 1995, ISBN 0261103288
Teen Recommended

Bilbo Baggins is a Hobbit, and this book narrates his adventures. One of the highlights of the book is that Bilbo meets Gollum, a nasty slimy creature who has possession of a marvelous ring. Bilbo gets the ring and soon realizes its amazing powers—like invisibility. This prequel to *The Lord of the Rings* presents a kind of epic journey. After his adventures, Bilbo returns to Bags End just in time to prevent his home from being sold; he was no longer considered respectable because of his adventurous nature.

Teaching Ideas and Resources

1. As in many fantasies, there are creatures, animal-types, who are given human characteristics. Ask students to describe the character in *The Hobbit* that they would most like to be and explain why.

2. The fantasy genre builds on allegory. *The Hobbit* can be used to teach allegory and makes a good parallel text with *The Odyssey*.
3. The following websites are helpful for working with Tolkien:

   www.tolkienonline.com/
   www.successlink.org/great2/g1156.html
   www.uni-giessen.de/tefl/seminarP/newMedia/muds/Prepare.html
   www.michigan.gov/scope/0,1607,7-155-13515_13516_13517-76619--00.html
   www.tolkiensociety.org/press/literacy.html
   www.berghuis.co.nz/abiator/unit/hobbit/hindex2.html
   gollum.usask.ca/tolkien/

Why Give This Book to Teens?

- Because the book has a way of presenting some of the universal qualities of human nature, but we can learn from these more enjoyably through fantasy.
- Because they might enjoy the adventures Bilbo takes.
- Because this is a wonderful work for the imagination.

Tolkien, J. R. R.: *The Lord of the Rings* (trilogy)
Published by HarperCollins, 1994, ISBN 06181129022
Teen Recommended

The Fellowship of the Ring; The Two Towers; The Return of the King—These works are filled with allegory; dominant themes include the addiction of power; the struggle of good and evil; the spirit of self-sacrifice; the self-destruction coming from revenge, jealousy, and ambition; and the redeeming qualities of true friendship and loyalty. The Hobbits are all protagonists, but Frodo and Sam are the ultimate heroes as they overcome every obstacle to rid the world of the Ring.

Teaching Ideas and Resources

1. Explore with your students the rich themes in the poem:

   Three Rings for the Elven-kings under the sky
   Seven for the Dwarf-lords in their halls of stone,
   Nine for Mortal Men doomed to die,
   One for the Dark Lord on his dark throne
   In the Land of Mordor where the Shadows lie.

> One Ring to rule them all, One Ring to find them,
> One Ring to bring them all and in the darkness bind them
> In the Land of Mordor where the Shadows lie.

2. Have students analyze the characters who are protagonists/positive figures and those who are antagonists/negative characters—including the range of creatures like Orcs, the Nazgul, and so on. What do these characters teach about humankind?
3. Explore with your students the symbolism of names of characters, mythic creatures, and places.
4. Teri Lesesne in "Beyond Camelot: Poetry, Song and Young Adult Fantasy" (chapter 12 in Kaywell, *Adolescent Literature as a Complement to the Classics*, vol. 2, 1995) uses the Trilogy as one of the YA novels to supplement this unit.
5. Teaching guides are available at:

   www.randomhouse.com/highschool/catalog/display.pperl?0-345-33971-1&view=tg
   www.randomhouse.com/highschool/catalog/display.pperl?isbn=0345339703&view=tg

6. This site is on C. S. Lewis and J. R. R. Tolkien:

   www.aslan.demon.co.uk/allegory.htm

7. A video series entitled *Rings, Kings and Things* providing an explanation of modern fantasy literature's debt to medieval literature is available from Cerebellum.com.

Why Give This Book to Teens?

- For the adventure, the imaginative tale.
- Because they can meet characters who portray true friendship and loyalty.
- Because they may need help to sort through the realities of life that include people who are power-hungry, jealous, and selfish.
- Because they need to find some heroic models.

Other books by J. R. R. Tolkien to consider reading: *The Hobbit*.

APPENDIX

Cross-Index of Books, Alphabetized by Author

Block, Francesca Lia
I Was a Teenage Fairy **Teen Recommended** Chapter 8

Blume, Judy
Are You There God? It's Me, Margaret **Teen Recommended** Chapter 4
Tiger Eyes **Teen Recommended** Chapter 5

Brashares, Ann
The Sisterhood of the Traveling Pants **Teen Recommended** Chapter 6

Bridgers, Sue Ellen
All Together Now Chapter 4
All We Know of Heaven Chapter 4

Card, Orson Scott
Ender's Game **Teen Recommended** Chapter 8

Coelho, Paulo
The Alchemist **Teen Recommended** Chapter 8

Colfer, Eoin
Artemis Fowl **Teen Recommended** Chapter 8

Cooper, Susan
The Dark Is Rising **Teen Recommended** Chapter 8
Over Sea, Under Stone **Teen Recommended** Chapter 8

Cormier, Robert
After the First Death Chapter 4
The Chocolate War Chapter 6
Fade Chapter 8

Covey, Sean
Seven Habits of Highly Effective Teens **Teen Recommended** Chapter 4

Creech, Sharon
Ruby Holler Chapter 4
Walk Two Moons Chapter 5
The Wanderer **Teen Recommended** Chapter 5

Greene, Bette
The Drowning of Stephan Jones Chapter 6
Summer of My German Soldier **Teen Recommended** Chapter 4

Guest, Judith
Ordinary People **Teen Recommended** Chapter 5

Haruf, Kent
Plainsong **Teen Recommended** Chapter 4

Hesse, Karen
Letters from Rifka Chapter 7
Out of the Dust Chapter 7
Witness Chapter 6

Highwater, Jamake
Anpao: An American Indian Odyssey Chapter 8

Hinton, S. E.
The Outsiders **Teen Recommended** Chapter 4

Houston, Jeanne Wakatsuki, and James D. Houston
Farewell to Manzanar Chapter 7

Kerr, M. E.
Night Kites Chapter 6

Kingsolver, Barbara
The Bean Trees **Teen Recommended** Chapter 4
The Poisonwood Bible **Teen Recommended** Chapter 4

Lamb, Wally
She's Come Undone **Teen Recommended** Chapter 4

Latifa
My Forbidden Face: Growing Up Under the Taliban—A Young Woman's Story Chapter 6

Napoli, Donna Jo
Song of the Magdalene Chapter 6

Nolan, Han
If I Should Die Before I Wake Chapter 7

Park, Barbara
Mick Harte Was Here **Teen Recommended** Chapter 5

Paterson, Katherine
Bridge to Terabithia **Teen Recommended** Chapter 8
Jacob Have I Loved **Teen Recommended** Chapter 4
Lyddie **Teen Recommended** Chapter 7

Paulsen, Gary
Hatchet **Teen Recommended** Chapter 7
Nightjohn Chapter 7
Sarny Chapter 7
The Transall Saga **Teen Recommended** Chapter 8

Pelzer, David
A Child Called It **Teen Recommended** Chapter 4
The Lost Boy **Teen Recommended** Chapter 4

Philbrick, Rodman
Freak the Mighty **Teen Recommended** Chapter 6

Reynolds, Marilyn
Love Rules Chapter 6

Rinaldi, Ann
Wolf by the Ears Chapter 6

Rowling, J. K.
Harry Potter and the Chamber of Secrets
Teen Recommended Chapter 8
Harry Potter and the Goblet of Fire
Teen Recommended Chapter 8

Twomey, Cathleen
Charlotte's Choice Chapter 4

Veciana-Suarez, Ana
Flight to Freedom Chapter 7

Voight, Cynthia
Homecoming **Teen Recommended** Chapter 7

Wells, Rebecca
The Divine Secrets of the Ya-Ya Sisterhood
Teen Recommended Chapter 4

White, Ruth
Belle Prater's Boy Chapter 5
Weeping Willow Chapter 4

Wojciechowska, Maia
Shadow of a Bull Chapter 7

Wolff, Virginia Euwer
Make Lemonade **Teen Recommended** Chapter 4

Yolen, Jane
Briar Rose Chapter 7

Zindel, Paul
The Pigman **Teen Recommended** Chapter 5
The Pigman's Legacy **Teen Recommended** Chapter 5

~

Bibliography

"About Shelly Mickle." www.shelleymickle.com/biography.htm.

Adair, Jan. "Tackling Teens' No. 1 Problem." *Educational Leadership* 57, no. 6 (2000): 44–47.

"Adolescent Literature: Making Connections with Teens." Special issue, *Virginia English Bulletin* 44, no. 2 (Fall 1994).

Albritton, Thomas, Patricia Turnbull, Carol Dreyer Yeazell, and Carl P. Dolan. "Facets: The Role of the English Teacher in the Development of Moral Values." *English Journal* 74, no. 8 (1985): 14–17.

Allen, Janet, ed. *Using Literature to Help Troubled Teens Cope with End-of-Life Issues*. Westport, CT: Greenwood Press, 2002.

American Pediatric Society & Society for Pediatric Research. www.aps-spr.org.

(Angel, Ann: biography) *ALAN Review*, Winter 2003.

Authors4teens. www.authors4teens.com. (YA author biographies.)

Baines, Lawrence. "Fist Fights, Guns, and the Art of Teaching English." *English Journal* 84, no. 5 (1995): 59–64.

Benjamin, Beth, and Linda Irwin-DeVitis. "Censoring Girls' Choices: Continued Gender Bias in English Language Arts Classrooms." *English Journal* 87, no. 2 (1998): 64–71.

Bogdan, Deanne, and Stephen Yeomans. "School Censorship and Learning Values through Literature." *Journal of Moral Education* 15 (1986): 197–211.

Bontempo, Barbara T. "Exploring Prejudice in Young Adult Literature through Drama and Role Play." *ALAN Review* 22, no. 3 (1995): 31–33.

Bowman, Cynthia Ann, ed. *Using Literature to Help Troubled Teens Cope with Health Issues*. Westport, CT: Greenwood Press, 2000.

Brady, Evelyn McLean. "How to Survive Urban Violence with Hope." *English Journal* 84, no. 5 (1995): 43–50.

Brandell, Jerrold R. *Of Mice and Metaphors: Therapeutic Storytelling with Children*. New York: Basic Books, 2000.

Bridgers, Sue Ellen. "Learning a Language of Nonviolence." *English Journal* 89, no. 5 (2000): 71–73.

Brinkley, Ellen H. "Faith in the Word: Examining Religious Right Attitudes about Texts." *English Journal* 84, no. 5 (1995): 91–98.

Bruce, Heather E., and Bryan Dexter Davis. "Slam: Hip-hop Meets Poetry—A Strategy for Violence Intervention." *English Journal* 89, no. 5 (2000): 119–127.

Bugniazet, Judith. "A Telephone Interview with Robert Cormier." *ALAN Review* 12, no. 2 (Winter 1985): 14–18. Reprinted in *Two Decades of "The ALAN Review,"* edited by Patricia P. Kelly and Robert C. Small Jr. Urbana, IL: NCTE, 1999. Page references are to the reprinted version.

Campbell, Laura Ann. *Storybooks for Tough Times*. Golden, CO: Fulcrum Resources, 1999.

Canada, Geoffrey. "Raising Better Boys." *Educational Leadership* 57, no. 4 (1999/2000): 14–17.

Cangelosi, Barbara R. "'Who You Dissin', Dude?' At-Risk Students Learn Assertive Communication Skills." *English Journal* 89, no. 5 (2000): 111–118.

Carbarino, James, and Ellen deLara. "Words Can Hurt Forever." *Educational Leadership* 60, no. 6 (2003): 18–21.

Carey-Webb, Allen. "Youth Violence and the Language Arts: A Topic for the Classroom." *English Journal* 84, no. 5 (1995): 29–37.

Carroll, Pamela S. *Using Literature to Help Troubled Teenagers Cope with Societal Issues*. Westport, CT: Greenwood Press, 1999.

Cheripko, Jan. *Rat*. Honesdale, PA: Boyds Mills Press, 2002. (Author biography on cover.)

Coghlan, Rosemarie. "The Teaching of Anti-Violence Strategies within the English Curriculum." *English Journal* 89, no. 5 (2000): 84–89.

Coles, Robert. *The Call of Stories*. Boston: Houghton Mifflin, 1989.

Cooper, Doug, and Jennie L. Snell. "Bullying—Not Just a Kid Thing." *Educational Leadership* 60, no. 6 (2003): 22–25.

Daisey, Peggy, and Cristina Jose-Kampfner. "The Power of Story to Expand Possible Selves for Latina Middle School Students." *Journal of Adolescent & Adult Literacy* 45, no. 7 (2002): 578–87.

Doll, Beth, and Carol Doll. *Bibliotherapy with Young People: Librarians and Mental Health Professionals Working Together*. Englewood, CO: Libraries Unlimited, 1997.

Frazel, Midge. midgefrazel.net/character.html.

Gill, David. "Giving Peace a Chance: Gandhi and King in the English Classroom." *English Journal* 89, no. 5 (2000): 74–77.

Gorrell, Nancy. "Teaching Empathy through Ecphrastic Poetry: Entering a Curriculum of Peace." *English Journal* 89, no. 5 (2000): 32–41.

Gregg, Gail, and Pamela S. Carroll, eds. *Books and Beyond: Thematic Approaches for Teaching Literature in High School*. Norwood, MA: Christopher-Gordon, 1998.

Gribbon, William. "Religious Conservatives and Public Schools: Understanding the Religious Right." *English Journal* 84, no. 5 (1995): 84–90.

Gullotta, Thomas P., Gerald R. Adams, and Carol A. Markstrom. *The Adolescent Experience*, 4th ed. San Diego, CA: Academic Press, 2000.

Hale, Lisa A., and Chris Crowe. "'I Hate Reading If I Don't Have To': Results from a Longitudinal Study of High School Students' Reading Interest." *ALAN Review* 28, no. 3 (Spring/Summer 2001): 49–57.

Hansen, J. Merrell, and John Childs. "Creating a School Where People Like to Be." *Educational Leadership* 56, no. 1 (1998): 14–17.

Holderer, Robert W. "The Religious Right: Who Are They and Why Are We the Enemy?" *English Journal* 84, no. 5 (1995): 74–83.

Holmes, Marsha Lee. "Get Real: Violence in Popular Culture *and* in English Class." *English Journal* 89, no. 5 (2000): 104–110.

Jonsberg, Sara Dalmas. "A Place for Every Student." *English Journal* 89, no. 5 (2000): 27–30.

Joshua, Janice Maidman, and Donna DiMenna. *Read Two Books and Let's Talk Next Week: Using Bibliotherapy in Clinical Practice*. New York: J. Wiley, 2000.

Kaplan, Jeffrey. *Using Literature to Help Troubled Teenagers Cope with Identity Issues*. Westport, CT: Greenwood Press, 1999.

"Karen Cushman." Education Place. www.eduplace.com/rdg/author/index.html.

"Karen Hesse." www.indiana.edu/~reading/ieo/bibs/hesse.html.

"Karen Hesse's Biography." Scholastic. www2.scholastic.com/teachers/authorsandbooks/authorstudies/authorhome.jhtml?authorID = 45&collateralID = 5183&displayName = Biography.

Kaywell, Joan, ed. *Adolescent Literature as a Complement to the Classics*. 4 vols. Norwood, MA: Christopher-Gordon, 1993, 1995, 1997, 2000.

Kelly, Patricia P., and Robert C. Small, Jr., eds. *Two Decades of "The ALAN Review."* Urbana, IL: NCTE, 1999.

Kessler, Rachael. "Initiation—Saying Good-Bye to Childhood." *Educational Leadership* 57, no. 4 (1999/2000): 30–33.

Kurtz, Ernest, and Katherine Ketcham. *The Spirituality of Imperfection*. New York: Bantam Books, 1992.

"Learning about Gary Paulsen." www.scils.rutgers.edu/~kvander/paulsen.html.

L'Engle, Madeleine. *An Acceptable Time*. Commemorative Edition. New York: Bantam Doubleday Dell, 1997.

———. "Is It Good Enough for Children?" *The Writer*, July 2000, 8-10.

———. *A Ring of Endless Light*. New York: Farrar, Straus and Giroux, 1980.

Lerner, Arthur, and Ursula R. Mahlendorf. *Life Guidance through Literature*. Chicago: American Library Association, 1992.

Lerner, Richard M., M. Ann Easterbrooks, and Jayanthi Mistry, eds. *Handbook of Psychology: Developmental Psychology*. Vol. 6. Hoboken, New Jersey: John Wiley & Sons, 2003.

McNulty, Raymond J., Daniel A. Heller, and Tracy Binet. "Confronting Dating Violence." *Educational Leadership* 55, no. 2 (1997): 26–28.

Mindich, Daniel. "The Ada Valley Simulation: Exploring the Nature of Conflict." *English Journal* 89, no. 5 (2000): 128–133.

Monseau, Virginia R., and Gary M. Salvner, eds. *Reading Their World: The Young Adult Novel in the Classroom*. 2nd ed. Portsmouth, NH: Boyton/Cook Heinemann, 2000.

Montemayor, Raymond, Gerald P. Adams, and Thomas P. Gullota, eds. *Personal Relationships During Adolescence*. Advances in Adolescent Development, Annual Book Series, Volume 6. Thousand Oaks, CA: Sage Publishers, 1994.

National Adolescent Health Information Center. youth.ucsf.edu/nahic.

National Institute of Mental Health. www.nimh.nih.gov.

National Mental Health Association. www.nmha.org/infoctr/factsheets/82.cfm.

Nelson, G. Lynn. "Warriors with Words: Towards a Post-Columbine Writing Curriculum." *English Journal* 89, no. 5 (2000): 42–46.

Noe, Laurie R. "Heard the One About the Principal Who Painted the Door?" *Journal of Staff Development* 23, no. 3 (2002): 20–22.

Olweus, Dan. "A Profile of Bullying at School." *Educational Leadership* 60, no. 6 (2003): 12–17.

Parks, Sandra. "Reducing the Effects of Racism in Schools." *Educational Leadership* 56, no. 7 (1999): 14–18.

Pass, Olivia McNeely. "Peace from Within: Teaching Texts That Comfort and Heal." *English Journal* 89, no. 5 (2000): 90–94.

"The Power of Story-telling: It Can Make a Difference in Our World." *Business Times*, November 8, 2002, Executive Arts section.

Quinn, Anna L. "Hopes of a New Harvest: Sowing Seeds of Understanding with Contemporary Literature." *English Journal* 89, no. 5 (2000): 100–103.

Radley, Gail. "Spiritual Quest in Young Adult Literature." *ALAN Review* 28, no. 3 (Spring/Summer 2001): 40–43.

Reed, Aretha J. S. *Reaching Adolescents*. New York: Macmillan College Publishing Company, 1994.

Rees, Linda W. "A Thousand Cranes: A Curriculum of Peace." *English Journal* 89, no. 5 (2000): 95–99.

Reid, Louann, and Jamie Hayes Neufeld, eds. *Rationales for Teaching Young Adult Literature*. Portsmouth, NH: Heinemann, 1999.

Remboldt, Carole. "Making Violence Unacceptable." *Educational Leadership* 56, no. 1 (1998): 32–38.

(Reynolds, Marilyn: biography.) www.morninggloryopress.com/pages/fictrite.html

Rolheiser, Ronald. *The Holy Longing*. New York: Doubleday, 1999.

"The Round Table: Should English Teachers Be Involved in the Teaching of Values in the Classroom? If So, How?" *English Journal* 76, no. 8 (1987): 55–58.

Ruggieri, Colleen A. "The Value of Voice: Promoting Peace through Teaching and Writing." *English Journal* 89, no. 5 (2000): 47–54.

Ryan, Michael. "Read a Book—Or Go to Jail." *Parade Magazine*, February 5, 1995, 16–17.

Salvner, Gary M. "Lessons and Lives: Why Young Adult Literature Matters." *ALAN Review* 28, no. 3 (Spring/Summer 2001): 9–13.

Schneider, Barbara, and David Stevenson. "The Ambitious Generation." *Educational Leadership* 57, no. 4 (1999/2000): 22–25.

The School for Ethical Education: www.ethicsed.org/resources/resource.htm.

Shakeshaft, Carol, Laurie Mandel, Yolanda M. Johnson, Janice Sawyer, Mary Ann Hergenrother, and Ellen Barber. "Boys Call Me Cow." *Educational Leadership* 55, no. 2 (1997): 22–25.

Shaw, Mikki. "What's Hate Got to Do with It? Using Film to Address Hate Crimes in the School Community." *English Journal* 87, no. 2 (1998): 44–50.

Shuman, R. Baird. "Big Guns, Thwarted Dreams: School Violence and the English Teacher." *English Journal* 84, no. 5 (1995): 23–28.

Smagorinsky, Peter. "Reflecting on Character Through Literary Themes." *English Journal* 89, no. 5 (2000): 64–69.

Stanford, Barbara. "Conflict and the Story of Our Lives: Teaching English for Violence Prevention." *English Journal* 84, no. 5 (1995): 38–42.

Stanley, Jacqueline. *Reading to Heal*. Boston: Element Books, 1999.

State of Louisiana Department of Health and Hospitals. "Suicide Third Leading Cause of Death for Adolescents in Louisiana." News Release, May 9, 2002. wwwsrch2.doa.state.la.us/news/submitArticles/20020930741/20020930741Suicideprevention.htm

Stein, Nan. "Listening to—and Learning from—Girls." *Educational Leadership* 57, no. 4 (1999/2000): 18–20.

Steinberg, Laurence. *Adolescence*. 5th ed. Boston: McGraw-Hill College, 1999.

Suhor, Charles, and Bernard Suhor. *Teaching Values in the Literature Classroom: A Debate in Print*. Urbana, IL: NCTE, 1992.

Tell, Carol. "Generation What? Connecting with Today's Youth." *Educational Leadership* 57, no. 4 (1999/2000): 8–13.

Thomas, Glen, and Caroline Roberts. "The Character of Our Schooling." *American School Board Journal* 181, no. 5 (1994), 33–35.

Thompson, Julian F. "An Underutilized Resource: Values Education and the Older YA Novel." *ALAN Review* 23, no. 3 (Spring 1996): 47–49.

Tighe, Mary Ann. "Character Education + Young Adult Literature = Critical Thinking Skills." *ALAN Review* 26, no 1 (Fall 1998): 57–63.

Valone, Keith. www.sanmarino.k12.ca.us/~smhs/FacultyResources/documents/TeenSuicidePrev/tsld003.htm (Power Point Presentation on teen suicide prevention).

Vaughn, Pamela Adams. "Keeping Our Schools Safe." *Creighton University Magazine*, Spring 2000, 12–19.

Wallace, Margaret. "Nurturing Nonconformists." *Educational Leadership* 57, no. 4 (1999/2000): 44–46.

Weissbourd, Rick. "Moral Teachers, Moral Students." *Educational Leadership* 60, no. 6 (2003): 6–11.

Wessler, Stephen L. "It's Hard to Learn When You're Scared." *Educational Leadership* 61, no. 1 (2003): 40–43.

White, J. Elaine. "Young Adult Literature as a Key to Literacy." *ALAN Review* 27, no. 3 (Spring 2000): 52–54.

Willinsky, John. "Recalling the Moral Force of Literature in Education." *The Journal of Educational Thought* 22 (1988): 118–131.

Wolfe, Denny. "Three Approaches to Coping with School Violence." *English Journal* 84, no. 5 (1995): 51–54.

Wright, Mary F., and Sandra Kowalczyk. "Peace by Piece: The Freeing Power of Language and Literacy through the Arts." *English Journal* 89, no.5 (2000): 55–63.

Wrye, Marion. "The Silent Classroom." *English Journal* 89, no.5 (2000): 79–83.

~

Author and Title Index

~

Subject Index

About the Author

Mary Warner has been teaching English to adolescents for almost thirty-one years—nine years at the high school level and twenty-two years at the postsecondary level. She currently teaches young adult and children's literature at San Jose State University, where she also works with the English credential programs and serves as associate director of the San Jose Area Writing Project. She is the editor and author of two chapters in *Winning Ways of Teaching Writing: A Practical Guide for Teaching Writing, Grades 7–12* and has also published numerous articles on literature as a source of meaning for teens and adults.

Mary is a member of the School Sisters of Notre Dame, an international congregation of religious women dedicated primarily to the education of women and youth.